America's England

OXFORD STUDIES IN AMERICAN LITERARY HISTORY

Gordon Hutner, Series Editor

Family Money
Jeffory A. Clymer

America's England
Christopher Hanlon

Writing the Rebellion
Philip Gould

America's England

ANTEBELLUM LITERATURE
AND ATLANTIC SECTIONALISM

Christopher Hanlon

OXFORD
UNIVERSITY PRESS

OXFORD
UNIVERSITY PRESS

Oxford University Press is a department of the University of Oxford.
It furthers the University's objective of excellence in research, scholarship,
and education by publishing worldwide.

Oxford   New York
Auckland   Cape Town   Dar es Salaam   Hong Kong   Karachi
Kuala Lumpur   Madrid   Melbourne   Mexico City   Nairobi
New Delhi   Shanghai   Taipei   Toronto

With offices in
Argentina   Austria   Brazil   Chile   Czech Republic   France   Greece
Guatemala   Hungary   Italy   Japan   Poland   Portugal   Singapore
South Korea   Switzerland   Thailand   Turkey   Ukraine   Vietnam

Oxford is a registered trade mark of Oxford University Press
in the UK and certain other countries.

Published in the United States of America by
Oxford University Press
198 Madison Avenue, New York, NY 10016

© Oxford University Press 2013

First issued as an Oxford University Press paperback, 2016

Library of Congress Cataloging-in-Publication Data
Hanlon, Christopher.
America's England : antebellum literature and Atlantic sectionalism / Christopher Hanlon.
p. cm.
Includes index.
ISBN 978-0-19-993758-5 (hardcover)—ISBN 978-0-19-993759-2 (e-book)
ISBN 978-0-19-049445-2 (paperback)
1. American literature—English influences. 2. American literature—19th century—History and criticism.
3. United States—Civilization—British influences. 4. English-speaking countries—Intellectual life—
19th century. 5. United States—Relations—Great Britain. 6. Great Britain—Relations—United
States. I. Title.
PS159.E5H36 2013
810.9'003—dc23
2012032190

9780199937585

To my families—northern and southern, English and American.

{ CONTENTS }

{ PREFACE }

This book argues that the decades prior to the U.S. Civil War bore witness to a cisatlantic contest over transatlantic connection, an American competition over English history, culture, and politics that coalesced the shifting resonance of those terms into a welter of U.S. sectional disputes. It contends that U.S. writers and public intellectuals of the period engaged in forms of transatlanticism that reconfigured the political tensions threatening the federal Union, positioning those forms of national friction as if continuous with much older antagonisms endemic to the political and cultural history of England. In making these arguments, it traces the history of a way of thinking and writing about England, a pattern of invocation made in witness to the state of political emergency building in America over the course of what U.S. cultural historians call the antebellum period, or what our colleagues in British Studies refer to as the early Victorian era.

A danger inherent in an undertaking such as this is that of offering merely another account of antebellum America's cultural embroilment with Britain. After all, the decades with which I am concerned have proven fruitful ground for scholars interested in the history of intellectual commerce between the two nations, through whose work students of the period have reaped a nuanced sense of the early nineteenth-century North Atlantic as a space of fecund transnational interaction. Transatlantic literary historians have taught us to understand the pace of literary exchange between the United States and Britain as having been accelerated by a culture of reprinting, wherein an absence of legal regulation spurred the migration of intellectual property between English-speaking domains around the Atlantic rim;[1] they have shown us that writers in both Britain and the United States worked within shared contexts of social reform entwining swaths of writers and readers in both countries within joint projects of organic intellectualism;[2] and they have made illuminating arguments for viewing antebellum U.S. public culture as a deferential space in which Americans looked to England for standards of taste; in which they sought out English books, plays, and fashion; and in which they indulged in reveries over England as the focal point of sublime associations.[3] All of this constitutes a richly complicating response to Robert Weisbuch's call, in 1986, for just such an outpouring of transatlantic literary study.[4] But this unfolding of transatlantic scholarship also supplants Weisbuch's depiction of nineteenth-century U.S. literary production—defined in Weisbuch's *Atlantic Double-Cross* primarily as having labored under a massive anxiety of influence—with an account of broader patterns of transnational exchange and collegiality conditioning the early decades of U.S. literary culture and its relationship with contemporaneous circles of writers and readers in Britain.

Our sense of the imagined communities of antebellum America—already the subject of decades of scholarship focused first upon the intellectual history of the elites of the American Renaissance and then upon broader cultural milieus those earlier treatments tended to gloss—has become more detailed as a result of transatlanticism, more aware of the extent to which the history of the era is enmeshed in a series of cultural antecedents concerning Britain. And yet, as enriching as this field of work has proven, what has been absent from its purview is a sense of the ways in which U.S. sectionalism itself, the very circumstance for which reason we continue to term this period "antebellum," determined the ways U.S. thinkers understood the transatlantic constellation. Strangely, what is missing from virtually all transatlantic studies of the antebellum period is a mindfulness of how sectionalism both shaped American apprehensions of England and configured itself in relation to these apprehensions.

America's England details the process through which American public intellectuals, politicians, journalists, and writers of travel narrative, poetry, and fiction formulated a transatlanticism outfitted to provide alternative accounts of the national breakup over slavery. My phrase "Atlantic sectionalism" names a habit of thought, developing among both northern and southern partisans through the decades preceding the Civil War and persisting well into the conflict itself, through which assertions of transatlantic connectedness entwined polemics over states' rights and federalism, northern and southern lineage, secession and union, slavery and freedom. Much of *America's England* describes the cultural work performed by northern and southern partisans whose appropriations of a conceptualized England tended to align themselves and their regional or political kindred with a kind of reconstituted mother country. Atlantic sectionalism, then, does not stem from some impoverished cultural confidence during the antebellum period, or represent some homage to Britain amounting to a stifling of native thought—in fact, I agree with Amanda Claybaugh that the history of literary appreciation in the Anglo-American world tends to discredit narratives of gradual American emergence from aesthetic dependence upon Britain, revealing a much more mutual cultural reciprocity that belies the old supposition of an a priori British condescension toward America even as it complicates accounts of an American need to stake out alternate cultural space.[5] Rather, Atlantic sectionalism describes the extent to which what is often taken as a reflexive deference to Britain, and especially England, functioned in a nationally solipsistic way during the antebellum period, providing northern and southern rhetorical combatants—fixated upon some core notion of an ancestral Nation—materials for an invidious national discourse.

As I say, this is not a story that has been told over the course of these particularly productive two decades of transatlantic and nineteenth-century studies, and so in this sense, I hope to reintroduce a political dimension into our sense of the transatlantic antebellum period. Though, for instance, Weisbuch and more recently Sam Haynes have elaborated the ways in which England represented for many Americans, at particular moments, a cultural hegemon; though Elisa Tamarkin has shown us the depth and resonance of Anglophilia, especially among northeasterners in the United States; and though Paul Giles and Paul Gilroy have taught us to view both British and American texts over two centuries as part of a singular if complex North Atlantic culture (taking us from the progressive model Weisbuch and Haynes espouse to show instead how each nation's literature "reveal[s], as in a crazy mirror, what is lacking in the other"[6]), what has been left out of this discussion over early nineteenth-century transatlanticism is the sense in which a protean idea of England channeled political energies among northern and southern opponents in the United States.[7] Public intellectuals in the United States could not but refer the terms of the national conflict over slavery to England—whose abolition of slavery throughout the empire in 1833 pressured conservative U.S. discourses as well as voices of liberal dissent—but rather than doing so directly and literally, these partisans tended to codify their antipathies for one another in terms of complicated engagements with various constructions of English history, race, geography, and political economy.

Describing those engagements as well as the reconfiguring effects they exerted back upon sectionalist thought comprises most of my purpose in this book. But that said, the story I tell also encompasses the ire with which sectional partisans eventually turned upon the England they had fashioned, denouncing its history, politics, and culture as suddenly inimical to the northern or southern cause. *America's England* ultimately describes both curves of this arc: the expressions of transatlantic esteem through which northerners and southerners rearranged their reciprocal aversions in terms of an imagined rapport with England; but also the wholesale recall of affection through which these same partisans finally came to recoordinate questions over federalism, slavery, and the future of the Republic around various expressions of Anglophobia. In one sense, I'm tempted to say that the story I offer charts the coming into being of a U.S. national consciousness unfettered by the example of England, in which the resolution of the slavery question relieved U.S. thinkers somewhat of the importance of feeling English. But it is probably more accurate to describe the act of recoiling itself as a part of the fantasy structure embroiling America with England. The fawning stories northerners and southerners told about England during the antebellum period also constitute a kind of impossible demand, an account to which no society, not even Victoria's empire, could at once conform. So the trajectory of this book plots a series of national and sectional fixations upon Englishness, but it is also an account of the ways those fixations undermined themselves, calling England to task for its betrayal of a special relationship that had in any case been conceived by Americans in order to serve American purposes.

"To say the truth," Emerson wrote in 1863, "England is never out of mind. Nobody says it, but all think and feel it. England is the model in which they find their wishes expressed. . . ."[8] As antebellum northerners such as Emerson, Nathaniel Hawthorne, Frederick Douglass, or Lydia Maria Child—and southern counterparts such as John Pendleton Kennedy, William Gilmore Simms, or George Fitzhugh—thought about England, they also thought through the fragmenting state of the Republic, and so expressed in their thinking about England increasingly divergent wishes over the future of Anglophone civilization in North America. My sense is that recovering their conversation helps us to reconstitute an historical and interpretive context in which some writers who have appeared outré might now seem more resonant. In charting the interstices and overlaps of the massively complex cultures of the antebellum United States and Victorian England, other transatlantic scholars have made it clear that satisfying accounts of the literary cultures of the era cannot be relayed through national canons alone, and so while I deal with several figures familiar in prior studies of antebellum U.S. literature and culture, I also spend extended time with writers whose names have been less ubiquitous. My procedure in this book is sometimes to depict the cultural fields I examine through a survey of many texts and cultural formations so as to establish their common conceptual lexis, but I also tend to place such surveys in the service of more extended examinations of single texts. If I sometimes tarry with examples of this latter group for extended periods, it is in order to pay due attention to the subtle dialogue through which literary texts constitute their complicated relations with the surrounding culture, and because I think this close attention becomes especially rewarding in the case of texts that have fallen from our memory as cultural historians. I think this facet of my method in this book may also be helpful in restoring a sense of standing for some of the writers toward whom I turn—especially those of the antebellum South. Writers such as Simms, Timrod, and Kennedy enjoyed broad readerships and were central to a conversation about U.S. sectional strife that produced a conceptual ether of the period, and so my account of that conversation tries to capture some sense of their often extensive resonance. At the same time, the story I tell concerns figures whose contemporary reputations are more widely established. Of these, Emerson is of abiding importance not only because of his nearly continuous connection to England (widely known in his day through his public connection to Carlyle but also evidenced in his journals, public lectures, and unpublished manuscripts of many sorts as well as his 1856 *English Traits*), but also in light of his position as a lightning rod for sectional resentment expressed in a twenty-five-year stream of hostile southern reviews.[9] But rather then issuing reminders about the contemporaneous reputations of the authors I treat, my hope is that *America's England* provides perimeter to what may otherwise appear as an atomized collection of political, journalistic, and literary voices. In the process, I hope to offer a perspective on antebellum America, and its relations with England, discerning of the usable pasts these voices concocted as well as the futures they projected.

{ ACKNOWLEDGMENTS }

While this book treats a broad pattern of affiliation as both the source of fiction and something like a form of false consciousness in itself, the affiliations behind this book are the most real thing I know, and leave me in an embarrassment of debt. I must first thank some of the people who have read and commented on portions of my manuscript, and others whose conversation has allowed me to improve it at so many turns: C. C. Wharram, Susan Ryan, Elisa Tamarkin, Angela Vietto, Tim Taylor, Richard Sylvia, Ruth Hoberman, Newton Key, Janet Marquardt, Suzie Park, Dana Ringuette, David Raybin. Though any remaining shortcomings are mine alone, other, anonymous readers brought to my project by Oxford University Press have alerted me to possibilities I had missed while saving me from mistakes and misstatements, from infelicitous phrasing, from my own limits. Over the course of two years, colleagues comprising my research group at Eastern Illinois University—including some of those I've named but also Dagni Bredesen, Terri Fredrick, Robin Murray, and Jeannie Ludlow—kept me on task. To Randall Knoper and Robert Paul Griffin, both of the University of Massachusetts, without either of whose influence I would never have begun this project, I must extend continual, if inadequate, gratitude. At various stages my project was supported by the Office of Research and Sponsored Programs at Eastern Illinois University, and I am also grateful to the Graduate School at Eastern for supplying me, over the course of two summers, crack research assistants in John Belleau and Brianne Bolin. Librarians at the Houghton Library at Harvard tend a sublime space in which I've happily spent days reading Emerson's manuscripts, and I have also benefited from the efficiency and professionalism of librarians at the University of Illinois, the American Antiquarian Society, the Boston Public Library, the British Library, and Booth Library at Eastern. Of the librarians who staff this last institution, Karen Whisler, Andrew Lenaghan, and Clifford Harrison have made enormous differences to the work I have been able to carry out.

Various colleagues have over the past few years offered me the supreme compliment of invitations to share portions of this work. From the University of Manchester, I once again thank Michael Bibler, Brian Ward, Natalie Zacek, Carolyn Broomhead, and Anke Bernau, all of whom arranged to bring me to Manchester's intellectually thrilling American Studies Group, Critical MASS. My colleague and friend Coleman Hutchison participated with me on a 2010 C19 panel of Southernists and invited me to share thoughts on Henry Timrod for his panel on the Civil War at the Society for the Study of Southern Literature in 2012. Laura Mielke, one of the most likable and generous people in our field, asked me to join her panel on public violence at C19 in Berkeley in 2012, along with our brilliant colleagues Sandra Gustafson and Glenn Hendler. The English Department at Oakland University entrusted me with the inaugural annual lecture of their American Studies program in 2012, for which I must extend special gratitude to Susan Hawkins, Lisa Czapski, Katy Bodenmiller, and my fellow Emersonian Andrea Knutson. Colleagues in the Civil War Caucus of the Midwest Modern Language Association (which one would have to invent had Kathleen Diffley not already done so, imbuing it with the same mixture of intellectual daring and affability characterizing all her work), have offered me their insight, and I am also grateful for the perspectives of fellow panelists and audience members at the 2009, 2010, and 2011 annual conventions of the American Literature Association, and at the 2010 and 2012 meetings of that wide community of wisdom and conviviality that has become C19.

In 2003, 2008, and 2011, teaching appointments at Harlaxton College—a place apart in the Tennysonian hills of Lincolnshire—provided the ideal setting for reading and meditating on the tendency of Americans to engraft their most deeply held selves into England. Of Harlaxton's faculty and staff I am especially grateful for the friendship and conversation of David Green, Edward Bujak, Helen Snowe, Phil Taylor, and Gordon and Suzanne Kingsley. Many Harlaxton students over the years have fired my enthusiasm for my subject, making it a pleasure to finish a day of classes only to return to my flat and write. Of these, I thank particularly students from my courses in transatlantic literature and the British novel, especially Rachel Cochran, Kelsey Gunderson, Kelsey Mattingly, Eliza Ingram, Shelby Koehne, Heather Gerrish, and Megan Werner, just as I am a better Americanist for the pleasure of having advised four brilliant graduate students in transatlantic and antebellum literature: Kim Hunter, Emily Ramage, Josh Sopiarz, and John Stromski. And for showing my students, and me, so many corners of his country and teaching us so much in the process, I am in much debt to David Greaves of Grantham, England.

A version of chapter 5 was published in *American Literature*, and I thank Priscilla Wald as well as Emily Dings and Liz Beasley, as well as two anonymous readers to whom I am grateful for having helped to hone the essay. A version of chapter 1 was published in *American Literary History*—a fact that brings me to Gordon Hutner, without whose wisdom this book would be much diminished. Many people reading these words know what a pleasure it is to take Gordon's advice, and too often, to take credit for the results of taking that advice. At Oxford University Press, Brendan O'Neil has steered the project through with efficiency and good humor, qualities for which I thank him as well as Stephen Bradley and Erica Woods Tucker—not least of all for putting my manuscript in the hands of Mary Anne Shahidi, the most thorough copy editor with whom I have worked.

My very first reader and most important interlocutor, upon whose judgment I have come to depend before all others, is Jeffrey Insko. Lacking him, this book would be the least of what I would be without. My parents, Fran and Walter, and my brother and sister, Greg and Leslie, along with their partners Sue and George and my nephew Sawyer, are constantly in my corner; among the ways they express love for me is the interest they take in my work. The rest of my family does that as well and has also left its imprint on this book: thank you Mac, Maureen, Alasdair, Pam, Ralph, Lordis, Terry, Nola, Bob, Joyce, Eddie, Peter, Ralph, Debbie, Tristan, Elsbeth, Kai, and Darcy. My daughter, Tilda, tells me she hopes this book will make me rich and famous, but doesn't yet grasp that she was the advent after which all further enrichment seems superfluous. All of that said, my greatest debt, for her unfailing eye, her buoyancy, her honesty, partnership, and her English and southern counterbalance to my American and Yankee ways, with whom I have spent all of my time in England and the best moments of my life, is to the medievalist Francine Phyllis Evelyn McGregor. I will meet you, my darling, where sleeps the crimson petal, and the white, where waves the cypress by the palace walk, and winks the gold fin in the porphyry font. Waken thou, darling, with me.

Introduction

1. Striking Roots

Departing his post as American consul to Liverpool in 1857, Nathaniel Hawthorne later described a meeting with his replacement, the appointee of the newly elected President Buchanan, as an encounter between representatives of two originary American lines conducting themselves affably, at least, while on English soil. The next appointee arrives, "a very genial and agreeable gentleman, an F. F. V."—that is, a member of a "First Family of Virginia," a descendant of one of the original James River settlers—"and, as he pleasantly acknowledged, a Southern Fire-Eater—an announcement to which I responded, with similar good-humor and self-complacency, by parading my descent from an ancient line of Massachusetts Puritans."[1] This meeting upon Hawthorne's departure from England, conducted between the descendants of "ancient line[s]" now at odds in North America, articulates the abiding concern of this book, which documents the effort among Hawthorne's contemporaries to recover England as an alternative conceptual space within which purportedly ancient lines of northerners and southerners might reconfigure the terms motivating sectional crisis in the United States. Placed near the outset of *Our Old Home* (1863), a memoir of England also depicting Hawthorne's resolution to strike his American "roots" into English soil—thus claiming, we might imagine, a substitute ground upon which ancient lines of Massachusetts Puritans and Virginia fire-eaters might reimagine their relations at transatlantic remove—Hawthorne's recollection of his meeting with Buchanan's appointee raises questions that also underpin the chapters to follow. What can it mean, for citizens of a nation less than eighty years old, to imagine regional affiliation as attachment to ancient lines of northerners or southerners? What do such assertions concerning ancient lineage announce during a period of national dissolution? How do such ancient lines triangulate with a still more ancient mother country out of whose genealogies these latter lines branch, and hence wherein—we might suppose—all otherwise divergent Anglo-American lineages must resolve themselves?

It is Hawthorne himself who juxtaposes the process of striking roots at oceanic distances from American points of origin, into the soil of our old home of England, alongside his own abiding rootedness in the ground of sectional turmoil at home. Even if, as Hawthorne now notes, "Since our brief acquaintanceship, my fire-eating friend has had ample opportunities to banquet on his favorite diet, hot and hot, in the Confederate service" (5: 38), Hawthorne refuses to view his Virginian replacement through the lens of sectional antipathy. Encountering one another far from the deepening acrimony of Washington, each man had been merely the representative of an "ancient line," similarly dislocated. And yet, transplanted as he may have been from the divisions over which these two lines now do battle in the United States, Hawthorne—now writing his memoir in abolitionist Concord during the very din of that conflict—describes his departure from the meeting and from England in terms of his inability to reconcile the displaced self with the one who now records that departure:

> For myself, as soon as I was out of office, the retrospect began to look unreal. I could scarcely believe that it was I, that figure whom they called a Consul, but a sort of Double Ganger, who had been permitted to assume my aspect, under which he went through his shadowy duties with a tolerable show of efficiency, while my real self had lain, as regarded my proper mode of being and acting, in a state of suspended animation.
>
> This same sense of illusion still pursues me. There is some mistake in this matter. I have been writing about another man's consular experiences, with which, through some mysterious medium of transmitted ideas, I find myself intimately acquainted, but in which I cannot possibly have had a personal interest. Is it not a dream altogether? (5: 38)

The sense of unreality to which Hawthorne later confessed infused his failed effort, after the Consulate, to crystallize in fiction the uncanny sensations attending his remembrance of this period of his life—a process that resulted in the abandoned "American Claimant" manuscripts of 1858–61.[2] Perhaps the ambience of dislocatedness permeating Hawthorne's activities as U.S. consul years before—perhaps, for that matter, his difficulty in distilling the impressions he fomented during those years to the form of romance—was a most recent instance of the decenteredness he had announced as early as the penultimate paragraph of "The Custom-House": "I am a citizen of somewhere else" (1: 44). Unlocatable in geographical space, this somewhere else of Hawthornian citizenship nevertheless marks a remove from both those roots he imagined himself to have struck in England and his situatedness within an "ancient line" of New Englanders, that other self whose animation England would suspend. Indeed, Hawthorne confesses that throughout his sojourn in England, "I was often conscious of a fervent hereditary attachment to the native soil of our forefathers, and felt it to be our own Old Home" (5: 40). In the notebooks he maintained over the course of his stay in England, he transformed that sense of fervent attachment, coupled with suspended animation, to an interregnum in his family's Anglo-American history, its departure from the mother country now hearkening toward Hawthorne's return as U.S. consul—his own family effectively bridging modern England to its feudal past. "My ancestor left England in 1635," he noted. "I return in 1853. I sometimes feel as if I myself had been absent those hundred and eighteen years—leaving England just emerging from the feudal system, and finding it on the verge of Republicanism. It brings the two far separated points of time very closely together, to view the matter thus."[3]

America makes the medieval seem contemporary, Hawthorne seems to say: it infuses the distant English past with a contemporary explanatory power. The placement of medieval England as if in prologue to the political structures of early America enjoyed increasing currency in the public sphere Hawthorne had temporarily left, as ensuing chapters will examine. But there is also in Hawthorne's musings an effort to displace America as a familial and political location, as if the defining historical setting of both the Hawthorne line and Republicanism itself lay within the English locale from which the family took its leave rather than in the North American spaces of Puritan New England or the Revolution, let alone of the unfolding national conflict of Hawthorne's day. Brenda Wineapple calls secession "the agonizing, unfathomable reality" from which, for Hawthorne, England became a "refuge."[4] Elisa Tamarkin, more attuned to his failures to form that refuge, nevertheless says that like the various American Claimant manuscripts, Hawthorne's reminiscence "is not only an escape from the 'uneasy, agitating Conflict' of the present but also a return to an older order—to the original, loyal feelings that at least aim to be a reparative and 'natural' response and in some circuitous way an assurance of 'reality.'"[5] In thus voicing the "fervent hereditary attachment" to which Hawthorne confesses himself sensible, the American descendant of English forefathers not only invigorates his own lineal attachments but also finds an alternate national stability leagues from the successive, seemingly unreal signs of American disintegration unfolding in his absence: Bleeding Kansas beginning in 1854, Preston Brooks and Charles Sumner in 1856, John Brown in 1859.

And yet the fact of the American crisis worms its way into Hawthorne's reminiscence at various moments, including his account of the meeting with the fire-eating Virginian President Buchanan had appointed as his replacement. If *Our Old Home* was, as some commentators have suggested, Hawthorne's attempt to remove himself from the sectional crisis through the vehicle of reminiscence, he also recalled the book to the scene of that strife through his dedication of the memoir to former president Pierce: an inscription attracting immediate reproach from northern reviewers angered not only by Pierce's conservative record as president, but, more infuriatingly, the revelation in 1863 of an 1860 letter to Jefferson Davis in which Pierce appeared to some to have commended the possibility of secession.[6] Urged by his publishers to remove the inscription, Hawthorne refused, calling Pierce a patriot, "faithful forever to that grand idea of an irrevocable Union" (5: 5). Addressing himself directly to his friend and fellow Bowdoin alumnus in the volume's introduction, Hawthorne alludes to his own prior attempts to romance the intertwining of Anglo-American bloodlines as he confesses, "I had once hoped, indeed, that so slight a volume would not be all that I might write" in drawing upon his time in England, that he had rather envisioned his English journals as the storehouse of "side-scenes, and back-grounds, and exterior adornment, of a work of fiction, of which the plan had imperfectly developed itself in my mind" (5: 3–4). "Of course, I should not mention this abortive project," he explains,

> only that it has been utterly thrown aside, and will never now be accomplished. The Present, the Immediate, the Actual, has proved too potent for me. It takes away not only my scanty faculty, but even my desire for imaginative composition, and leaves me sadly content to scatter a thousand peaceful fantasies upon the hurricane that is sweeping us all along with it, possibly, into a Limbo where our nation and its polity may be as literally the fragments of a shattered dream as my unwritten Romance. (5: 4)

The present, the immediate, the actual—the developing catastrophe of national dissolution, Hawthorne explains, recalls him from his imaginary English space, and the shattering of his literary effort, indeed, reduplicates the shards of a federal Union whose passing makes the nation itself a kind of failed narrative experiment. That shattered dream of Union permeates Hawthorne's description of his consular office, what Hawthorne calls this "little patch of our nationality imbedded into the soil and institutions of England" (5: 8). The office, he explains, was "duskily lighted by two windows looking across a by-street at the rough brick-side of an immense cotton ware-house" (5: 7), a repository of the material product of slavery through which the Confederacy—at least up until the approximate moment of Our Old Home's publication—attempted to leverage recognition and assistance from Britain. On the wall of the office, Hawthorne tells us, "hung a large map of the United States, (as they were, twenty years ago, but seem little likely to be, twenty years hence,) and a similar one of Great Britain, with its territory so provokingly compact, that we may expect it to sink sooner than sunder" (5: 7). Pessimistic about his own nation's prospects, Hawthorne delivers his prediction of its dissolution with an air of studiedly detached conjecture, and then juxtaposes the image of the faltering Union—its geography yet cohered even if upon the very moment of national schism—with an enticingly "compact" Britain.

The consular office is adorned with other symbols of national flux as well, such as "a colorless, life-size lithograph of General Taylor, with an honest hideousness of aspect, occupying the place of honor above the mantel-piece" (5: 7–8). Looming over the consulate, Taylor's image calls to mind Hawthorne's earlier account of his political appointment as surveyor of customs in Salem—a post Hawthorne lost, just as he would later depart the Liverpool consulate, as a result of a change in presidential administration. With Zachary Taylor's inauguration in 1849, Hawthorne was forced out of the Custom House, a fate of political decapitation he had described in *The Scarlet Letter* in similarly distant tones alternating between bemusement and stupefaction. There he explained that Taylor's election was a "remarkable event," a development seeming almost providential, since Hawthorne had already "endeavored to calculate how much longer I could stay in the Custom-House, and yet go forth a man" (1: 40, 39–40). "To confess the truth," Hawthorne explains, "it was my greatest apprehension,—as it would never be a measure of policy to turn out so quiet an individual as myself, and it being hardly the nature of a public officer to resign,—it was my chief trouble, therefore, that I was likely to grow gray and decrepit in the Surveyorship" (1: 40). So it would be with Hawthorne's replacement as American consul in Liverpool, a result of Buchanan's election, by which time Hawthorne claims, "I disliked my office from the first, and never came into any good accordance with it," such that "I was quite prepared, in advance of the inauguration of Mr. Buchanan, to send in my resignation" (5: 37, 38). Indeed, the whole of the first chapter of *Our Old Home* resonates with "The Custom-House" inasmuch as both affect such ambivalence, as if Hawthorne would purport indifference to the bequeathal upon him of a series of appointments he had nevertheless been happy to accept.

For although Hawthorne had maneuvered for the Liverpool position (which may have been a reward for his campaign biography of Pierce, a work the *New York Herald* had ridiculed, upon its release in 1852, as Hawthorne's latest romance), he presents his appointment in *Our Old Home* standoffishly, as if he had simply resolved to make the best of an unsought turn of events. "So I settled quietly down," Hawthorne explains, "striking some of my roots into such soil as I could find, adapting myself to circumstances, and with so much success, that, though from first to last I hated the very sight of the little room, I should yet have felt a singular kind of reluctance in changing it for a better" (5: 9). Striking his roots into English soil—or rather, into this "little patch of our nationality imbedded into the soil and institutions of England"— Hawthorne repeats the act of nativization he had ascribed to Hester Prynne well after her condemnation by the Puritan magistrates of *The Scarlet Letter*, where Hester's "sin, her ignomiry, were the roots which she had struck into the soil" (1: 80). Like Hester—of whom Hawthorne explains, "It was as if a new birth, with stronger assimilations than the first, had converted the forest-land, still so uncongenial to every other pilgrim and wanderer, into Hester's wild and dreary, but life-long home" (1: 80)—Hawthorne strikes roots into a soil as simultaneously English and American as Hester's "forest-land" where, as Laura Doyle points out, it bears noting that none of the Puritans can claim nativity at all. "All other scenes of the earth," *The Scarlet Letter* explains, "even that village of rural England, where happy infancy and stainless maidenhood seemed yet to be in her mother's keeping, like garments put off long ago— were foreign to her, in comparison" (1: 80).[7]

The striking of transatlantic roots becomes the controlling trope in Hawthorne's account of his consular experiences. Upon his daily arrival to the consulate, Hawthorne navigates crowds of appellants, penniless American wanderers appealing for passage back to North America. Among these, Hawthorne depicts a nameless old man claiming to be from Philadelphia, "who was in the habit of visiting me every few months, and soberly affirmed that he had been wandering about England for more than a quarter of a century" (5: 13), and whom Hawthorne finally decides he cannot assist homeward since surely, to him, Philadelphia would by now have "become more like a foreign land to him than England was now" (5: 15). Others buffet this westward path of return, seeking instead the consul's assistance in reestablishing an English nativity. Recollecting another case, Hawthorne describes a Connecticut shopkeeper who believes himself the heir of an English estate and title, a delusion Hawthorne also ascribes to "a great many other" Americans (5: 18). Having named his children after Queen Victoria and Prince Albert, and having received polite thanks from the queen's secretary for sending photographs of his offspring, this would-be noble now asks Hawthorne's assistance in securing an interview with the queen, through whose aid he intends to recover his title. To this example of "this diseased American appetite for English soil" (5: 20) Hawthorne adds another, this time of a "respectable-looking woman, well-advanced in life . . . decidedly New Englandish in figure and manners" who offers "evidences of her indubitable claim to the site on which Castle-street, the Town Hall, the Exchange, and all the principle business part of Liverpool, have long been situated" (5: 20). Such fantasies of aristocratic and English lineage are common enough among many Americans, Hawthorne opines, and yet, offering what may be a précis for the now-abandoned romances, he supposes that "even absurdity has its rights, when, as in this case, it has absorbed a human being's entire nature and purposes" (5: 17). Better, Hawthorne imagines, that the queen had never acknowledged receipt of the first claimant's tribute. "I submit to Mr. Secretary Seward," Hawthorne offers, wryly, "that he ought to make diplomatic remonstrances to the British ministry, and require them to take such order that the Queen shall not any longer bewilder the wits of our poor compatriots by responding to their epistles and thanking them for their photographs" (5: 18). England, Hawthorne imagines, can become for Americans a kind of madness—it bewilders one's wits. Under the nurturance of an American imagination, it becomes an absurdity, but one that can absorb a human being's entire nature and purpose.

There is, Hawthorne decides, among many Americans "still an unspeakable yearning toward England":

> When our forefathers left the old home, they pulled up many of their roots, but trailed along with them others, which were never snapt asunder by the tug of such a lengthening distance, nor have been torn out of the original soil by the violence of subsequent struggles, nor severed by the edge of the sword. Even so late as these days, they remain entangled with our heartstrings, and might often have influenced our national cause like the tiller-ropes of a ship, if the rough gripe of England had been capable of managing so sensitive a kind of machinery. (5: 18–19)

Stretched taut across the Atlantic, Anglo-American roots constitute an oceanic pathway, spliced with the heartstrings of Americans venturing in a latitudinal search for home. In his unfinished manuscript for *The Ancestral Footstep*, Hawthorne's protagonist, Middleton, discerns in England "a thread, to which the thread that he had so long held in his hand—the hereditary thread, that ancestor after ancestor had handed down—might seem ready to join in. He felt as if they were the two points of an electric chain, which being joined, an instantaneous effect must follow" (12: 8). The broken thread or electric chain of heredity Middleton is unable to splice—something like the dormant transatlantic telegraphic cable that, after having carried messages of jubilation and goodwill for a few tantalizing weeks in the late summer of 1858, suddenly malfunctioned at the North Atlantic depths, where it would lay silent throughout the war—remains enticingly if barely connected in *Our Old Home*. There, hereditary threads also make up a kind of "machinery," a marionette device or form of rigging through which, Hawthorne imagines, a more canny England might exercise influence over "our national cause." Certainly the romances Hawthorne attempted after his return to America present the claim to Englishness as an effect of self-deception or even outright conspiracy: of these, only in *Septimius Felton* does the American protagonist discover that he is actually, rightfully, English. How could such popular fantasies of aristocratic lineage not but tamper with the republican sensibilities of American parvenus venturing back to the mother country?

Again, Hawthorne is perhaps the most susceptible to the hallucination he derides. Unable to draw home from England the romance he had envisioned, he instead seems to export the terms of his American preoccupations literally into England itself. Middleton, himself a former congressman who has abandoned America in disgust "with the fierceness of political contests in our country," and now investigating the familial mystery that has drawn him across the Atlantic, discovers it to consist of "dissension and bloodshed between the sons of one household," a house as violently divided as the Washington he has quitted (12: 51, 29). Middleton's ancestors, as Hawthorne has it in his nearly free-associative manuscript, are usually New Englanders, but at other moments Hawthorne rethinks the possibilities: perhaps they had "emigrated to New England with the Pilgrims; or perhaps, at a still earlier date, to Virginia with Raleigh's colonists," he supposes (12: 49).

Whatever Middleton's more recent geographical affiliations, the important thing for Hawthorne is that his ancestral English past activate his present antipathies. "Many footsteps," Middleton explains to the present occupant of the manor he would claim—a man to whom he also refers as his "hereditary foe" (12: 45)—"the track of which is lost in England, might be found reappearing on the other side of the Atlantic; aye, though it be hundreds of years since the track were lost here" (12: 66). And though Hawthorne makes it clear throughout the manuscript that no good can come of the claimant's meddling in the familial past, the draw of affiliation is simply too inexorable for Middleton to resist placing his own foot in the bloody impression. "What have you to do here?" demands Alice, the Englishwoman whom Hawthorne envisions as Middleton's potential savior. "Your lot is in another land. You have seen the birthplace of your forefathers, and have gratified your natural yearning for it; now return, and cast your lot with your own people, let it be what it will." Alice understands, more than anyone else in the manuscript, that Middleton's compulsion to claim an English past has everything to do with his dissatisfactions with his homeland. "I fully believe," she insists, "that it is such a lot as the world has never yet seen, and that the faults, the weaknesses, the errors of your countrymen will vanish away, like morning-mists before the rising sun" (12: 56).

Here it is not the English who manipulate that machinery of which *Our Old Home* speaks; Americans affiliate or disaffiliate with England, Alice understands, as a way of negotiating their own national and cisatlantic situation. But they hardly ever experience it that way. When Middleton actually steps within his ancestral home, his initial experience is of the same sort that conditions Hawthorne's in the consular office, the sensation "of being in one dream, and recognizing the scenery and events of a former dream" (12: 27). The house divided to which Middleton now returns—that site of hereditary violence from which once ventured that "emigrant" Hawthorne describes in "The Custom-House" as "the original Briton, the earliest emigrant of my name" (1: 8)—remains, finally, wrested from English hands but unclaimed by the American's. All that is left in the end is the bloody footprint on the threshold, a stain resembling the evidence of that original Briton who, as "The Custom-House" explains, has also left the mark of blood upon Hawthorne himself (1: 9).

2. America's England

Hawthorne preoccupies me at this opening moment not only because his accounts of his own and of others' removals to England are so thoroughly conditioned by his mindfulness of the sectional crisis in America and its implications for a certain kind of vagabond transatlantic personality. I also take Hawthorne's conflictedness over England as an exemplary case because it has been the focus of many of his best readers, scholars who understand Hawthorne's ambivalence over the mother country to portend something essential for America, but who tend to isolate that ambivalence from the disintegration of the federal Union of which, after all, Hawthorne was an esteemed governmental representative as well as a citizen. This trend reaches back to Henry James, who critiques what he calls "the weak side of Hawthorne's work—his constant mistrust and suspicion of the society that surrounded him [in England], his exaggerated, painful, morbid national consciousness," but who has little to say of the crisis of the Union except that the war itself was for Hawthorne "not a propitious time for cultivating the Muse."[8] In his condescending assessment of Hawthorne as the type of American "addicted to the belief that the other nations of the earth are in a conspiracy to undervalue" him, who looked "at all things, during his residence in Europe, from the standpoint of that little clod of Western earth which he carried about with him as the good Mohammedan carries the strip of carpet on which he kneels down to face toward Mecca," James inaugurated a view that has since developed in less supercilious ways.[9]

Most illustrative here is Frederick Newberry, whose classic treatment of Hawthorne's relationship with England describes Hawthorne as "intensely aware of how New England Puritans disinherited themselves from the cultural tradition of the mother country," a disavowal which, Newberry argues compellingly, Hawthorne essentially romanced throughout his career.[10] In some ways like Laura Doyle—who has more recently found in *The Scarlet Letter* an account of North American nativity narrated so as to erase the violence of British colonization[11]—Newberry understands Hawthorne's historical meditations as simultaneously trained upon an English past and arrested in consideration of what abandonment of that past entails. For Newberry, the Puritans' expulsion of a monarchical, Anglican cultural influence constitutes what Hawthorne regarded as an historical process extending well beyond the Puritans (indeed, the decapitation of Charles I in 1649, as Doyle and Larry Reynolds point out, is in "The Custom-House" made to resonate with Hawthorne's own 1849 figurative decapitation by the Whigs),[12] and the consequences of that expulsion—including a gradual intensification of an iconoclastic strain in American cultural life—both deny America its inheritance and provide for "secular redemption" in the establishment of representative democracy.[13] And so Hawthorne laments the loss and theorizes the redemption, leading Newberry to read Hawthorne's English notebooks, as well as *Our Old Home*, as expressive of his desire "to settle his lifelong tension between political allegiance to America and aesthetic loyalty to England."[14]

Newberry's is obviously a masterful reading, but it bears pointing out that the phrase "political allegiance to America" can have a vacuous ring to it in the late 1850s, as Hawthorne was compiling his English notebooks, and certainly during the early 1860s, as he was arranging the materials of *Our Old Home*. Long prior to that period of national disbanding, political allegiance to America may have meant, as for Washington Irving during his own political appointment in England, a broadly conceived preference for republican institutions over the constitutional monarchy to which Britain had evolved well before American independence. In Irving's sketchbook of 1820, that sort of political allegiance can lead him to chide the English for their superior airs in nearly the same breath as he hails the United States as "one of the greatest political experiments in the history of the world," and, unbelievably, "a society where there are no artificial distinctions."[15] Even when Hawthorne complains about the English, he never allows himself quite the sort of complacency in which Irving can indulge, but then, how could he? By 1863, such invocations of America as a society that brooked no artificial distinctions would have been, at least, more complicated; and what Irving calls one of the greatest political experiments in world history was as of the publication of *Our Old Home* yielding up the horrific violence of Shiloh, Antietam, Gettysburg. As attentive as Newberry's study of Hawthorne's relationship with England may be, even he doesn't quite capture its ambivalence, because he abstracts from that relationship the pressures of sectional crisis and national dissolution.

Perhaps an apparent polarity between the sectional and the transnational informs a broader tendency in the field over the past decade or so. Transatlanticism draws to a nexus a multiplicity of traditions, constituting a frame of reference that disperses the explanatory power of formerly salient national categories. Within this more fluid scope, U.S. sectionalism and the Civil War to which it led seem less centrifugal than for prior generations of Americanist scholars who were more inclined to situate the history of American literary production along cisatlantic trajectories. Paul Gilroy, for instance, is interested in the Civil War only as it opened the possibility of a multiracial United States for black intellectuals of the 1860s.[16] Though Amanda Claybaugh takes as her subject a group of Anglo-American social reformers virtually all of whom stood in some relation to antislavery campaigners of the United States and Britain, her purpose is not to configure this network of reformers in relation either to proslavery rhetoric or to sectionalist discourse.[17] Doyle, in *Freedom's Empire*, is spellbinding on the subject of slavery within the larger sweep of racialized freedom her book investigates, but she does not include in her investigation the various and explicitly Atlantic theories of race or freedom that northern and southern sectionalists hurled at one another over the course of the 1840s, '50s, and early '60s. Or perhaps the problem is that sectionalism is *too* centrifugal a force. It may be that sectionalism has seemed external to the transatlantic frames of reference that have redefined the field over the past two decades because sectionalism appears so clearly a stateside issue, so obviously a domestic preoccupation between 1820 and 1865, so patently a lynchpin of the very cisatlantic accounts of antebellum nationhood beyond which transatlantic scholarship has challenged us to think.

In *Atlantic Republic*, Paul Giles presents the Civil War as a massive overdetermination, a blockage impeding Americanists from imagining those decades in other, less nationally bound ways. "The territorial instability that characterized the United States in the 1840s has often been overlooked by American scholars, who have chosen instead to concentrate on the country's own Civil War of the 1860s," he explains, before describing that pattern as "an indirect way of asserting the primacy of traditional American ideals of federal unity and freedom." In allowing the Civil War to eclipse the war with Mexico or the conflict with Britain over the Northwest, Giles complains, too many Americanists reify the national boundaries upon whose fluidity those prior disputes turned, and in this way obscure the degree to which those conflicts "raised the distinct possibility of the geography of the United States being organized quite differently from the 'sea to shining sea' model that later became established."[18]

The Civil War, Giles would remind us, was among a series of nationally formative geopolitical struggles unfolding during the period we nevertheless decide to call antebellum, events we submit to a collective amnesia in a tendency to imagine the period as if always hurtling toward Fort Sumter. Another way to get at the problem Giles broaches here is to say that, abstracted from the nation-building conflicts of the 1840s, the Civil War appears as an "internecine struggle," a domestic crisis wherein, since both warring sides defined themselves as American, the controlling terms are also imagined as if quarantined from internationally circulating concerns. This is what it means, truly, to foreground the Civil War and its buildup as "an indirect way of asserting the primacy of traditional American ideals of federal unity and freedom," since the foreclosure of foreign influence entailed in such foregrounding of the sectional crisis tends to heighten rather than challenge a widely held sense that the United States has always in some divinely appointed way stood apart. One might add to Giles's list of undertreated 1840s international crises the observation that Americanist scholars of the Civil War era have found little of interest in the fact that during the third year of the secession, two major European powers, France and Britain, invaded and occupied almost half of Mexico. This was an act that flouted the so-called Monroe Doctrine, which the European powers since the 1820s had actually honored in measurable ways. Yet such events have simply not registered for antebellum literary historians. Possibly this neglect is legible as what Giles describes as a compulsive return to the Civil War, a persistent myopia among antebellum scholars concerning events and texts that do not seem readily incorporable into the narrative of sectional crisis and racial polarity this compulsive return has entailed.

It may be that this book is guilty of the same incessant return to the house divided against itself. But while my subject is situated within the sectional crisis and Civil War, my interest in this period concerns precisely that dimension most suited to dislodge study of the antebellum period from the theorems of national isolation and unity against which Giles lodges his true complaint. In taking up the Civil War and the period of sectional strife that led to it as almost continuously embedded in a series of struggles over Englishness, I depict the conflict over sectional preeminence as it was articulated through terms that bound the United States to a larger and more complex North Atlantic entity. The sectional crisis was not *simply* codified as an internecine struggle by antebellum Americans, who tended to speak of it in transnational ways. To be sure, the English formations at play in the processes through which northerners and southerners reimagined their differences bear a resemblance to what Giles has called, in a more recent work, objects of "virtual focus" in that they assume a shape and texture "as if the observer were seeing native landscapes refracted or inverted in a foreign mirror"[19]—hence Middleton's sensation, upon stepping into the ancestral manor to which he imagines himself claimant, "of being in one dream, and recognizing the scenery and events of a former dream" (12: 27). And yet, though such refractions of the English represented tautologically, serving sheerly American ideological objectives even when they most claimed for themselves a sort of cosmopolitan consciousness, observing their circulation within sectional discourses of the era helps us to see these decades in terms apart from other narratives of antebellum U.S. nationalism that have emphasized westward expansion, manifest destiny, or an insular Monroe Doctrine as the dominant tropes of U.S. nationhood.

In its larger curve, *America's England* examines the rhetorical and conceptual uses to which sectional partisans in the United States put England, and presents those multiple uses in terms of an imagined ethnic past, a conflation of English and American space, and fraught engagements with a contemporaneous England brought suddenly closer through technological and economic development. The opening arc of this curve, encompassed in chapters 1 and 2, describes the draw toward Englishness felt in both North and South, where a compulsion to identify with England intensified as the sectional crisis deepened, and where northern and southern partisans tended to refract through English culture, character, and history their own positionalities within the national ordeal. The northern and southern spokespeople I examine in chapter 1 claimed narrowly configured categories of Englishness as their own biological inheritance, delineating categories of English lineage outfitted to provide hereditary and historical coordinates by which to plot the crisis between the states along longer curves than those provided by the national politics of the era. In particular, the period generated competing accounts of the Norman Conquest, the aftermath of which was imagined by many Americans to pit ruthless Norman conquerors against vanquished Saxon subjects, both of whose descendants had renewed the age-old conflict on the North American continent. In the move to redescribe their own national tensions as the expression of ethnic struggles afflicting England since the Norman Conquest, northern and southern racial theorists and public intellectuals not only conscripted particular renditions of English history into their considerations of contemporaneous American struggles; they often foregrounded their refined notions of English lineage as the engine of those struggles, rendering political concerns over the expansion of slavery into the territories, the rights of fugitive slaves, or the meanings of particular articles of the Constitution merely topical, subordinate to the underlying ethnic mechanisms of national dissolution.[20] Emerson, I argue, both participated in such rhetorics and, in his 1856 *English Traits*, attempted to deconstruct the racial partitions they entailed by reconceiving England—and by proxy the antebellum United States—as a study in ameliorative racial genealogy.

On the other hand, in chapter 2 I examine alternate American appropriations of the Norman Conquest as an historical precursor to southern modes of domination over African-American slaves. Through the 1840s and '50s, repeated analogies between twelfth-, thirteenth-, and fourteenth-century Saxon serfs and nineteenth-century American slaves configured much more specific polemics over the very political struggles often eclipsed by white sectionalists who tended to view themselves as latter-day Normans or Saxons. Even as many northern and southern public intellectuals pitched readings of ancient English history as a template for understanding contemporaneous antagonisms between North and South as the fruit of biological descent, others—including Frederick Douglass, Lydia Maria Child, and the historical romancer Henry Herbert—attended to the same periods of English history in order to generate sympathy for Saxons enslaved under the Conquest, thus augmenting abolitionist discourses over the evils of U.S. slavery. Under such renditions, the lessons of English history not only served a broad polemic against slavery itself, but also honed expressions of dissent over the fugitive slave law as a violation of habeas corpus and the right of jury trial for captured slaves—rightful inheritors, in Wendell Phillips's phrase, of the "old Saxon privilege" of due process.[21]

To some extent, these transatlantic reconceptualizations of sectional antagonism polarized the imagined ethnic and cultural bases of the American polity, undermining the notion that white citizens of the United States formed a unified biological community from which African-American slaves stood absolutely apart. But in still other ways, a continued reference to English historical, cultural, and political formations allowed antebellum public intellectuals and authors to configure an era of developing national acrimony along longer historical trajectories that situated domestic controversies at transatlantic remove. Such antebellum efforts to understand the political turmoil of the American present through recourse to an imagined English past conditioned a widespread capitulation, over the first half of the century, to English landscape aesthetics, both as formulated by first-generation eighteenth-century picturesque theorists such as William Gilpin and Uvedale Price and by nineteenth-century adherents to the picturesque mode in the United States. In their broad tendency to view American geographies through English standards of natural beauty, northern and southern appreciators of landscape resembled one another: a nearly wholesale reimagination of the New England landscape as a form of English countryside was mirrored, from the 1820s through the 1850s, by a similar rendering of southern lands from the Chesapeake Valley through the Old Dominion and still southward. But the epistemological and political ramifications extending from such engagements with the picturesque varied considerably by section. In chapter 3, I draw out one such set of implications by turning again to Emerson, whose 1836 *Nature* percolates views on natural variety forming in part out of Emerson's concern over his national culture's enthrallment with English ways of looking at the natural world. The picturesque conditioned Emerson's sense of the transcendent unity of nature, especially in its emphasized phenomenology of the grand sweep and an otherwise unified natural world, and in this way—for Emerson and for others—it intimated a continuum between aesthetically and politically divided lands.

In chapter 4, I continue to study the influence of the English picturesque upon the U.S. antebellum scene by turning to the aesthetic's influence upon artists and writers in the upper South. In particular, the picturesque presented a dialectic between distance and propinquity, a point of emphasis that helps to generate a conflicted sense of southern aura permeating John Pendleton Kennedy's 1832 *Swallow Barn*, a book whose sunny views of plantation life are finally unsettled by the very picturesque energies it channels. For both Emerson and for Kennedy, the picturesque carried far-reaching ramifications for the phenomenologies of natural perception rooting both *Nature* and *Swallow Barn*, even if these works have come to stand, respectively, for regional literary modes relatively unconversant with one another. But in *Swallow Barn*, the picturesque impels Kennedy toward an ontology of racial difference that unsettles the habit of rendition through which natural space in the United States was being reimagined as English land, even as this unsettling contributes to a further loosening of Kennedy's commitment to slavery as a social system.

Distance and propinquity enter into a different sort of negotiation in my final pair of chapters, which take up U.S. sectional engagements with a contemporaneous Britain brought suddenly near through the advent of subaqueous telegraphic technology and increasingly globalized free-market economic structures. The controversy surrounding South Carolina congressman Preston Brooks's assault on Massachusetts senator Charles Sumner in 1856, I argue in chapter 5, became implicated in the public mind with further debates occasioned by the laying of transatlantic cable between the United States and Britain. Even as the assault called upon more broadly circulating equations between oration and public violence, it drew the body of an abolitionist, northeastern politician into relation with a set of anxieties emerging over the prospect of telegraphic communication with Britain: for instance, the contraction of international distance for which telegraphy was in other quarters celebrated. Sumner had come to represent a style of information delivery increasingly associated not only with telegraphy but also, for southern members of the U.S. Senate particularly, the circulation of "rumor and speculation" through which telegraphically expressive northern merchants threatened to dispossess southern planters. All of this, I argue, compressed in the Sumner assault a spectacle of anxieties over transatlantic telecommunication coupled with sectional grievances over the cotton trade with England. And the cotton trade itself, I argue in chapter 6, prompted public intellectuals such as Henry Timrod and Emerson to articulate their own prophesies for globalized trade as either providing future space for Confederate slavery or virtually guaranteeing its end. While free-trade leaders in England imagined dilating global markets as a broadening of international cooperation and diplomacy, commentators across both the southern and northern U.S. discerned in the mechanisms of free trade the outline of a British policy of support for a southern secession. In the South, such prophesies brought prior assertions of an alignment with England to a pitch; but in the North, many observers turned upon England in ways that presaged similar revocations of esteem in the South in 1863, after which the British policy of neutrality appeared to most Americans to have become permanent.

This broad reversal of attitudes toward England, I suggest in my conclusion, charts an abiding cycle in a certain U.S. psychology where England is concerned, a perennial demand followed an equally recurrent disavowal. Looming in the backdrop of the sectional conflict was the question of whether England was prepared to lend not only salient rhetoric but also economic support to the abolition of slavery in the United States; after the outbreak of hostilities, for that matter, the question of whether Britain would extend diplomatic recognition to the Confederacy long remained open. Over the course of this latter irresolution, especially, it would be a strain to describe American attitudes toward the English, either on the North or the South, as an expression of deference or of Anglophilia.[22] "The truth is," Hawthorne wrote to Ticknor in October 1855, "I love England so much that I want to annex it."[23] But by the time he gave up his abortive English romance, Hawthorne wrote him again, now proclaiming "I HATE England."[24] It was a recall of affection Hawthorne shared with Emerson, who had lauded England, in *English Traits* (1856), as "the land of patriots, martyrs, sages, and bards," the progenitor of "original right which make the stone tables of liberty,"[25] only then to urge his audiences of 1863: "Put down your foot, and say to England . . . We have seen through you. Henceforth, you have lost the benefit of the old veneration which shut our eyes to the altered facts."[26] This reversal of a prior tendency to adulate resolves the long-standing habit of thought by which northern and southern spokespeople in the United States had reconcocted their own politics through recourse to a set of purportedly English formations, now seeming to hate England precisely for having adored it so.

Beholding what appeared as the apocalypse of the American Republic from their own patrician distance, many English commentators would, as Emerson declaimed, express a kind of delight. "When the occasion of magnanimity arrived," he railed, "you had none: you forgot your loud professions, you rubbed your hands with indecent joy, and saw only in our extreme danger the chance of humbling a rival and getting away his commerce."[27] Other English witnesses to the war would regret what they saw as the waning of a de facto English state, the self-immolation of "a nation gifted with [England's] own courage, intelligence, and enterprise, an imperishable population, however divided or subdivided, or however ruled, possessing her arts, her morals, her literature, and her religion,"[28] a nation whose "roots," in one English journalist's Hawthornian expression, "grow beneath the Atlantic."[29] But this book is not about England. By reconfiguring American bloodlines, geographies, and political economies in ways suggested by further renditions of English example, the thinkers I examine reimagined their national community at a time when the polity at hand seemed irreparably fractured. Resituated at the intersections of various American and English topoi, the sectional conflict assumed a coherence for many of the figures I examine in the pages to follow, and in the process reversed the more famously westward gaze of American nationality back along the path of its oceanic roots—yearningly fixed, as Hawthorne would say, upon the farther shores of the Atlantic rim.

Transatlantic Bloodlines and English Traits

1. The Blood of an Englishman

In the third volume of his *Vicissitudes of Families*, published in 1863, the London genealogist John Bernard Burke reminisced over an American vogue for British pedigree in full swing during the decade prior to the outbreak of the American Civil War. Burke recalled that during those years, "the most intelligent and zealous of my genealogical clients were from the other side of the Atlantic, all yearning to carry back their ancestry to the fatherland, and to connect themselves in some way with historical associations."[1] Placing Massachusetts and particularly Boston as having been "more genealogical" than either Yorkshire or London, Burke also recalls "that a very large sum was given at New York or Washington—I forget which—for the purchase of a perfect series of our English county histories, as the best sources of American genealogy."[2] Burke's remembrance reveals much about the fluctuating cultural capital through which transatlantic genealogists and their clients transacted business during the 1840s and '50s. While complimentary of his American clientele as "intelligent and zealous" in their drive to situate themselves within an English lineage, Burke also jabs these intelligent and zealous clients for their provinciality, as registered in his own (provincial) inability or disinclination to distinguish New York from Washington ("I forget which") and in his mention of the "yearning" that marked these clients' aspiration to Anglicize themselves by hook or by crook, "in some way." It is their de facto provinciality that might produce Burke's clients' wish to claim English peerage, but that also renders droll their longing to connect or concoct "historical associations" betwixt themselves and some stratum of Englishness.

An 1856 reviewer of the ten-volume *New England Historical and Genealogical Register* at first seems to sneer at the growing appetite for English genealogy as un-American and un-democratic: "What, in this land of equality, where every man is as good as every other, can it be possible that any man believes his ancestors to have been greater and better than himself and his friends?"[3] But while imagining that "the subject of pedigree" rankles some irreducible republican bent among Americans, the reviewer also attempts to rationalize the vogue for "historical associations" upon which transatlantic genealogists like Burke built their careers; after all, "there is but little danger in acknowledging our taste for the noble and gentle science of heraldry and genealogy" since "no man ever rejoices in the fact that his grandfather made his exit with a hempen collar upon his neck."[4] Like Burke, the reviewer notes "the number of family records, or genealogical monographs, now extant in print, is much larger in America than in aristocratic England" even as he remarks, "How many there are, who have always classed genealogy and heraldry among the most senseless and offensive exhibitions of feudal pride! But since sober and practical America is the largest present producer, there must be in these documents some hidden elements of interest. . . ."[5] During the late 1840s and especially the 1850s, American genealogies tracing family names back to English ancestry mushroomed: the writer for the *North American Review*, for example, lists ninety-eight genealogies—"such of the genealogies that have appeared in print in this country as we have been able to discover"—published in the United States between 1816 and 1855, with seventy-one of these appearing after 1840.[6]

So Hawthorne did not need to go to Liverpool in order to encounter an American yearning for English reconnection, since a widespread effort to re-affiliate with English bloodlines underlay even less eccentric projects than those *Our Old Home* describes. At one level, as Hawthorne supposes, the burgeoning desire for English pedigree among many Americans of the 1840s and '50s would seem simply to register a heightening of American regard for England during the period. But it would be more accurate to notice in these decades a marked ambivalence in American attitudes toward England, and not simply for genealogists and their clientele. It is true that England exerted a fascination over many northeastern abolitionists who admired it not only for its opposition to slavery, but as worth emulating in some more essential sense. Abolitionists from England and indeed across Britain not only underwrote the political agendas of their American counterparts by offering financial support, eager audiences for British lecture tours, and a seasoned symbology; they also came to incarnate some fundamental rectitude—what Elisa Tamarkin calls "*Englishy* English"[7]—around which many abolitionists came to build an intense esteem. Such was the case, for instance, when Charles Sumner wrote to a friend, "In England, what is called society is better educated, more refined, and more civilized than what is called society in our country. You understand me to speak of society,—as society,—and not of individuals. I know persons in America who would be an ornament of any circle anywhere; but there is no class with us that will in the least degree compare with that vast circle which constitutes English society."[8] Thus Tamarkin points out, "The 1840s and 1850s are filled with rhapsodies on just how clever Britain is—it is Britain that has spread an 'intellectual empire' across the globe and that has, says Ralph Waldo Emerson, 'inoculated all nations with her civilization, intelligence and tastes.'"[9] Indeed, in his journal of 1850, Emerson recounts having confessed to Thoreau, "I like the English better than our people, just as I like merchants better than scholars; for, though on a lower platform, yet there is no cant, there is great directness, comprehension, health, and success. So with the English," while also recording, "My own quarrel with America, of course, is that the geography is sublime, but the men are not."[10]

Still, affinities between British and American abolitionists did not produce in America a larger, unqualified regard for Britain during the 1840s and '50s. Indeed, it would be just as true to say that the period witnessed a rising Anglophobia in the United States. Especially after the 1844 election of James Polk, with relations between the two nations straining over competing claims to the Oregon territory and with former president Jackson issuing public warnings about Britain's plan to encircle the United States within an "iron hoop" by recolonizing the continent through the southwest, England became for many Americans a detested adversary.[11] John O'Sullivan's famous coinage "manifest destiny," though it first appeared in an essay for the *Democratic Review* in 1839, gained currency only later in the context of the Oregon dispute, when O'Sullivan invoked America's "claim . . . by the right of our manifest destiny to overspread and to possess the whole of the continent which Providence has given us. . . ."[12] Even New England abolitionists' good opinion of England would ebb with the onset of the war and Parliament's declaration of neutrality, among other signs that in spite of its often stridently abolitionist tone, the empire remained practically uncommitted to the goal of emancipation for American slaves.

The variance in America's posture toward England during the 1840s and '50s is recapitulated in Emerson's conflictedness about England in *English Traits* (1856), and hence it makes sense to think of the book as one expression of the wider culture's wavering outlook on England. Other readers of Emerson, such as Richard Bridgman, Carl Hovde, and Julie Ellison, tend to view the book as Emerson's attempt to emphasize that "the *only* place for mankind's hope was on the American continent" by elaborating his own "fundamental skepticism about England's position of leadership, a skepticism enunciated at the height of her industrial and imperial power."[13] Indeed, this assessment has become the dominant response to *English Traits* over the past three decades (though Hovde also calls *English Traits* "perhaps the most ingratiating of Emerson's major works"[14]). The tendency to treat *English Traits* as denunciation rather than homage owes much to Robert Weisbuch's thesis that American writers throughout the nineteenth century experienced both the plenitude of English history and culture and the apparent newness of America as an impediment to their legitimacy as creative artists. Following Weisbuch's central claim "that the American writer begins from a defensive position and that the achievements of British literature and national life are the chief intimidations against which he, as American representative, defends himself,"[15] readers of *English Traits* have built a consensus that Emerson's purpose, especially when he seems to valorize, is actually to subvert, to double-cross. How else to square the passages of *English Traits* that gush over England—"the land of patriots, martyrs, sages, and bards"—with the Emerson who had once complained that England had "Shakspearized now for two hundred years"?[16] Weisbuch's reading of the Emerson of the 1850s places him on a continuum with the Emerson of the 1830s, as if to suggest that twenty years after his first Phi Beta Kappa address, Emerson still viewed England first of all as a cultural hegemon from under whose shadow American artists and intellectuals must struggle to emerge.

Even prior to Weisbuch, the most sustained study of *English Traits*, Philip Nicoloff's *Emerson on Race and History* (1961), anticipates later transatlantic studies by positioning the book as "one of the significant services Emerson performed in his lifelong battle to promote America's intellectual independence."[17] Though Nicoloff sees *English Traits* as "very much the product of a particular era of American national experience," as part of a national moment of "passage," for him this moment of passage grew out of "international controversy over America's present achievements and future expectations," and especially the question over "whether Americans could, in time, so free themselves from cultural bondage to England as to produce an independent flowering of their own" (11). Nicoloff acknowledges that the "particular era of American national experience" out of which *English Traits* emerged was also an era of national disintegration, but insists that the book was a vehicle through which Emerson attempted to disavow the sectional crisis in the United States—much the same way as Brenda Wineapple views Hawthorne's American Claimant manuscripts.[18] "The American political scene," Nicoloff explains of Emerson, "was growing more painful to him, and he now lay not so much in danger of being pulled from the world of thought into the world of affairs as of having public affairs so blight his search after the higher laws as to leave him without occupation" (23–24). Although Nicoloff acknowledges Emerson's preoccupation with the sectional crisis during the months he compiled *English Traits*, he regards this preoccupation as an obstacle, rather than an impetus, for his meditations on England.

It is true enough that *English Traits* begins with a chapter in which Emerson permits himself to dismiss Coleridge and Wordsworth as products of the Old World. Emerson finds Coleridge "old and preoccupied," a man who "could not bend to a new companion and think with him"; Wordsworth "made the impression of a narrow and very English mind; of one who paid for his rare elevation by general tameness and conformity" (*W* 5: 14, 24). At such moments, one might discern in Emerson umbrage toward the elevated reputation of English men of letters. But rather than some kind of subversion of England's perceived cultural supremacy—or even a kind of mental holiday abroad for Emerson, a way of disavowing the cisatlantic turmoil at home—*English Traits* appeared in the midst of other expressions of American interest in England enunciated during the 1840s and '50s, artifacts of a discourse that make it more interesting to discern the book in other ways, and indeed, that *English Traits* can help us to understand. By entwining itself with an account of British ethnicity developed first by American abolitionist intellectuals during the decade prior to the Civil War, *English Traits* engages a process, already underway among many northern and southern intellectuals of the same period, through which various portions of the white U.S. population became affiliated with specific and nominally racial categories of Englishness within the "father country" Burke found so many American clientele so eager to rejoin.

As I see it, reading *English Traits* within this context of deliberation over Anglo-American bloodlines tends to undercut the account according to which Emerson found the sectionalism of the late 1840s and '50s too painful to engage, or according to which America's chief interest in England was in overcoming her cultural productivity. But reading *English Traits* in this way also adds nuance to our conception of antebellum understandings of race, the complexity of which had everything to do with the desires animating many Americans to associate with and also distance themselves from various strata of Englishness. These understandings of race not only allowed Americans to transport themselves, genealogically, toward particular English bloodlines; they also engaged British discourses over race that had formed at a remove from the taxonomies—Caucasian, Negro, Indian, and so on—more familiarly at play in antebellum America. At the same time, however, British understandings of bloodline offered themselves up within the horizon of U.S. debates over racial politics that appeared, to many Americans, inherent in the sectional crisis, providing a schema to which American thinkers like Emerson could attach their own cisatlantic currency.

It bears mention that other readers have viewed *English Traits* as Emerson's attempt to think through the constitution of American character, in ways that reveal the book as only ostensibly cosmopolitan. Dana Phillips, for instance, explains that in *English Traits*, "Emerson's true subject is America and the racially determined American character."[19] So far as it goes, this line of argument intimates the solipsism of *English Traits*, the sense in which its examination of the English is ultimately geared toward the affirmation of a certain American bent Emerson imagines to find its roots in England. But at the same time, Emerson doesn't simply shore up this American character as essentially and unproblematically English. Rather, *English Traits* engages a larger project resembling what Werner Sollers calls the "process of ethnic dissociation" key to the formation of nationhood and in which literature obviously plays a crucial role (290). Part of this wider project of ethnic dissociation rests upon the use of British history as a kind of typology for the domestic situation unfolding in America at the mid-century, a typology we see especially at work in Emerson's depiction of the Norman Conquest as the primordial struggle between the two great ethnic strains of the English makeup—the Saxon and the Norman—whom *English Traits* casts as the progenitors of opposed political sensibilities. The political narrative *English Traits* offers interweaves what Emerson alternatively calls "character" or "temperament" with race in a way that is on the one hand typical of antebellum ethnology but which, on the other, is grounded in a broader transatlantic racial historiography underlying what genealogists like Burke saw as the "yearning" of his many clients, national and sectional agents who were determined to find in English history "the best sources of American genealogy." The book is embroiled, in other words, in a form of Atlantic sectionalism: rather than charting an escape from the cisatlantic conflict, Emerson understands questions about English constitution and character to have everything to do with questions concerning U.S. sectional strife. Understanding how that domestic context forms circumference for Emerson's longer understanding of English traits requires an account of how others of his era configured English history with regard to North/South relations in the United States, for this history of discourse also provides context for Emerson's earlier writings on England and New England prior to the second trip abroad *English Traits* documents.

2. Saxons and Normans, North and South

Race is, of course, everywhere in *English Traits*. In his gloss of British prehistory as a sequence of compromised or failed attempts to settle Britain by Celts, Goths, and Romans, Emerson explains, "The island was a prize for the best race" (*W* 5: 74), and finally extols the Saxons as those who "seriously settled in the land," providing the island with an ethnic and cultural bulwark against the Norman invasion of 1066. Emerson explains that a century after the Conquest,

> it came out that the Saxon had the most bottom and longevity, had managed to make the victor speak the language and accept the law and usage of the victim; forced the baron to dictate Saxon terms to Norman kings; and, step by step, got all the essential securities of civil liberty invented and confirmed. The genius of the race and the genius of the place conspired to this effect. . . . The power of the Saxon-Danes, so thoroughly beaten in the war that the name of English and villein were synonymous, yet so vivacious as to extort charters from the kings, stood on the strong personality of these people. (*W* 5: 75)

In some ways, Emerson's account of Saxon England as the birthplace of "all the essential securities of civil liberty" resonates with a much older form of ancient constitutionalism according to which the political achievements of representative democracy, and indeed of the U.S. Constitution itself, were already inherent in the Magna Carta of 1215. But in passages such as this, it is clear that Emerson has in mind not only the political legacy of English institutions, but more pressingly another form of constitution: the congenital temperament—his term, frequently, is "genius"—of the Saxon character. Having more "bottom and longevity" than other groups that settled or invaded England, Emerson's Saxons provided the basis for British "character," a term encompassing both the cultural and the biological skein of the island. Since "it is in the deep traits of race that the fortunes of nations are written" (*W* 5: 134), Emerson spends much time in *English Traits* elaborating the racial temperament of the Saxons. Although "formally conquered" by the Normans, the Saxons nevertheless achieved what Emerson describes as a form of biological counterconquest carried out under the auspices of the "elastic organization" of the Saxon's superior makeup, which could not but emerge from beneath the Normans' merely military victory:

> [I]t is in the deep traits of race that the fortunes of nations are written, and however derived,—whether a happier tribe or mixture of tribes, the air, or what circumstance that mixed for them the golden mean of temperament,— here exists the best stock in the world, broad-fronted, broad-bottomed, best for depth, range and equability; men of aplomb and reserves, great range and many moods, strong instincts, yet apt for culture; war-class as well as clerks; earls and tradesmen; wise minority, as well as foolish majority; abysmal temperament, hiding wells of wrath, and glooms on which no sunshine settles, alternated with a common sense and humanity which holds them fast to every piece of cheerful duty; making this temperament a sea to which all storms are superficial; a race to which their fortunes flow, as if they alone had the elastic organization at once fine and robust enough for dominions; as if the burly inexpressive, not mute and contumacious, now fierce and sharp-tongued dragons, which once made the island light with his fiery breath, had bequeathed his ferocity to his conqueror. They hide virtues under vices, or the semblance of them. (*W* 5: 134)

Other portions of *English Traits* lionize the Saxons as "the hands of mankind . . . [who] have a taste for toil, a distaste for pleasure or repose, and the telescopic appreciation of distant gain" (*W* 5: 76). Even in Emerson's contemporary England, "to set [the Saxon] at work and to begin to draw his monstrous values out of barren Britain, all dishonor, fret and barrier must be removed, and then his energies begin to play" (*W* 5: 76). But while Emerson's tendency in *English Traits* is to praise Saxons and their progeny for their work ethic, honesty, eloquence, ingenuity, and perseverance, the Normans come in for some of the most scathing invective found anywhere in Emerson's corpus, tirades approached in tone only in Emerson's later writings against the South in such lectures as "The Assault upon Mr. Sumner" (1856), "The Fugitive Slave Law" (1854), "American Civilization" (1862), and "The Emancipation Proclamation" (1863). Emerson describes the Norman conquerors as "greedy and ferocious dragoons, sons of greedy and ferocious pirates," barbarians who nearly destroyed everything worthy—that is, everything Saxon—about England:

> The Normans came out of France into England worse men than they went into it, one hundred and sixty years before. They had lost their own language, and learned the Romance or barbarous Latin of the Gauls; and had acquired, with the language, all the vices it had names for. The conquest has obtained in the chronicles, the name of the "memory of sorrow." Twenty thousand thieves landed at Hastings. These founders of the House of Lords were greedy and ferocious dragoons, sons of greedy and ferocious pirates. They were all alike, they took every thing they could carry, they burned, harried, violated, tortured, and killed, until every thing English was brought to the verge of ruin. Such, however, is the illusion of antiquity and wealth, that decent and dignified men now existing boast their descent from these filthy thieves, who showed a far juster conviction of their own merits, by assuming for their types the swine, goat, jackal, leopard, wolf, and snake, which they severally resembled. (W 5: 60–61)

For Emerson, the descendants of the "filthy thieves" who carried out the conquest of Saxon England, though now "decent and dignified men," are nevertheless at odds with the democratic political and social sensibilities of Saxon England (*English Traits* passes in silence the Saxons' brutal conquest and treatment of the Celts, it bears noticing). Here Emerson admits his contentions are without solid historical footing, since "[h]istory does not allow us to fix the limits of the application of these names with any accuracy." Nevertheless, "from the residence of a portion of these people in France, and from some effect of that powerful soil on their blood and manners, the Norman has come popularly to represent in England the aristocratic, and the Saxon the democratic principle" (W 5: 74). This political and temperamental opposition has shaped the democratic composition of American intellectual and political life within a larger and polarized North Atlantic, since "England tends to accumulate her liberals in America, and her conservatives at London" (W 5: 52). For Emerson, the most important residuum of the Norman conquest was to drive democracy-loving Saxons to the United States, making North America the repository of England's most egalitarian energies.

That said, we might ask: To what "popular" conceptions of Norman and Saxon "blood and manners" does Emerson refer in 1856? On the one hand, Emerson's valorization of the Saxons hearkens back to a revolutionary-era schema through which American colonists had configured the break with England as a return to Anglo-Saxon democracy.[20] But by the 1850s, nostalgia for Saxon civilization had taken a new resonance for Americans who saw themselves on the verge of a different moment of political dissolution. Six years prior to the publication of *English Traits*, but precisely within the period after Emerson's second voyage to England as he considered the volume, H. D. Kitchell's "The Anglo-Saxon Element in England and America" (1850) idealized Saxon inhabitants of England prior to the Norman conquest for "their native passion for absolute personal independence . . . the grand element which they contributed to modern civilization."[21] As would Emerson, Kitchell lauds the Saxon's passion for independence, a quality that made him a precursor to the similarly independent American New Englander: "Altogether," Kitchell explains, "the Saxon was your real savage Yankee, untamed, some fifteen centuries before his time" (108). In fact, Kitchell regarded the Norman conquest as an interregnum in a Saxon project of global uplift, since "[t]here was a great mission assigned to this race" and "it was reserved for this people to pour themselves down over the earth, to infuse their vigorous life and earnest character into the decaying nations" (104). In the United States, this infusion of Saxon life and character was carried out under the auspices of what Kitchell calls "*Saxon Puritanism*," "what God had been preparing to bring forth as the right seed wherewith to plant a new world" (111; emphasis original). In this way Kitchell rehearses the ancient constitutionalist argument according to which the American Revolution appears as a chapter of Saxon manifest destiny, figuring the northern colonists who carried it out (Kitchell is mute upon southerners such as Jefferson and Washington and the role they played in the Revolution) as latter-day Saxons themselves.

Kitchell's vision of Saxon "vigorous life and earnest character" as a form of global infusion, a tonic for "decaying nations," anticipates Emerson's similar metaphor from *English Traits*, according to which "England has inoculated all nations with her civilization, intelligence, and tastes" (*W* 5: 36). More resonant with Emerson's specification of purportedly Norman and Saxon political antipathy is Kitchell's depiction of the Normans as "a totally different people from the Saxons" and the progenitors of an "Absolute monarchy . . . which it took ages for the Saxon Commons to tame down into the constitutional monarchy of the present English system" (109). "[A]ll that is liberal and hopeful," Kitchell explains, anticipating Emerson, "even all that is tolerable, in the British condition and constitution, has been wrested inch by inch from the Norman crown and nobility from the Saxon commonalty" (109). But Kitchell also goes on to explain that "the contest is not yet ended" (109), since for him, the differences of "life and . . . character" dividing Normans from Saxons have formed the basis for divisions between inhabitants of the northern and southern United States from the seventeenth century onward:

> There was a wide difference of origin, purpose, and character between the first planters of our Southern States and the founders of New England—a difference which has perpetuated itself, and gives to this hour the tone to our northern and southern sentiment. The South was colonized very much as we

are now colonizing California. . . . [F]or a long period the ruling purpose of the southern colonial companies was traffic, gain, speculation, and the search for precious metals. How different from this was the high and holy purpose that peopled New England! And the same year that witnessed the approach of the May-Flower to the shore of New England, saw also the first slave-ship on its way to Virginia, with its cargo of human chattels, the first of a long succession of wretched bondmen! (116–17)

The transatlantic genealogies Kitchell charts—contrasting a southern mercantile class of colonists with northeastern Puritans animated by a more "high and holy purpose" than mere commercial benefit—duplicates the arguments of the first volume of George Bancroft's *History of the United States* (1834). Bancroft had valorized the New England Puritans as "the harbingers of revolution," "a class of men, as remarkable for their qualities and their influence on public happiness, as any which the human race has ever been diversified," energized by "a higher principle than that of the desire of gain."[22] Virginia, in contrast, was settled by "vagabond gentlemen and goldsmiths, who, in spite of the remonstrances of [John] Smith, gave a wrong direction to the industry of the colony," having "believed they had discovered grains of gold in the glittering earth, which abounded near Jamestown" (1: 148). Bancroft's *History* juxtaposes the northern and southern colonies along lines that anticipate Kitchell's, though for the latter historian, the "wide difference of . . . character between the first planters of our Southern States and the founders of New England" would eventually energize the sectional conflict. Moreover, this difference of character emerged not simply out of discrete regional cultures or imperial objectives but more saliently out of the heterogeneity of Norman and Saxon "stock." Put simply, as Kitchell explains, "They were not of the same race" (117).

Political disagreements between the abolitionist Northeast and the slaveholding South were ultimately biological in origin, for Kitchell. "The Saxon common people"—whom Kitchell considers the lifeblood of the Puritan project—"had no share in [the] movement" to colonize Virginia, which is more properly considered "a Norman colonization" (117). In the southern colonies, among the descendents of the Norman conquerors, "slavery found an early and congenial and permanent home," since such an institution would flourish among those possessed of "[t]he Norman pride, his scorn of labor, his high blood, despotic temper, and aristocratic temper":

The leading Virginia companies were of English nobility—the favorites and retainers of the Crown; and the colonists themselves were mainly of the same class—decayed noblemen—gentlemen adventurers—the aristocratic loungers in the courts of Elizabeth and James. The Saxon common people had no share in that movement. It was a Norman colonization. And this gave character and direction to the enterprise. . . . And these have prevailed to retain and cherish there the institution of slavery, long after the Saxon spirit in the East had thrown off the uncongenial appendage. And that spirit, as it more and more pervades our land, is fast undermining this alien institution. (117)

Slavery is thus for Kitchell "the dark spot on our fame," "the shame of our country, the fountain of misrule, confusion, and danger" insofar as it represents a kind of Norman beachhead in North America (116). Antithetical to the "great mission assigned" the Saxon race to usher a burgeoning of global democracy, American slavery reactivates an historic enmity between ancient opponents. The political controversy over slavery, however, is subordinate to Kitchell's ethnological contention that considers slavery uncongenial to Saxon "life and . . . character," which in any case "is fast undermining this alien institution" (117) in execution of the "great mission assigned" and presently advanced by the Saxon race.

Emerson's own tendency to view England as a conglomeration of "stocks" predated Kitchell's, as did his interest in depicting U.S. regional cultures as *some* form of English racial inheritance. In his New England Lectures of 1843, Emerson had spoken of a "New England race," an Anglo-Saxon bloodline conditioning "the more ideal character" prevalent in the New England states. Here Emerson presented the Puritan settlers of Massachusetts as "precisely the idealists of England, the most religious in a religious era."[23] The religious idealism of the Puritans was for Emerson the wellspring of New England social and political idealism. "The new is only the seed of the old," he explained. "What is this abolition, non-resistance, and temperance but the continuations of Puritanism" (*LL* 1: 12). In his second lecture of the series, he only hinted toward an invidious comparison with the South: "I hope New England will come to have its pride in being a nation of servants, and not like the planting states, a nation of the served" (*LL* 1: 34).[24]

A similar valorization of the New England Puritans would activate George P. Marsh's argument in his address entitled "The Goths in New-England," delivered at Middlebury College seven months after Emerson's New England lecture series. Marsh was a philologist just beginning a six-year tenure as U.S. representative for Vermont when he delivered his address, arguing that New England civilization formed as a result of an exodus from England of "Gothic" political liberals and revolutionaries. "It was the spirit of the Goth," Marsh suggested, "that guided the May-Flower across the trackless ocean; the blood of the Goth, that flowed at Bunker's Hill."[25] Though Marsh did not refer his account of the Gothic strains of English civilization to U.S. sectional contests, he configured his scheme as the engine of growing political tensions besetting Britain in 1843. "The restoration of the Stuarts having accomplished the total overthrow of British liberty, the mind of England slept" since Cromwell's execution, he stated before referring to "a strife between the aristocracy and the people" as "a struggle between the discordant elements of the English character."[26] As in Kitchell, Marsh's account displaces the political with a "conflict of principles" that in turn gathers infelicitous strains within "the English character," rendering ethnic what might otherwise be thought of as ideological, political, or economic discord.

Neither Emerson nor Marsh sharpen their racial contentions about New England in 1843 toward anything like the sectionally driven critique of Kitchell's 1850 manifesto. Certainly, in the 1843 lectures, Emerson's use of the word "race" seems in keeping with Lawrence Buell's assessment of the word's broader meaning for Emerson, a "casually elastic" term encompassing anything from national origin to regional or even religious affiliation and not necessarily biological makeup.[27] But by his 1852 lecture entitled "The Anglo-American," delivered at the approximate moment he was writing to his brother William that his notes on England were fast expanding to a book,[28] Emerson echoes Kitchell in now specifying "Anglo-Saxon" as "Saxon," a type he depicts as "nature's democrat," human civilization's standard-bearer for human rights:

> Rather, it is right to esteem without regard to geography this industrious liberty-loving Saxon wherever he works,—the Saxon, the colossus who bestrides the narrow Atlantic,—with one foot on England, and one on America,—at home on all land,—at home on all seas, asking no leave to be of any other,—formidable, conquering and to conquer, with his nervous and sufficient civilization weaponed already far beyond his present performing. At least I infer that the decided preference of the Saxon on the whole for civil liberty is the security of the modern world. He is healthy;—nature's democrat, nature's worker;—his instincts and tendencies, sound and right. (LL 1: 293)

Bestriding the narrow Atlantic, resolving the United States and England within one wider, English-speaking civilization, Emerson's Saxon not only arches that expanse but imbues it with tendencies toward "civil liberty." Further, the impending conflict between the North and the South now appears, as with Kitchell's treatment two years earlier, as the antagonism of opposing "principles" that alternately compose the "compound English race" and constitute "races" in themselves:

> Still a portion of both races come, and the old contest of feudalism and of democracy renews itself here on a new battlefield.
>
> That makes sometimes, and, at this moment, the vast interest of American history. Which principle, which branch of this compound English race is here (and now) to triumph? The liberty-loving, the thought-loving, the godly and grand British race, that have fought so many battles, and made so many songs, and created so many reverend laws and charters, and exhibited so much moral grandeur in private and poor men;—or, the England of

Kings and Lords; castles and primogeniture; enormous wealth and fierce exclusion? Which is to be planted here? It is wonderful with how much rancour and premeditation at this moment the fight is prepared. (*LL* 1: 293)

Emerson's sense that the sectional crisis was a continuation of age-old hostilities—indeed perhaps the decisive moment in a history of strife between two variants of English temperament—steeped the conflict in bloodline and ancestry. In his August 1 lecture of 1844, "Emancipation in the British West Indies," Emerson had made a similar gesture in proclaiming, "The genius of the Saxon race, friendly to liberty; the enterprise, the very muscular vigor of this nation, are inconsistent with slavery" (*W* 11: 147). This was a maneuver akin to Kitchell's assessment of the Saxon and Norman biological roots beneath the "differences . . . of character" dividing North from South. It was, moreover, a conception that would enjoy a wider currency on both sides of the Mason-Dixon.

3. From the Norman Conquest to the Confederacy

In depicting Normans and Saxons as antagonistic racial groups, Emerson and Kitchell enjoined a trend exemplified in various English histories published within a decade of *English Traits*. Thomas Babington Macaulay's first volume of *The History of England* (1848), indeed, represented the division between Saxon and Norman in comparison to the color line in America. "The Battle of Hastings, and the events that followed it," he wrote, "not only placed a Duke of Normandy on the English throne, but gave up the whole population of England to the tyranny of the Norman race."[29] Pointing out that "[t]he Conqueror and his descendants to the fourth generation were not Englishmen [since] most of them were born in France," Macaulay reports that "[o]ne of the ablest among [the Normans] indeed attempted to win the hearts of his English subjects by espousing an English princess. But, by many of his barons, this marriage was regarded as a marriage between a white planter and a quadroon girl would now be regarded in Virginia" (11). Six years after Macaulay went to press, H. E. Garland would reiterate the *History*'s analogy between Norman rule of the Saxons and the South's domination of African slaves—or rather, depict both forms of mastery as part of the same historical continuum— explaining that in England, "[t]he Norman was the master, the Saxon was the slave—a constant apprehension of revolt and revenge filled the mind of the one—while a spirit of hatred and a thirst for retaliation filled the bosom of the other." Though eventually "all traces of two distinct and hostile people were lost in the common appellation of Englishmen," Garland also points out that "[t]wo hundred years ago and for a century afterward, the continuous act done was the importation of Negro slaves into the North American colonies by the British government."[30]

In the year following Macaulay's *History*, John Mitchell Kemble published *The Saxons in England: A History of the English Commonwealth till the Period of the Norman Conquest*. Kemble was the first modern editor of *Beowulf*, a revolutionary who in 1830 joined an expedition to overthrow the regime of Ferdinand VII of Spain, and a renowned Anglo-Saxonist who collected the texts of the entire corpus of Anglo-Saxon charters, published as the *Codex Diplomaticus Ævi Saxonici* (6 vols., 1839–48). *The Saxons in England* lauded a Saxon predilection for civil liberty (codified in the Magna Carta) as the basis for England's Victorian stability, while elsewhere in Europe

> thrones totter, and the deep foundations of society are convulsed. Shot and swell sweep the streets of capitals which have long been pointed out as the chosen abode of order. . . . Yet the exalted lady who wields the scepter of these realms, sits safe upon her throne, and fearless in the holy circle of her domestic happiness, secure in the affections of a people whose domestic institutions have given to them all the blessings of an equal law.[31]

In his journal early in 1851 (close to his most impassioned entries concerning the Fugitive Slave Law), Emerson quoted approvingly from *The Saxons in England*: "A nation never falls until the citadel of its moral being has been betrayed and becomes untenable" (*J* 8: 205).

None of this is to say that the intellectual history of the period reveals a consistently Saxonist bent. Rather, works such as Kitchell's, Macaulay's, and Kemble's appeared within a context of deliberation over the constitutions of Saxons and Normans. George L. Craik and Charles MacFarlane's *Pictorial History of England* (4 vols., 1841–44), for instance, had lauded the Normans as more decorous and delicate than their Saxon subjects, who

> were a people of large and gross appetite, who spent the chief part of the day at feasts, in which excess was considered to compensate for elegance; while their thirst was at least commensurate with their hunger; so that drunkenness had become their national reproach. The Normans, on the other hand, notwithstanding their Danish descent, appear to have, in a great degree, renounced the coarse habits of their ancestors; so that at their arrival in England, their moderation and refinement in eating and drinking, distinguished them from the natives.[32]

Similarly, the Scottish genealogist Robert Knox's *The Races of Men: A Philosophical Enquiry into the Influence of Race over the Destinies of Nations* (1850) depicted the Saxons as having never progressed beyond a state of barbarism before being vanquished by their racially superior Norman conquerors. The first large section of *The Races of Men* took up "the history of the Saxon or Scandinavian race" as an instantiation of Knox's thesis that "human character, individual and national, is traceable to the nature of that race to which the individual or nation belongs."[33] Unlike Macaulay and Kemble, who valorized the Saxons against their Norman conquerors, and certainly unlike Kitchell, who looked to Saxons "to pour themselves down over the earth, to infuse their vigorous life and earnest character into the decaying nations," Knox depicted the Saxons as a shiftless, congenitally doomed people. "What the race had been doing since the beginning of time it is impossible to say," he writes, "but being without inventive genius, I do not see how they could originate any but the lowest forms of civilization, such as I have seen in Southern Africa amongst the Dutch, that is, Saxon, Boors, and such as I have heard prevails in 'the far west'" (61–62).

In the United States, such thinking found purchase among a series of southern statesmen with varying degrees of investment in figuring the Normans' supremacy over the Saxons. In his 1852 address at the opening of the Richmond Atheneum, at about the moment Emerson was calling the Saxon race the best hope for "the security of the modern world," the Reverend John Robertson spoke of "the piratical Saxons" as "mere barbarians" whose "ignorance" had made the Norman Conquest inevitable.[34] By the early years of the Civil War, a discourse over the ethnic supremacy of the Normans over the Saxons had evolved to a form of propaganda serving an emergent Confederate national and racial mythos. Between June 1860 and August 1863, a number of prominent southern magazines ran articles by a series of writers describing the political rift between North and South as the product of a more profound biological division, what William Archer Cocke described as "the radical and irreconcilable difference" dividing North from South, Puritan from Cavalier.[35] The idea that southern Confederates were not simply at ideological logger-heads with northeastern abolitionists but in fact constituted a discrete bio-logical lineage was built on an account of English history structurally similar to Kitchell's, though for the later Confederate racial theorists, "Saxon blood" constituted the degenerate strain in England's ethnological makeup. For instance, the author of an 1861 *De Bow's* essay entitled "The Conflict of Northern and Southern Races" described "an original antagonism existing between the North and the South, as a necessary sequence of their radical difference in race, ever active and growing, and which has resulted in the complete disruption of every tie which ever bound them together," and went on to locate the origins of this racial antagonism in the rift between Norman and Saxon.[36] Explaining that "[t]he Athenian and the Spartan were not more unlike than the Saxon and the Norman" (393), the author reasons that "[o]ne of these elements, the Saxon, sought the rigid climate of New England, and the other, the Norman, the genial and sunny South, as the proper spheres for their peculiar manifestations" (393).

Other southern commentaries honed this revision of Kitchell's racial and sectional thesis. In "The Differences of Race Between the Northern and Southern People," William Falconer of Alabama explained that since the Norman Conquest, Britain had been divided between a Norman aristocracy and a Saxon-descended "common people" who now resent their Norman superiors with the fury of a vanquished race (a contumely that ran amok, for instance, in the person and symbol of Cromwell).[37] Saxon descendents now removed to the northeastern part of the United States, Falconer argued, have been historically unable to govern themselves: "Here again [in seventeenth-century New England], they measurably became their own rulers, and continued to exhibit those severe traits of fanaticism which had ever marked their own history" (404). As Falconer describes them, these Puritans born of Saxon stock "instinctively pursued the same path, in the general outline of their lives—squabbling, fighting, singing psalms, burning witches, and talking about liberty—until George III lost the brightest jewel of his colonial diadem, when the English Parliament passed the Boston port bill" (404). In another essay published in *De Bow's* (along with the *Southern Literary Messenger*, one of the most frequent organs for this sort of Confederate racial theory during the opening years of the Civil War), and echoing Macaulay's statement in the first volume of *The History of England*, George Fitzhugh aligned Saxon-born northerners in their biological alterity with African slaves: "The peasantry [of England] are Anglo-Saxons, and they occupy a social position quite as low as that of our slaves, and never emerge from that position."[38] Indeed, as one writer in the *Southern Literary Messenger* put it, since the Saxon was "Never capable, in their best days, of self-government, it is frightful to think of the doom awaiting [them] at the end of this war."[39]

In two intriguing scholarly investigations, historians Richard B. Bonner and Ritchie Watson describe such sectionalist discourse strictly as a Civil War phenomenon, and more particularly as an invention of the Confederate intelligentsia.[40] Indeed, Bonner suggests "there was hardly any serious effort prior to 1860 to extend this historical antagonism into an irreconcilable conflict of race" while supposing that "[e]xplicit racialization of the sectional conflict" arose out of the radicalization of the Northeast in the wake of John Brown's attack on Harper's Ferry (39). But in fact the argument according to which inhabitants of the northern and southern states were traceable to discrete genetic pools predated the Civil War by at least eleven years, when Kitchell put it to use in order to elevate northeastern abolitionists over southern slaveholders. For that matter, other writers appropriated Kitchell's taxonomies prior to the Civil War. A review essay on Kemble's *The Saxons in England*, published within a month of Kitchell's *Wellman's* essay, criticizes the Normans for being a race of "oppressors" while also explaining that "the struggle between the Puritan and the Cavalier was, in its leading features, marked by an original distinction between Saxon and Norman."[41] "Like the fugitives from burning Troy"—Norman-dominated England—Saxon émigrés "brought the Palladium of their liberty with them across the Atlantic" to New England, where they established the governmental structures that formed the basis for American civilization (48). As with Kitchell, the essay ends in marvel at the prospect of a North American nation founded in Saxon liberty and lineage.[42] Other authors made the point more implicitly. For instance, a hostile reviewer of Nehemiah Adam's *The Southside View of Slavery* (1855) criticized the curfewing of southern slaves through the increasingly familiar Saxonist historical analogy: "The Norman tyrants found the *curfew* a very fine device for keeping the Saxon people in their place. But the question arises, where is the boasted confidence of the whites in the blacks, if such laws must be enforced?"[43] Garland's 1854 essay "England and the Slave Trade" asserts that the Norman temperament, though nominally "lost [along with the Saxon] in the common appellation of Englishmen," becomes like "a seedgrain that cannot die— unnoticed, today, it will be found flourishing as a banyan-grove (perhaps also as a hemlock forest) after a thousand years" (415). American slavery, now akin to the oak Emerson found no greater than the acorn, is the outgrowth and extension of the earlier catastrophe of the Norman Conquest, which Garland describes in this way:

> Seven hundred and eighty-eight years ago, the act done was the landing of William of Normandy on the shores of England with sixty thousand men under his command—the result was the battle of Hastings—the death of Harold and the conquest of England. These sixty thousand men with their wives and children stalked into the houses of the defenseless Saxons and turned them out and took possession of their estates. The Normans built castles, wore coats of mail, bore arms, rode on Horse-back, and formed a compact order from the prince to the retainer completely organized for defense—while the Saxons, driven from their mansions, stripped of their arms, and, dwelling in exposed huts, were compelled to till for others the land they had once called their own—or reduced to starvation, or driven to the green forests to find a scanty subsistence on hunting and robbing. (415–16)

A more diffuse attempt to ground sectional antipathy in English heredity predates such commentaries by decades. As early as 1837, one writer in the *Southern Literary Messenger* argued, "We, too, of the South, and especially we of Virginia, are descendants, for the most part, of the old cavaliers—the enemies and persecutors of those old puritans—and entertain, perhaps, unwittingly something of an hereditary and historical antipathy against the children, for the fathers' sakes."[44] This alignment of southern cavaliers against northern puritans represented a much less honed effort to configure English history as the wellspring of hostilities between the U.S. North and South than would emerge during the 1850s and reach a pitch during the opening years of the Civil War. But the eventual sharpening of a sectionalist account of the Norman Conquest provided the context within which the racialist passages of *English Traits* would assume urgency and force.

Nor was this rendition of Atlantic sectionalism some marginal phenomenon passing unnoticed by the cultural mainstream. Indeed, accounts such as these, according to which the Norman Conquest provided the template for the unfolding sectional crisis in America, achieved enough prominence during the decade prior to the Civil War to be reiterated in the English press as the war unfolded. The London *Times*, for instance, noted in 1863 that military conflict between the northern and southern American states "has long been brewing," having "had its rise in the elementary minds of the races" holding sway in New England and in the South.[45] The New England "Puritan," the *Times* explained in terms by now familiar to many North Atlantic readers, "is the ultra liberty man of the world," "not willing to be under authority of God or man." Possessed of an "extreme" "pride of individual right," "he admits government only as he likes it." Left to their own devices in the political vacuum of New England, latter-day Saxons have "contended for that idea of liberty which claims a perfect equality for each individual of the human species" (a sensibility the *Times* denounced as an "anarchy" whose "final despotism . . . was developed just as soon as it gained the ascendency in the election of Mr. Lincoln").[46] In a piece more sympathetic to the northern cause, *Blackwoods Edinburgh Magazine* contested the frequent American insistence "that foreigners are incapable of judging of their disputes, because they know nothing of the political institutions of America." Such correctives notwithstanding, the anonymous writer insists that the sectional crisis

> has been a matter not of sudden creation, but of slow growth. It is compounded of very ancient laws, of customs still more ancient, or concessions wrung from arbitrary power, or rights claimed by immemorial usage, of the settlement of revolutions, and of incessant legislation aiming to adapt what was already established to the changed conditions of English life in successive generations. It bears the impress of the Saxon race and of their Norman conquerors: in its texture are interwoven the threads of chivalry, of feudalism, of the Reformation, and of the Revolution.[47]

4. Melioration and Union

Emerson's own accounts of the Norman Conquest, and the struggles of ethnicity and temperament he believed it activated, were bound to similar accounts being generated by others, and because of this *English Traits* could not but appear as a related effort to enlist English ancestry in the conflict between the states. While *English Traits* stands as perhaps the most canonically prestigious instance of this version of Atlantic sectionalism—configuring opposed English temperaments as the engine of political conflict in the United States—understanding *English Traits* within that context helps to advance other, contemporary conversations about Emerson's position within larger North Atlantic conversations about race.

Placing *English Traits* within the context of antebellum deliberation over Norman and Saxon bloodlines further complicates what has already become in recent years an intricate conversation over Emerson's attitudes toward the racial ideologies of his day. Anita Patterson, for instance, has argued that Emerson's great shift from *Nature* (1836) and the first two series of essays (1841, 1844) to the more obviously topically energized lectures following the 1844 address on the West Indies consists in a swing "from a concept of obligation that is essentially religious to one that is primarily racialist." This shift, Patterson maintains, entails a divide between Emerson's early "belief in political obligations that result from Lockean, rational, voluntary acts of consent" and "obligations that are to some extent involuntarily born into or found."[48] Such notions of involuntary or congenital politics certainly circulate throughout the various attempts to place the Norman Conquest and its genealogical aftermath as a primal scene that U.S. partisans were now compelled to repeat through the instrument of sectional conflict—through not only renditions of the conflict itself as a legacy of biological discord but also, in the case of either Saxonist or Normanist historians, an understanding of certain English descendants as more fit than others to be free. These historiographies of biological transmission form a part of the cultural setting of *English Traits*—and in some significant ways, the book is at home with such notions of a racially circumscribed politics.

But there is also much in *English Traits* to unsettle its position alongside contemporaneous discourses on English race and U.S. sectionalism. Gregg Crane has suggested that even when Emerson speaks of "blood" or "stock," he does so figuratively, as when he converts the "literal figure of ancestry and blood into a metaphor for national unity created through moral consensus,"[49] a reading to which Ian Finseth offers cautious assent. Still, even if Emerson finds mainly metaphoric potential in the racial discourses of his day—and even if he remains skeptical of their accuracy—it is surely a mistake to forget that Emerson also takes racialist science very seriously. In view of Emerson's cautious engagement with contemporaneous racial theory, Finseth insists that only as we begin to do justice to "Emerson's shifting, subtle responses to contemporaneous debates about race" can we come closer toward "a full understanding of . . . the history of racial thought in the United States."[50] *English Traits* might serve as an exemplum of Finseth's thesis, for the book not only participates in but also complicates the discourse on race and English history that was developing within transatlantic culture of the 1840s and '50s.

One of the most salient instances of this occurs at the outset of the chapter entitled "Race," where Emerson cites the work of Robert Knox, the "ingenious anatomist" to whom Emerson refers as having "written a book to prove that races are imperishable, but nations are pliant constructions, easily changed or destroyed" (*W* 5: 44). The book Emerson means, of course, is *The Races of*

Men, one of the more sustained considerations of the Saxon racial makeup. Knox had depicted the Saxons in illustration of his larger thesis that racial amalgamation leads to mass sterility and ultimately extinction (echoing the common polygenetic wisdom of his day, Knox wrote that "nature produces no mules; no hybrids, neither in man nor animals") (v, 65), and it bears mention that, at least initially, Emerson took Knox's work on hybridity and racial amalgamation in earnest. In "Fate" (1860), he would call him "a rash and unsatisfactory writer" whose book proffers "unpalatable conclusions," but which was nevertheless "charged with pungent and unforgettable truths" (*W* 6: 16). Earlier, in his journal of 1851, he cited approvingly "Knox's law of races, that Nature destroys hybrids, and extinguishes them; that the colony detached from the race deteriorates to the crab" (*J* 8: 222).

But in *English Traits*, Emerson would criticize Knox, whom he complains "did not found his races on any necessary law, disclosing their ideal or metaphysical necessity; nor did he on the other hand count with precision the existing races and settle the true bounds. . . ." The "true bounds" of any racial pool seem to Emerson impossible to chart, since "[t]he individuals at the extremes of divergence in one race of men are as unlike as the wolf to the lapdog. Yet each variety shades down imperceptibly to the next, and you cannot draw the line where a race begins or ends" (*W* 5: 44). Against Knox's warnings that miscegenation leads to degeneration and sterility, Emerson now insists that the English belie taxonomical analysis precisely because they instantiate a successful fusion of types. The English do not "appear to be of one stem, but collectively a better race than any from which they are derived. Nor is it easy to trace it home to its original seats. Who can call by right name what races are in Britain? Who can trace them historically? Who can discriminate them anatomically, or metaphysically?" (*W* 5: 51)

Emerson's critique of Knox elaborated his long-standing view of nature as a chain of being wherein elementary life forms beget those of greater complexity. "The lowest organizations are the simplest; a mere mouth, a jelly, or a straight worm," Emerson explains. But for him the increasing biological complexity of nature betokens not simple diversity but a greater degree of "gradation," a "resolution of races," since "nature loves inoculation." "A child," he explains, "blends in his face the faces of both parents and some feature from every ancestor whose face hangs on the wall. The best nations are those most widely related; and navigation, as effecting a world-wide mixture, is the most potent advancer of civilizations" (*W* 5: 50). The "inoculation" that "nature loves" is now one with that inoculation of "all nations" Emerson had attributed to the British Empire, which has "inoculated all nations with her civilization, intelligence and tastes."

We might notice the extent to which this Emersonian great chain of being recapitulates the "subtle chain of countless rings" Emerson had portrayed in the epigram to *Nature* he added in 1849: "A subtle chain of countless rings/Each one unto the farthest brings;/The eye reads omens where it goes,/And speaks all languages the rose;/And, striving to be man, the worm/Mounts through all the spires of form" (*W* 1: 1). Written under the influence of Robert Chambers's *Vestiges of a Natural History of Creation* (1844), which Emerson had read in 1845, the 1849 epigram replaced the quotation of Plotinus that had adorned the 1836 edition of *Nature* ("Nature is but an image or imitation of wisdom, the last thing of the soul; Nature being a thing which doth only do, but not know" [*W* 1: 403–404]) and reflects Emerson's shift toward an evolutionary view of human constitution.[51] The 1849 epigram also anticipates *English Traits'* scoffing attitude toward what Emerson calls "the legend of pure races": for Emerson, diversity leads not to rigid taxonomy but to "resolution," which is to say that increasing orders of biological complexity entail increasing orders of "melioration." In striving to be man, the worm of *Nature* as well as the mere mouth, jelly, or worm of *English Traits* transmogrifies as it amalgamates; ring "brings" unto other rings, commingles with and merges into adjacent and concentric strata of life, belying the alleged "fixity or incontrovertibleness of races as we see them" (*W* 5: 49). Thus do lines of racial demarcation appear as "frail boundaries," links within a "subtle chain." Did not Emerson once proclaim of circles that "throughout nature this primary figure is repeated without end"? (*W* 2: 301)

Emerson's configuration of nature as a progression toward melioration comprises an attempt to destabilize a series of allegedly fixed biological categories, including those taken to compose English races and by proxy the American regional identities that were being configured in his day as the outgrowth of these categories. This is not to say that Emerson abandons race as a viable category; nor does he successfully distinguish himself against the tendency of antebellum American racial theorists to congratulate themselves as genetically destined to prevail over others. "It is race, is it not?" he asks, "that puts the hundred millions of India under the dominion of a remote island in the North of Europe" (*W* 5: 47). But even as he asks such rhetorical questions, Emerson recognizes the superciliousness behind them, even if comprised of suppositions he does not always avoid replicating. "Men hear gladly of the power of blood or race," he notes. "Every body likes to know that his advantages cannot be attributed to air, soil, sea, or to local wealth, as mines and quarries, nor to laws and traditions, nor to fortune; but to superior brain, as it makes the praise more personal to him" (*W* 5: 46). However powerful the inducements to fix race as the ultimate source of character and temperament, such accounts are belied by the shifting "gradation and resolution of races," the "inoculation" "nature loves" and which close observation detects:

The fixity or inconvertibleness of races as we see them is a weak argument for the eternity of these frail boundaries, since all our historical period is a

point to the duration in which nature has wrought. Any the least and soli-
tariest fact in our natural history, such as the melioration of fruits and of
animal stocks, has the worth of a *power* in the opportunity of geologic periods. Moreover, though we flatter the self-love of men and nations by the
legend of pure races, all our experience is of the gradation and resolution of
races, and strange resemblances meet us everywhere. It need not puzzle us
that Malay and Papuan, Celt and Roman, Saxon and Tartar should mix,
when we see the rudiments of tiger and baboon in our human form, and
know that the barriers of race are not so firm but that some spray sprinkles
us from the antediluvian seas. (*W* 5: 49–50; emphasis original)

Discerning the rudiments of one species within others, Emerson hearkens
back, yet again, to the essay on *Nature*, where he had once marveled over how,
"In a cabinet of natural history, we become sensible of a certain occult relation
and sympathy in regard to the most unwieldy and eccentric forms of beast,
fish, and insect."[52]

Still more striking is the resonance between the passage from *English Traits*
and the 1833 notebook entry out of which this passage from *Nature* developed,
where Emerson recorded his impressions at the Jardin des Plantes, whose
multitude of preserved biological specimens struck him for its "upheaving
principle of life everywhere incipient." "Not a form so grotesque, so savage,
nor so beautiful but is an expression of some property inherent in man the
observer,—an occult relation between the very scorpions and man. I feel the
centipede in me,—cayman, carp, eagle, and fox" (*J* 3: 163). The theory of racial
"fixity" Emerson would later encounter in Knox could not account for such
"occult relation[s]" as Emerson had long espied in the natural world, where
biological barriers were constantly shifting, always permeable, fringes of variation rather than lines of absolute division.

Such a vision of gradation, resolution, and inoculation is of course antithetical to the suppositions about race informing those many others who
during the 1840s and '50s were writing about Saxons and Normans, northerners and southerners, England and America. Emerson's ameliorative maneuver in *English Traits* cuts against the sectionalist pitch of those arguments
making the case for a form of ethnic dissociation that seemed to many to
provide a biological basis for political and national division. None of this necessarily contradicts other readings of *English Traits* forwarded by readers like
Cornel West or Peter Field, both of whom view Emerson's interest in Norman
and Saxon bloodlines almost strictly in terms of his own struggles with polygenetic discourses on the biological constitution of Africans and Caucasians.
This emphasis, for instance, causes West to view *English Traits* as an instance
of the fact "that Emerson's conception of the worth and dignity of human
personality is racially circumscribed; that race is central to his understanding
of the historical circumstances which shape human personality; and that this

understanding can easily serve as a defense of Anglo-Saxon imperial domina-
tions of non-European land and peoples."[53] But while no one would deny that
the paramount racial controversies of the 1850s concerned African-American
slaves first of all, the controversy over Saxons and Normans was not *simply* a
metaphor for relations between Americans of European and of African descent. It was this, but it was also a site for a process of national recharting that
seemed to its participants to go a long way in providing a biological account
for tensions between the states.

This is to say that within its transatlantic context, *English Traits* becomes
Emerson's way of redescribing the nation itself as a process of melioration and
resolution, rather than envisioning North America—as he had in the 1852 lecture "The Anglo-American"—as the latest stage upon which Saxons and Normans would clash. The biological principles of melioration and admixture
Emerson deploys in his critique of Knox thus become the principal guarantor
of America's national future. These ramifications remained clear to Emerson
even so far as his 1878 iteration of the lecture "The Fortune of the Republic,"
where Emerson drew from the Civil War an entire "history of Nature" as an
"incessant advance from less to more, from rude to fine organization," a process that "spends individuals and races prodigally to prepare new individuals
and races" (*W* 3: 525).

Indeed, such possibilities also condition the closing lines of *English Traits*,
which end the book by returning to the beginning of Emerson's second
voyage to England and to a speech he gave upon his arrival at the Manchester
Athenæum. All of Britain was at this moment in the midst of a commercial
crisis following the repeal of the Corn Laws and the sense of upheaval occasioned in the Chartist movement, and so the gracious guest complimented
his hosts on the qualities he now imagined would see them through the crisis,
all of which he pinned to the Saxon temperament. "That which lures a solitary
American in the woods with the wish to see England," Emerson told his Manchester audience, "is the moral peculiarity of the Saxon race,—its command-
ing sense of right and wrong, the love and devotion to that,—that is the imperial trait, which arms them with the scepter of the globe" (*W* 5: 310–11). This
moral peculiarity of the Saxon race, the bottom and longevity of all English
traits, would surely carry the day. "If it not be so," Emerson promised, "if the
courage of England goes with the chances of a commercial crisis, I will go
back to the capes of Massachusetts and my own Indian stream, and say to my
countrymen, the old race are all gone, and the elasticity and hope of mankind
must henceforth remain on the Alleghany ranges, or nowhere" (*W* 5: 314). Of
course Emerson's point was that "the courage of England" would *not* dissi-
pate, and yet these final lines of *English Traits* seem to announce the upshot
of Emerson's commentary on Knox and on the amelioration of races, the end
of "the legend of pure races" this commentary strives to undermine. In the
last moments of *English Traits* and the first moments of the voyage his book

documents, Emerson imagines his homecoming to America, his return from the historical and racial site of origins toward which America so often peers, the end of his sojourn in the father country with which genealogists such as Burke assisted their American clientele in reassociating themselves. Returning to Massachusetts with the revelation that "the old race are all gone," Emerson imagines himself to reverse that retrospective and genealogical gaze, severing the roots Hawthorne would yet discern from the vantage of the Liverpool consulate, projecting new histories for an old bloodline, now relocated out upon the Alleghany ranges, or nowhere.

Feeling Free in Medieval America

1. Black Saxons

On August 2, 1847, over four thousand people gathered on the grounds ad-joining the village academy of Canandaigua, New York, in order to commem-orate the ninth anniversary of the liberation of the British West Indies in 1838. The day's speakers would include Samuel Ward, Henry Highland Garnet, and Henry Johnson, the last of whom would read from the British Parliament's Act of Emancipation by means of which over 800,000 Caribbean slaves had been freed nine years earlier. Taking the podium at the day's outset, Frederick Douglass initiated the ceremonies by extolling "the impression made nine years ago upon the tablets of our memory by that magnanimous act of British legislation," which was itself, he said, only an instance of a broader historical tendency toward emancipation—"proof," he said, of a "sentiment as useful as it is universal."[1] After all, Douglass reminded his white listeners, they too were descended from slaves. "Who were the fathers of our present haughty oppres-sors in this land?" he asked.

> They were, until within the last four centuries, the miserable slaves, the degraded serfs, of Norman nobles. They were subjected to every species of brutality which their fiendish oppressors could invent. They were regarded as an inferior race,—unfit to be trusted with their own rights. They were not even allowed to walk on the public highway, and travel from town to town without a written permission from their owners. They could not hold any property whatever, but were themselves property, bought and sold. They were not permitted to give testimony in courts of law. They were pun-ished for crimes which, if committed by their haughty masters, were not deemed worthy of punishment at all. They were not allowed to marry with-out the consent of their owners. They were subjected to the lash, and might

even be murdered with impunity by their cruel masters. But, Sir, I must not dwell here, though a profitable comparison might be drawn between the condition of the coloured slaves of our land, and the ancient Anglo-Saxon slaves of England. (*FD* 2: 73)

The comparisons between Saxon and American slaves Douglass imagined in 1847 had indeed, for at least one crucial moment during the prior century, proven profitable for one American slave as well as perhaps fifteen thousand of his brethren in the United Kingdom. In his closing argument for James Somersett, who had escaped his Boston master while traveling in London in 1771 (nine years prior to the abolition of slavery in Massachusetts), Francis Hargrave had built much of his case around just such a correspondence as Douglass would later indicate. Hargrave's line of reasoning in 1772 had won from Lord Mansfield a decision effectively outlawing slavery in England—and indeed forming the legal basis for the eventual abolition of slavery throughout the empire—in contending that English common law had disallowed slavery since the enfranchisement of Saxon villeins near the end of Elizabeth's reign. Describing the conditions of villenage under the Norman Conquest, Hargrave had pointed out,

> The condition of a villein had most of the incidents I have before described, in giving the idea of slavery in general. His service was uncertain and indeterminate, such as his lord thought fit to require; or as some of our ancient writers express it, *he knew not in the evening what he was to do in the morning, he was bound to do whatever he was commanded.* He was liable to beating, imprisonment, and every other chastisement his lord could devise, except killing and maiming. He was incapable of acquiring property for his own benefit . . . [but] was himself the subject of property; as such saleable and transmissible.[2]

The villeins' state of subjugation was steadily eroded, Hargrave argued, by the English legal system itself, the "courts of justice," which "always presumed in favor of liberty, throwing the *onus probandi* upon the lord, as well in the writ of *homine replegiando*, where the villein was plaintiff, as in the *nativo habendo*, where he was defendant" (29). Under the stringent requirements of the English legal system from the eleventh to the sixteenth centuries, Hargrave had insisted, "Manumissions were inferred from the slightest circumstances of mistake or negligence in the lord, from every act or omission which legal refinement could strain into acknowledgement of the villein's liberty" (32).

The Somersett case, in which an English litigator drew an American slave into historical analogy with Saxon serfs of centuries before—winning through that juxtaposition the liberation of all slaves in England—provided American abolitionists throughout the antebellum period with a favored phrase often misattributed to Lord Mansfield, who was frequently said to have stated in his decision that "[t]he air of England is too pure for a slave to breathe" (the phrase actually appears in Hargrave's argument).[3] Beyond the circulation of this rhetorical fragment from *Somersett*, the analogy between African slaves and Saxon serfs was beginning to appear in American public deliberation over slavery by the time Douglass supposed such comparisons might prove useful for American abolitionists. In 1840, for instance, George T. Davis, a state senator from Franklin, Massachusetts, had delivered a lengthy speech in the Massachusetts General Court drawing Norman "barons and chevaliers" into historical correspondence with nineteenth-century apologists for slavery. At issue was a proposed resolution calling for the abolition of the slave trade in Washington, a measure some representatives regarded as a provocation of the South. Rejoining those worries, Davis reminded his fellow senators that

> [f]ive centuries ago, the leading truths of our Declaration of Independence were proclaimed by the serfs and villeins of England; and the Norman slaveholders of that day put in the same plea that is now put in by the gentleman from Worcester. When called upon by the King (in 1381) to say whether they would subscribe charters of enfranchisement, "God preserve us," answered the barons and chevaliers, "from subscribing to such charters, though we should all perish in one day; for we would rather lose our lives than our inheritance." In the progress of time, the instinct of liberty prevailed against the selfishness of tyranny, and raised up the ignorant and degraded serf into the brave, intelligent, free Anglo-Saxon. We, of all races in the world, should be the last to dispute the importance or the truth of the principle which has made us what we are.[4]

Davis's speech was shaped by transatlantic genealogies similar to those transmitted by Kitchell in "The Anglo-Saxon Element in English and American Society," Garland in "England and the Slave Trade," Marsh in *The Goths in New-England*, and, in an eventually more complicated way, Emerson in *English Traits*. Of all races of the world, Davis reprimanded his more recalcitrant fellow New Englanders, "we" should adhere to the Saxon principles that have "made us what we are," principles including the "leading truths of the Declaration of Independence" and which were, in the fourteenth century, "proclaimed by the serfs and villeins," the vanquished Saxons of Norman England. Themselves descended from English slaves, Davis argued, New Englanders ought not suffer difficulty in imaginatively identifying with African-American subjects of southern bondage.

Douglass himself would pursue the homology over course of two decades following his Canandaigua address. The summer after that appearance, Douglass reminded a Boston audience "of the degradation of the Anglo-Saxon race in England, under their Norman conquerors; yes, of that very race which boasts itself of superiority to all others, and assumes to plunder or enslave all others" (*FD* 2: 131).[5] At the end of the year, writing in the *North Star*, Douglass identified southern bigotry with Norman "tyranny" as he declaimed,

"'An inferior species of the race of men'! This is the same old trick of tyranny. The haughty Norman once looked down upon the degraded and subjected Anglo-Saxon as an inferior species of the race of man. The Americans now look down upon the Mexicans as an inferior species of the race of man; and so, we suppose, it will ever be with successful tyrants."[6] Speaking in New York in May 1854, he declared that "The doctrine of the hour . . . that the negro is inferior to the white man, and that the superior race has a right to enslave the inferior" was "not new. . . . No doubt the proud Anglo-Saxon heard it from the lips of their Norman master within the past five centuries" (*FD* 2: 488). In May 1857, again in New York, he would once again point out that "[t]he Anglo Saxons themselves had once been slaves. Twelve centuries ago this proud Anglo Saxon race was brought over from England to Ireland and sold in the market of Wexford. Thomas Francis Meager talked of his ancestors having owned fairhaired, blue-eyed Saxon slaves. Well, I am glad of it. You have risen since that time. Come along! Come along! We will come up, too, by-and-by" (*FD* 3: 146). And in Boston on January 26, 1865, he mused,

> This charge of inferiority is an old dodge. It has been made available for oppression on many occasions. It is only about six centuries since the blue-eyed and fair-haired Anglo-Saxons were considered inferior by the haughty Normans, who once trampled upon them. If you read the history of the Norman Conquest, you will find that this proud Anglo-Saxon was once looked upon as of a coarser clay than his Norman master, and might be found in the highways and byways of old England laboring with a brass collar on his neck, and name of his old master upon it. *You* were down then! (Laughter and applause.) You are up now. I am glad you are up, and I want you to be glad to help us up also. (Applause.) (*FD* 4: 65)

Tapping the transatlantic genealogies that had circulated through his national culture since at least 1850, Douglass assumes his white northeastern audience to regard themselves as the descendants of those Saxon serfs ("You were down then!"), and plumbs that habit of identification for its further implications. The resemblances Douglass elaborated between Saxon and American slaves were observed by other commentators as well. In his New York Central College lecture on June 22, 1852, professor of classics William G. Allen stated,

> In the veins of English and Americans; the freest of men—flows the blood of slaves. At the Norman Conquest, and the close of the Saxon Heptarchy, two-thirds of the population of England were held in different degrees of servitude. One person in every seven was an absolute *slave*, and a marketable commodity, in every sense of the word. Slaves and cattle were legal tender and the law was, that one *slave* should be held in value as equivalent to four oxen. A little consolation is better than none; so I would say to the black man, therefore—*Take courage, friend, you are only taking your turn.*[7]

Such commentaries provided a transatlantic and transhistorical variation upon the moment Stowe would narrate, in her 1851 serialization of *Uncle Tom's Cabin*, as Eva and Topsy's first encounter: "They stood the representatives of their races," Stowe wrote. "The Saxon, born of ages of cultivation, command, education, physical and moral eminence; the Afric, born of ages of oppression, submission, ignorance, toil and vice!"[8] Eva's relationship with Topsy ultimately erodes the barriers separating the Saxon from the "Afric," providing both girls confirmation that, whatever cultural institutions may separate them, they are in some broader sense sisters. Indeed, an imagined continuum between Saxon serfs and African slaves would not be lost upon southern spokesmen engaged in the construction of their own mythos of Norman descent. Arguing that "[t]he Norman cavalier cannot brook the vulgar familiarity of the Saxon Yankee," an editorial published in an 1862 issue of the Louisville, Bowling Green, and Nashville *Courier* hazarded that through the election of Lincoln, "the Puritans emancipated themselves, and are now in violent insurrection against their former owners. . . . A few more Bull Run thrashings will bring them once more under the yoke as docile as the most loyal of our Ethiopian 'chattels.'"[9] And when in the midst of the war, William Wells Brown quipped over having been "sorry that Mr. Lincoln came from such a low origin," as the president's Saxon ancestry comprised, he too maneuvered ancient English history so as to produce a discursive crisis within contemporaneous U.S. discourses of racial stature and purity. Lincoln's ancestors hadn't simply been slaves, Brown pointed out: they were the product of amalgamation between Romans, Normans, and Saxons, a subjugated people reputed among Romans to have been runtish and incorrigible. "Ancestry is something which the white American should not speak of, unless with his lips to the dust," Brown wrote.[10]

Six years prior to Douglass's address at Canandaigua, Lydia Maria Child dramatized the analogy between Saxon serfs and African-American slaves through a story set on a Charleston plantation in the midst of an impending insurrection. "The Black Saxons," which Child placed in the January 1, 1841, issue of *The Liberty Bell*, articulates its multiple historical frameworks as the algorithm of a transnational process of emancipation. While clearly addressing itself to contemporaneous anxieties over slave revolt, the story is set during the War of 1812, as British forces threaten to land on the South Carolina coast. Moreover, the story's principal character, Duncan, redoubles his own historical moment through his absorption in a history of the Norman Conquest, a narrative of subjugation that—despite his position as a holder of slaves—excites what Child describes as Duncan's reflexive democratic sympathies. "From the natural kindliness of his character, and democratic theories, deeply imbibed in childhood," Child explains, Duncan's "thought dwelt more with a nation prostrated and kept in base subjugation by the strong arm of violence, than with the renowned robbers, who seized their rich possessions, and haughtily trampled on their dearest rights."[11] The Normans of Duncan's imagination are those who would later populate Emerson's *English Traits*: pirates, dragoons. And mindful of his own precarious position on the frontline of an imminent British invasion, Duncan is inclined to identify with the Saxon victims of foreign occupation, whose fate he opines: "'And so that bold and beautiful race became slaves!' thought he. 'The brave and free-souled Harolds, strong of heart and strong of arm; the fair-haired Ediths, in their queenly beauty, noble in soul as well as ancestry; these all sank to the condition of slave;—and tamely submitted to their lot, till their free, bright beauty passed under the heavy cloud of animal dullness, and the contemptuous Norman epithet of 'base Saxon churl' was but too significantly true'" (20). What is most stirring, for Duncan, is that the Saxons "did not relinquish freedom without a struggle," a fact "proved by Robin Hood and his bold followers . . . brave outlaws of the free forest, and the wild mountain-passes, taking back, in the very teeth of danger, a precarious existence from the rich possessions that were once their own" (20–21). Truly, Duncan muses, "Troubled must be the sleep of those who rule a conquered nation!" (21)

Duncan's process of transatlantic identification is interrupted by a slave who requests a pass to attend a Methodist meeting, and after granting his leave, Duncan flies into a pique at the inconvenience. Possibly, he supposes, he has grown too lenient with his slaves. "It is a hard case, too," he decides, "to force a man to be a tyrant, whether he will or no" (21). Through some process of association, Duncan recalls the looming threat of British invasion, but then conjures a vision of Big-boned Dick, a recently escaped slave now reported to maintain "a rendezvous for runaways in the swampy depths of some dark forest" (23). Suddenly Duncan's prior identification with Saxon resistance fighters dissolves as he apprehends his true role in the emergent historical analogy—as Big-boned Dick comes, "unbidden and unwelcome, like Banquo's Ghost, into incongruous association with his spontaneous sympathy for Saxon serfs" (24). Clearly, Child informs us, Duncan's "republican sympathies, and 'the system entailed upon him by his ancestors,' were obviously out of joint with each other; and the skilfullest soldering of casuistry could by no means make them adhere together" (24). Now convinced that his slaves are confabulating with insurrectionists in the woods, Duncan waits for the next "Methodist meeting," which he attends after having donned "a complete suit of negro clothes, and a black mask well fitted to his face" (27).

So Duncan's identification with Saxon serfs of yore becomes continuous first with a form of minstrelsy, but then brings him into a space of brewing insurrection. The meeting place is set in the swamp, a traditional setting in southern literature—from Kennedy to Faulkner to Morrison—for the no-man's land between order and disintegration, slavery and freedom, white and black.[12] In Child's story, the swamp near Duncan's plantation becomes a transatlantic space as well, "a scene of picturesque and imposing grandeur" set "in richly fantastic resemblance to some Gothic cathedral" (29), as if some medieval sanctum has now opened in the backwoods where Duncan's slaves meet in order to deliberate. Some slaves advocate killing their masters in Nat Turner-style, wholesale slaughter, while others advocate mercy and Christian forgiveness. Eventually, to Duncan's relief, the insurrectionists decide to spare their white masters. But Duncan's prior sense of the meaning of his own English ancestry is permanently altered; taking leave from the insurrectionists' meeting, "he recurred to Saxon history, and remembered how he had thought that troubled must be the sleep of those who rule a conquered people" (42). While stopping short of viewing himself as a contemporary Norman conqueror, he nevertheless acknowledges his slaves' more convincing claim to the legacy of Saxon resistance:

> "And these Robin Hoods, and Wat Tylers, were my Saxon ancestors," thought he. "Who shall so balance effects and causes, as to decide what portion of my present freedom sprung from their seemingly defeated efforts? Was the place I saw to-night, in such wild and fearful beauty, like the haunts of the *Saxon* Robin Hoods? Was not the spirit that gleamed forth there as brave as theirs? And who shall calculate what even such hopeless endeavors may do for the future freedom of their race?" (43; emphasis original)

Duncan's realizations as he departs the meeting in the swamp voice the arguments Child would also publish in an essay appearing a year later in the *Philanthropist*, where Child dispelled the myth of Anglo-Saxon invincibility while further specifying her comparison between serfs and slaves. Quoting liberally from Sharon Turner and other historians of the Norman Conquest, Child argued that "[t]he punishments they suffered, were like those inflicted on the Africano-American slave.—Whether the thumb-screw, stocks, and other gear of a Southern plantation, were in vogue in those times, we are not appraised. But, our Anglo-Saxon forefathers, were subject to be put in bonds, whipped, branded, and at times were actually yoked."[13] "When, therefore, we affect to despise [the African slave] for his servility," Child warned, "let us remember that our ancestors were once as mean-spirited as he now is" (2). Child also hints at such transnational linkages in "The Black Saxons," where regardless of their impulses to either spare or execute their white masters, *all* the insurrectionists of the earlier tale plan to "join the British" once his Majesty's forces commence their invasion (30). Indeed, in an attempt to dissuade his confederates from their plans for bloody retribution, one unnamed insurrectionist suggests that such acts of violence are ultimately impotent: real power, he argues, adheres in mastery of the English language, since it is through literacy and the political agency it betokens that "by'm bye, you be de British yourselves!" (39)

But becoming British oneself is not simply a matter of enrobing oneself in any particular historical mythos, any more than Duncan's donning of

costume and blackface—or his prior assumption of some legacy entailed in
the myth of Robin Hood—can efface his status as a master of slaves. As he
tells the assembly of his own successful stratagem to alert a distant ally of the
coming English invasion, the unnamed slave describes a ruse conjoining the
economic material of American slavery with the geopolitical stance between
Britain and America, all within a discursive rendition of British conquest:

> You know Jim, massa Gubernor's boy? Well, I want mighty bad to let Jim
> know British going to land. But he lib ten mile off, and old boss no let me go.
> Well, massa Gubernor he come dine my massa's house; and I bring he horse
> to de gate; and I make my bow, and say massa Gubernor, how Jim do? He
> tell me Jim berry well. Den I ax him, be Jim good boy? He say yes. Den I tell
> him Jim and I leetle boy togeder; and I want mighty bad send Jim some-
> thing. He tell me Jim hab enough of ebery ting. Oh, yes, massa Gubernor, I
> know you bery good massa, and Jim hab ebery ting he want; but when leetle
> boy togeder, dere is always something *here*, (laying his hand on his heart). I
> want to send leetle backy to Jim. I know he hab much backy he want; but
> Jim and I leetle boy togeder, and I want to send Jim something. Massa Gu-
> bernor say, bery well Jack. So I gib him de backy, done up in de bery bit o'
> newspaper dat tell British going to land! And massa Gubernor *himself* carry
> it!! (40–41; emphasis original)

It is a remarkably compressed semiotic moment. A black Saxon himself,
whom Duncan will presently decide is possessed, more than he, of the "spirit
that gleamed forth" from "the *Saxon* Robin Hoods," swaths tobacco, itself an
economic product of North American slavery, within printed discourse an-
nouncing an impending British invasion, a new Norman conquest whose success would—in reversal of prior historical trajectory—liberate these black
Saxons from their white overseers. Unwitting as Duncan himself, who at the
beginning of Child's story exults in an historical narrative he will only later
recognize as indictment, the governor of South Carolina is made the vehicle
for the transmission of a message that, in the fashion of Paul Revere if with
inverted significance, announces that the British are coming. Indeed, the message Jim receives resembles "The Black Saxons" itself, inasmuch as it enfolds
the system of chattel slavery within another story of British incursion, a narrative of conquest commandeered, by Child and other commentators of the
1840s, with libratory purpose.

2. Twelfth-Century Plantation Fiction: Henry Herbert's Saxon Slaves

Curfews, corporeal punishment, forced displacement, arbitrary prosecution—
these are the historical afterimages of political disenfranchisement sustaining
such discourses through which the plight of African slaves became, for many

abolitionist commentators of the 1840s and '50s, the contemporary projection of Saxon serfdom. In the writings of contemporaneous historians of the Norman Conquest, there was significant disagreement concerning the true scope of Saxon rights and privileges throughout the Middle Ages: according to Sharon Turner, Saxons under William the Conqueror enjoyed legal rights preventing them, for instance, from being set to labor beyond defined parameters or from being transported outside of the country, whereas Macaulay maintained that Norman domination was so thorough as to constitute a kind of dark age: "During the century and a half which followed the Conquest," he wrote, "there is, to speak strictly, no English history."[14] During the early nineteenth century, multiple characterizations of Saxon resistance competed throughout historical and popular accounts of the Conquest. For some historians, the story of Saxon slavery was most remarkable for its lesson in the gradual efficaciousness of moral right; according to Macaulay, for instance, the Saxons were liberated "neither by legislative regulations nor by physical force. Moral causes noiselessly effaced first the distinction between Norman and Saxon, and then the distinction between master and slave. None can venture to fix the precise moment at which either distinction ceased."[15] And yet, this gradual renewal of Saxon citizenship notwithstanding, Normans lived under the constant threat of retribution dealt under cover of night by righteously aggrieved Saxons—Macaulay also described a 150-year insurgency through which "the subject race, though beaten down and trodden underfoot, still made its sting felt" by waging "a predatory war against their oppressors" in which "Many Normans suddenly disappeared leaving no trace."[16] A constant motif throughout these accounts, and also circulating within abolitionist descriptions of Saxon serfdom, presented the Saxons as victims of an unjust occupation, exemplars of integrity under trial.

The most sustained literary treatment of this historical construction appears in Henry Herbert's 1855 novel *Wager of Battle: A Tale of Saxon Slavery in Sherwood Forest*, which adapts its historical focus to narrative conventions emergent in abolitionist texts such as Stowe's *Uncle Tom's Cabin* and Douglass's *The Narrative of the Life of Frederick Douglass* while yet sharpening the analogies between southern slavery and Saxon serfdom that had by then preoccupied other commentators for a decade and a half. Herbert, an émigré from England, graduate of Cambridge, and son of a former M.P. and dean of Manchester, had come to the United States in 1831 and founded, with A. D. Patterson, the *American Monthly Magazine*, serving as editor for the journal from 1833 to 1835. More widely known to American readers though his pen name Frank Forester, through which he initially secured renown as a sporting writer, Herbert was also a prolific author of historical novels dealing with classical and English episodes and settings—his novel *Marmaduke Wyval* (1843) went through fourteen editions within ten years, while *The Roman Traitor*, which enjoyed more limited success in the United States, found broad acclaim in London. As a result of these successes and of Herbert's networking in New York and Philadelphia, he served as New York correspondent for the *National Intelligencer* during 1846 and won a solid reputation among editors in New York and Washington. One of these, Gamaliel Bailey of the *National Era*—then flush with the success of the *Era*'s serialization of *Uncle Tom's Cabin*—approached Herbert in 1853 with the idea of another serial illustrating the evils of slavery.[17] Herbert initially balked, and then reconsidered, commencing serialization of *The Saxon Serf: A Tale of English Slavery in the Twelfth Century* in the *Era* with the November 3, 1853, issue.[18]

In a career of considerable output, *The Saxon Serf* and its redux *Sherwood Forest* constituted the only periodical writing to which Herbert attached his real name. After appearing between covers in 1855 by Mason Brothers of New York as *Wager of Battle*, the novel was for the most part favorably reviewed. *The Albion*, for instance, announced, "Few writers combine in greater degree than Mr. Herbert the essentials required of one who would carry us back into the olden days," while lauding the novel's depiction of "the remarkable state of laws under Henry II" as "at once curious and instructive."[19] *Godey's Lady's Book* called the novel "beautiful and deeply absorbing" in its depiction "of the manners, customs, and institutions of the Saxon and Norman inhabitants of England in the twelfth century," while the *Plough, the Loom, and the Anvil* called it "one of the most entertaining volumes ever published."[20] Discerning in the novel a larger relevance to the domestic political situation in 1855, the *Evangelist* supposed that "the moral impression which [Herbert] would leave, no reader will escape," while *Peterson's Magazine*, equally impressed, confessed "a predilection for the historical novel, because, if honestly and capably written, it not only affords intellectual pleasure to the reader, but gives as in a mirror, the very spirit of the past."[21] Though Bailey had remarked in the January 4, 1855, issue of the *Era* that "Herbert's Story of Anglo-Saxon Serfdom is deservedly attracting much attention," adding that "[a]nti-Slavery readers will be particularly interested in it,"[22] Herbert disavowed the novel's association with contemporary slavery in the preface to his 1855 edition. There, Herbert explains, "[W]hile the gist of my tale lies on the adventures and escape of a fugitive Saxon Slave from the tyranny of his Norman Lord, my work contains no reference to the peculiar institution of any portion of this country, nor conceals any oblique insinuation against, or covert attack upon, any part of the inhabitants of the Continent, or any interest guaranteed to them by the Constitution."[23] The disclaimer did not appear in the first installment of *The Saxon Serf* in the *National Era*, nor in the novel's reserialization as *Sherwood Forest*, where presumably it would have strained credulity amongst readers of a newspaper which, even by the time of its serialization of *Uncle Tom's Cabin*, was replete with antislavery argument and imagery.[24]

Though Herbert distances himself from the accelerating sectional crisis in his preface to the 1855 text, he also backpedals in his explanation: "Nevertheless,

I would recommend no person to open a page of this volume, who is prepared to deny that slavery *per se* is an evil and a wrong, and its effects deteriorating to all who are influenced by its contact, governors alike and the governed, since they will find nothing agreeable, but much adverse to their way of thinking" (vi). Whatever similarities the reader of *Wager of Battle* may discern between twelfth-century Saxon serfs and nineteenth-century African-American slaves, the novel proclaims itself agnostic with regard to institutions rooted in particular "portion[s] of this country." But Herbert also aligns his narrative with larger problematics that cannot help but to draw the text into the very welter he would purportedly avoid. Herbert's oblique assertion of contemporary relevance for his narrative—stopping short of sectional polemic and yet implying a moral universe patently applicable to the conflict over southern slavery (so much so that anyone "prepared to deny that slavery *per se* is an evil," he warns, should not bother reading the novel at all) also conditioned his presentist introduction to *The Brother in Arms*, his 1853 novel concerning the English Civil War:

> It is the saddest of all the considerations which weigh upon the candid and sincere mind of the true patriot, when civil dispute is on the eve of degenerating into civil war, that the best, the wisest, and the bravest of both parties are those who first fall victim for those principles which they mutually, with equal purity and faith, and almost with equal reason, believe to be true and vital; that the moderate men, who have erst stood side by side for the maintenance of the right and the common good . . . are set in deadly opposition, face to face, to slay and be slain for the benefit of the ultraists. (3–4)

Moderate men, marshaled out of sober restraint by "ultraists," might otherwise doubt "whether it be not better to endure all endurable assaults on liberty—all, in a word, short of its utter extinction—than to defend it through the awful path of civil war" (4). But nearly as soon as he raises such pressing stakes for his 1853 narrative, Herbert turns away from his present-tense musings—"This sad and terrible truth was never more clearly demonstrated than in the opening of the great English civil war between the first Charles and his Parliament" (4)—seemingly opting out of the fray of contemporary politics. In a similar move, the bound version of *Wager of Battle* seems anxious to preclude its own reception as an unflattering allegory of southern society (and hence, possibly, secure a broader market beyond the readership of the *Era*); and yet Herbert encourages his reader in the very direction he waves off, indicating that his novel will be uncongenial to any reader unprepared to acknowledge that slavery per se is an evil and a wrong.

For that slavery is an evil, its effects deteriorating to all, is the point *Wager of Battle* drives home most repeatedly through its story of Kenric and Eadwulf, two Saxon serfs, brothers who begin the novel in thrall to the Norman Lord Philip de Morville, lord of the manor of Waltheofstow near Sherwood Forest. Both serfs live as chattel who "could be sold at any time, or to any

person, or even swapped for an animal, or gambled away at the slightest ca-
price of his owner" (23). Kenric is in some ways the novel's eponymous Saxon
serf: noblesse incarnate even throughout a life of slavery, a man whose few
earned privileges have become for him "the cause of something more real—of
a sentiment of half independence, a desire of achieving perfect liberty" (24).
Eadwulf, on the other hand, degraded by his serfdom, is "animated by no ambition, no hope, perhaps scarce even by fear" (25).

The first half of the novel narrates the realization of Kenric's desire of
achieving "perfect liberty" after he throws himself, selflessly, between an en-
raged stag and the daughter of the Norman lord Yvo de Taillebois. In recognition of Kenric's bravery and at Yvo's request, Philip manumits Kenric and his
family. Plotting a course from enthrallment to liberty through a scheme of
compensated emancipation contracted between agreeable and ultimately up-
standing slaveholders, Wager of Battle also indicts Norman attitudes toward
their Saxon underlings. Both Yvo and Philip, for instance, regard the Saxon
"as a dull, soulless, inanimate, stupid senseless animal, with the passions only,
but without the intellect of the man" (59). Their biases notwithstanding, Herbert explains that neither Norman lord "was in any respect a tyrant, individu-
ally cruel, or intentionally an oppressor; but both were, as every one of us is at
this day, used to look at things as we find them, through our own glasses, and
to seek rather for what is the custom, than for what is right, and therefore
ought to be; for what suits us, and is permitted to us by law to do to others,
than for what we should desire others do unto us" (59). Didactic asides such as
this tend to undermine Herbert's earlier proclamation that Wager of Battle is
unintended as a commentary on American slavery. Neither Philip nor Yvo—
nor many of their nineteenth-century American equivalents, one might
assume—are congenital oppressors; their lack of regard for their serfs is due to
"no hardness of nature or cruelty of disposition" (60). Rather, it is the legal
institution of serfdom that blunts Christian sensibilities that would otherwise
permit each man to recognize, at a minimum, "that a Saxon had a soul to be
saved" (61). This deadening of empathy, Herbert opines,

indeed, is the great real evil of slavery, wheresoever and under whatever
form it exists, that it is not more, but less, hurtful to the slave than to the
master, and that its ill effects are in a much higher and more painful degree
intellectual than physical; that, while it degrades and lowers the inferiors
almost to the level of mere brutes, through the consciousness of degradation, the absence of all hope to rise in the scale of manhood, and the lack of
every stimulus to ambition or exertion, it hardens the heart, and deadens
the sensibilities of the master, and renders him, through the strange power
of circumstance and custom, blind to the existence of wrongs, sufferings,
and sorrows, at the mere narration of which, under a different phase of
things, his blood would boil with indignation. (62)

Slavery's most damnable effect, for Herbert, is in its numbing of the slave-holder's sensitivity to suffering, through which masters come to see the world in terms congenial to their ownership of other human beings. In one of many instances of the phenomenon, Yvo and Philip walk through the village of Saxon dwellings at Waltheofstow, structures that are, "for the most part, superior to the miserable collection of huts, liker to dog-houses than to any form of human habitation, which generally constituted the dwellings of this forlorn and miserable race" (62–63). Though the inhabitants themselves suffer no physical abuse under Philip, "there was a dull, sullen, dogged expression on all their faces—a look not despairing, nor even sorrowful, but perfectly impassive, as if they had nothing to hope for, or regret, or fear" (64–65). The Saxon children, whom Herbert describes as "[h]alf-naked, sturdy-limbed, filthy little savages," are barely capable of communication, "utterly untaught and untamed, scarcely capable of making themselves understood, even in their own rude dialect . . . subject to no control or correction, receiving no education, no culture whatsoever . . . ignorant of every moral or divine truth—ignorant even that each one of them was the possessor of a mortal body, far more of an immortal soul!" (66). Herbert's narrative voice registers in full horror the degradation of Philip's serfs, all of which is lost on the two Norman lords. Herbert explains that "not a thought of these things ever crossed the mind of the stately and puissant Normans," who through custom and habit have become desensitized to Saxon suffering. Only in meeting Kenric's family at close quarters—particularly, in bearing witness to their sorrow at the death of Kenric's young nephew—do Yvo and Philip begin to entertain more emphatic notions about their Saxon serfs. In one sense, *Wager of Battle* documents the longer process through which Yvo frees himself from the false consciousness imposed upon him by the institution of medieval English slavery. But Kenric himself, of all the characters in Herbert's novel, seems immune to the demoralizing circumstances surrounding him. Unlike Eadwulf and the other "dull, sullen" Saxons, Kenric retains a dignity that seems to register his fitness for freedom.

Herbert distinguishes Kenric from the other serfs, in this regard, by attributing to him a democratic bent amplified by the fact of his superior stock. Kenric is Herbert's twelfth-century enlightened democrat, convinced of the existence of "self-existing and immutable rights" (149), or "certain rights . . . natural and political . . . co-existent with himself, inalienable, indefeasible, immutable, and eternal" (154). In linking Kenric to a Jeffersonian discourse of inalienable rights, Herbert rehearses a mythology of ancient constitutionalism that had enjoyed currency among revolutionary Americans including Allan Ramsay, whose 1771 pamphlet *Historical Essay on the English Constitution* had described preconquest Saxon England as a virtual democracy: "[I]f ever God almighty did concern himself about forming a government for mankind to live happily under," Ramsay suggested, "it was that which was established in England by our Saxon forefathers."[25] Jefferson had shared in a similar adulation of Saxon England as the cradle of democratic institutions, once writing in a August, 13, 1776, letter to Edmund Pendleton, "Are we not the better for what we have hitherto abolished of the feudal system? Has not every restitution of the antient Saxon laws had happy effects? Is it not better now that we return at once into that happy system of our ancestors, the wisest and most perfect ever yet devised by the wit of man, as it stood before the 8th century?"[26]

In documenting Kenric's liberation, the opening chapters of *Wager of Battle* also narrate a Jeffersonian "restitution of the antient Saxon law" of individual freedom. Once manumitted by Philip, Kenric and his family accompany Yvo to his estate in Cumbria, where Kenric will serve as the free steward of Yvo's forests. The narrative follows the group as they traverse England on their way to the new life in the Lake District, a passage to freedom Herbert extends through picturesque narration of an English countryside whose heady effects inspire repeated excursus on the nature of liberty. "Here and there," Herbert tells us, "in the neighborhood of some ancient borough . . . through which they lay their route, they came upon broad oases of cultivated lands, with smiling farms and pleasant corn-fields and free English homesteads, stretching across the fertile valley of some blue brimful river" (138). Such "pleasant interchanges of rural with forest scenery, occurring so often as to destroy all monotony, and to keep up a delightful anticipation in the mind of the voyager, as to what sort of view would meet his eye on crossing yon hill-top" also include within their picturesque composition the sight of other free Saxons: "There, it would be a knot of sun-burned Saxon woodmen, in their green frocks and buckram hose, with long bows in their hands, short swords and quivers at their sides, and buckler of a span-breadth on their shoulders, men who had never acknowledged Norman king, nor bowed to Norman yoke" (141–42). All of this, for Herbert, spurs much meditation on the example of Saxon freedom, since "Life was in England, then, as it was in France up to the days of the Revolution, as it never has been at any time in America . . . unless we return to the primitive, social equality, and manful independence of patriarchal times; when truth was held truth, and manhood manhood, the world over; and some higher purpose in mortality was acknowledged than the mere acquiring, some larger nobleness in man than the mere possessing, of unprofitable wealth" (142–43). Indeed, Herbert hazards that in the twelfth century, "the real division . . . between man and man, of the noble and the common . . . was a mere nothing then, to what it is to-day" (143). The Arcadian splendor of Kenric's and Edith's journey to Cumbria thus articulates a visual language revealing the artificiality of all caste systems. Such ambience, for Herbert, renders the English countryside more beautiful than that of nineteenth-century America, and also provokes Kenric's various considerations of his own inalienable rights.

This is because, Herbert explains, "the careless, unconventional, equalizing life of the forest was felt as giving a stronger pulsation to the free heart, a wider expansion to the lungs, a deeper sense of freedom and power" (148–49). Within such a bucolic setting, Kenric and Edith stand "ready to be enkindled by a passing breath into a devouring flame, the sacred spark of liberty" (150). Kenric is "fit to be free," Herbert explains, since he "became free, with no fierce outbreak of servile rage and vengeance, consequent on servile emancipation, but with calm although enthusiastic gladness which fitted him to become a freeman, a citizen, and, as he is, the master of one half the round world" (150). Kenric's fitness for freedom measures his "calm" determination, his aversion from insurrectionist violence or forcible liberation. Fitness for freedom, Herbert seems to illustrate, requires a serenity, a giving over of oneself to a pulsation of the heart and a spirit of equality also manifested in the picturesque landscape; it is inimical to revolutionary violence, unachievable "at the expense of . . . floods of noble blood . . . as marked the emancipation alike of the white serfs of revolutionized France, and the black slaves of disenthralled St. Domingo" (153). Rather, it is to be secured through the passive determination of those who are sensitive to "the sacred spark of liberty," those as composed and tranquil as the countryside through which Kenric and Edith conduct their middle passage.

But Kenric's and Edith's journey across picturesque England provides contrast for a second journey of liberation traversing alternate geographies, though through the same territory: that undertaken by Eadwulf, who escapes Waltheofstow in an attempt to reach his brother in Cumbria. Eadwulf makes his decision to flee only after a neighboring Norman lord, Sir Foulke d'Oilly, murders Philip, taking over the estate and instituting a brutal regime over the villeins and serfs working its lands. The ensuing chapters narrate Eadwulf's arduous escape through a landscape bearing little resemblance to the picturesque countryside serenading Kenric and Edith during their departure from East Anglia. After eluding d'Oilly's henchmen through the midlands, Eadwulf "strode onward across the barren heath and wild moors into which the forest now subsided" (189), making his way toward the sands of the Lune estuary near Lancaster. Along the way, he gains the assistance of free Saxons, but unlike the agrarian types who populate the meadows of Kenric's journey, these are fugitives who conduct themselves through the wilderness in a constant state of armed alert.

Eadwulf's crossing of the sands of the Lune makes up the most dramatic portion of *Wager of Battle*, bringing his fugitive's narrative to a climax ridden with biblical typology and an elemental symbolism resonant with *Uncle Tom's Cabin*. With Norman pursuers close behind, Eadwulf enters the estuarial plain as the tide turns, the sands underfoot in the process of transforming to a soupy, untreadable quicksand. All, Herbert tells us, is "a brooding calm," "ominous of a storm, but . . . calm, tranquil, and peaceful," though betokening "something awful, something that seemed to whisper of coming horror" (199). Rushing across the sands in a delirium of exertion, Eadwulf at first finds "the sands were hard, even, and solid, yet so cool and damp under the worn and blistered feet of the wretched fugitive" (201). Pausing to gaze "southward, in the direction of the sea," Eadwulf imagines he can "hear the moaning roll of its ever restless waves" as the estuary refills prior to the "gradual and at first imperceptible conversion of the solid sands into miry and ponderous sludge, into moving quicksand, into actual water" (206–207).

This intermingling of elements marks the no-man's land between slavery and freedom in *Wager of Battle*, the liminal space to which Eadwulf commits himself in becoming a fugitive, and in this sense engages a broader motif among many 1850s fugitive slave narratives. Eadwulf's journey from Waltheofstow, in fact, proceeds from the solid ground of East Anglia up to the barren heights of the Peaks, but then downward into moors, indistinct places of "green, oozy morasses" (189) where Eadwulf can throw the hounds off his scent, but that lead to this place where land and liquid vie for preeminence. Like the journey into the swamp depicted in Child's "The Black Saxons," but indeed also in so much southern plantation narrative throughout the nineteenth century and beyond, Eadwulf's traversal of dry land into the uncertain territory of bogs and moors attends his crossing over from a state of subjugation to something else—not actual emancipation, since even after crossing the sands he will remain a de facto fugitive, but rather a tentative, temporary escape. On the sands of the Lune, this symbolic code merges with an Exodus narrative in which d'Oilly's men, heedlessly pursuing Eadwulf over the sands, succumb to the tide of a churning Atlantic. Of those pursuing horsemen, Herbert tells us that

> [e]very rein was drawn simultaneously, every horse halted where he stood, almost belly-deep in the sands . . . and now the soil, every where beneath them and about them, was melting away into briny ooze, with slimy worms and small eels and lampreys wriggling obscenely, where a little while before, the heaviest war-horse might have pawed long and deep without finding water; and the waves were gaining on them, with more than the speed of charging cavalry, and the nearest shore was five miles distant. (208–209)

As if by divine intervention, Eadwulf finds first an island, then a skiff, but his pursuers are lost in the miasma, succumbing to "the fate of Pharoah and his host, when the Red Sea closed above them" (214).

Indeed, then, slavery produces effects deteriorating to all. There is in the apocalypse engulfing d'Oilly's slave hunters a form of jeremiad familiar to American readers since at least Nat Turner; like Pharoah and his host pursuing the Israelites across the bed of the Red Sea, d'Oilly's men find their just desserts in a virtually supernatural eruption of death. Jane Tompkins has demonstrated the extent to which water imagery in *Uncle Tom's Cabin*

enjoins a similar sort of rhetoric, simultaneously linking abolitionist rebuke to
a vision of moral redemption conditioning not only little Eva's prophesy of
the next world beyond the fiery surface of Lake Pontchartrain, but also in
Elisa's death-defying crossing of the deteriorating ice of the Ohio River.
Tompkins explains:

> Bodies of water mediate between worlds; the Ohio runs between the slave
> states and the free; Lake Erie divides the United States from Canada, where
> runaway slaves cannot be returned to their masters; the Atlantic Ocean divides
> the North American continent from Africa, where Negroes will have a nation
> of their own; Lake Pontchartrain shows Eva the heavenly home to which she
> is going soon; the Mississippi River carries slaves from the relative ease of the
> middle states to the grinding toil of the southern plantations; the Red River
> carries Tom to the infernal regions ruled over by Simon Legree. (138)

Eadwulf's passage across the liquefying Lancastrian sands partakes in Stowe's
symbolic pattern even as it foregrounds that pattern's source in Exodus. "The
most memorable day in the history of human emancipation from slavery," the
Liberator had proclaimed in 1841, "since the overthrow of Pharoah and his
hosts in the Red Sea, is the *First of August*—on which eight hundred thousand
chattels were transformed by the touch of LIBERTY into human beings in the
British West India Colonies."[27] Eadwulf is the beneficiary of no such transforming act of legislation as those West Indian slaves, nor of such legal manu-
mission as liberates his brother, but the site of his passage to Cumbria, nevertheless, becomes the locale of a righteous Judgment, a day of reckoning and of
violent political redemption.

3. Saxon Trial and the Fugitive Slave Law

The first half of *Wager of Battle* suspends itself between these dual narratives
of liberation: Kenric's release through the legal process of compensated
emancipation, and then Eadwulf's flight from bondage and the subsequent
extermination of his pursuers as if through the intervention of the English
landscape itself, energized by the "sacred spark of liberty" that can either en-
kindle the Saxon heart or immolate his persecutors. As a form of antislavery
narrative, *Wager of Battle*'s opposition of Kenric and Eadwulf resonates with
other pairings of obedient slaves and their defiant or even insurrectionary
counterparts: one thinks of the stoic perseverance of Uncle Tom, for instance,
versus the defiant self-determination of Eliza or George Harris. Expressions of
Saxon adulation during the 1850s drew upon similarly bifurcated accounts of
the Saxons' supposed posture toward their own enslavement: on the one hand,
there was the "indomitable Saxon" who resisted his subjugation with liberty-
loving ferocity; on the other, there was the example of gradual, bloodless

emancipation taking place through irresistible moral correctness, but at a pace that spanned the course of centuries.

So far as it goes, *Wager of Battle* performs the same sort of cultural work undertaken by other northern critics of southern slavery as they referred the institution to the history of Saxon serfdom. But *Wager of Battle* also hones its commentary much further than these other yokings of the medieval and the antebellum, because in the second half of the novel Herbert explores the reaches of the analogy and its ramifications for the legal treatment of American slaves. This latter portion of the novel comprises a drama of mistaken identity wherein the agents of Sir Foulke d'Oilly (perhaps willfully) confuse Kenric for his fugitive brother, seizing him in his Cumbrian home and thus executing an illegal arrest and transport. This turn brings *Wager of Battle* into the fray of debates over the constitutionality of the Fugitive Slave Law under way throughout the 1850s, but that reached a pitch as Herbert was completing his novel for the *National Era*. Offering its account of the fundamental injustice of the Normans' enslavement of Saxons, *The Saxon Serf* resonated broadly with earlier comparisons between twelfth-century Saxon serfs and nineteenth-century African-American slaves broadcasted by Child, Douglass, and other northern abolitionists. But in its second serialized rendition as *Sherwood Forest*—and then in binding as *Wager of Battle*—the novel reoriented itself around much more specific renditions of Saxonist and abolitionist discourses concerning the illegality of the Fugitive Slave Law, often described by abolitionists as a usurpation of two cornerstones of constitutional, and Saxon, jurisprudence: habeas corpus and the right of trial by jury.

Well prior to the 1857 *Dred Scott* decision, the Fugitive Slave Law had been criticized by abolitionists for its suspension of the right to trial by jury. Speaking at Faneuil Hall on March 25, 1850 (less than three weeks after Daniel Webster's infamous "Seventh of March" speech supporting the omnibus compromise bill of which the Fugitive Slave Law was a part), Wendell Phillips pointed out that "any person claiming that he is wrongfully held may have a *jury trial*. But the Massachusetts man mistakenly seized, in Boston, cannot have this old Saxon privilege! He must be surrendered whenever any one office underling is satisfied, on paper evidence, that the slave claimant is right."[28] In describing jury trial as a civil right with "Saxon" origins, Phillips echoed Theodore Parker, who in his 1848 "Letter to the People of the United States Touching the Matter of Slavery" had similarly hailed the jury of peers, along with habeas corpus, as a specifically Saxon inheritance. Even under the coercive system of Norman enslavement, Parker had argued, "among the institutions inherited from England were the trial by jury of twelve men in all matters affecting liberty and life; the presumption in favour of life, liberty, and innocence; the right of every man under restraint to have a legal reason publicly shown for his confinement, by a writ of Habeas Corpus."[29] Echoing Hargrave's argument in *Somersett*, Parker pointed out that in Norman England,

[t]he slave could make a contract with his lord, binding as that between peer and peer. He could in his own name bring an action against any one; in some cases even against his master. He could, in all cases and in his own name, demand a trial by jury, in a court of record, to determine if he were born a slave, or free. . . . Did the slave flee to another borough or shire, a jury of that place—except in certain cases, when the trial must take place in another county—must not only convict him as a slave before the master could recover his body, but must convict him of being the slave of that special claimant. (63)[30]

Written two years prior to the passage of the Fugitive Slave Law, Parker's letter drew southern statutes into invidious comparison with Norman common law, since

in South Carolina, Virginia, and Louisiana, the slave is not allowed a jury trial, even when his life is in peril. . . . But in every slave state he may be beaten to the extent of 'thirty-nine lashes well laid on,' without the verdict of a jury, but by the decision of a body of justice of the peace, varying in members from two to five. In all cases he is tried by men who regard him only as a thing, never by a jury of his peers—not even a mixed jury of slaveholders and slaves. (64)

Moreover, in a passage from his open letter republished in an April 1848 edition of the *North Star*, Parker had characterized Article 4, Section 2, of the Constitution (whereby those accused as fugitive slaves may be "carried back to slavery without the intervention of a Trial by Jury to determine whether the man is a *slave*") as "a departure from the Customs of your Fathers; a departure which the common law of England would not justify at any time since the Norman conquest." Trial by jury, Parker went on to say, has proven "the great safeguard of personal freedom; even in the dark ages of English law it was the Right of every man, of every fugitive slave, when his person was in peril."[31] By the time of Phillips's March 1850 address at Faneuil Hall, such concerns over the endurance of the "old Saxon privilege" had assumed urgency in light of the new federal law, which annulled what Parker had described as the Saxon right of the fugitive slave to be tried at his or her place of capture. Phillips hypothesized,

Suppose the claimant, either through malice or carelessness, has taken the wrong person, taken a Massachusetts freeman: how shall the victim be righted? Why, it is said, by appealing to some court in New Orleans, when he arrives. . . . How is he to get friends in New Orleans, where he never was before, to bring his case before a tribunal? Months may pass ere that, and meanwhile the poor, friendless one is melting fast into the indistinguishable mass of slaves, and may be sold and passed on from hand to hand, till redress is impossible. . . . The Southerners tell us, that the right of trial by jury is inconsistent with slavery. They tell is that if the Southerner is obliged to

prove his title to his slave, he would be very much inconvenienced! . . . But
if he be inconvenienced, who is to suffer, he or liberty? (51)

Such arguments drawing the Fugitive Slave Law into invidious comparison
with English Common Law were broadly resonant during the 1850s. On the
one hand, the era witnessed a call from legal reformers such as David Dudley
Field to codify all American statute so as to extricate it from English precedent.[32] But at the same time, the charge that the Fugitive Slave Law constituted
a violation of habeas corpus was taken seriously enough for attorney general
John Crittenden, acting in September 1850, to advise President Fillmore to
sign the congressional bill into law, offering his endorsement in a letter waving
off charges that the law would circumvent civil rights to trial by jury or habeas
corpus. "It is well known and admitted," Crittenden stated, "historically and
judicially, that [Article 4, Section 2] of the Constitution was made for the purpose of securing to the citizens of slaveholding States the complete ownership
of their slaves, as property, in any and every State or Territory of the Union
into which they might escape."[33] Thus, "[t]here is nothing in all this that does
not seem to me to be consistent with the Constitution, and necessary, indeed,
to redeem the pledge which it contains, that such fugitives 'shall be delivered
up on claim' of their owners" (378). Emphasizing "that there is nothing [in the
Fugitive Slave Law] which conflicts with or suspends, or was intended to suspend, the privilege of the writ of *habeas corpus*," and pointing out that "the bill
says not one word about that writ; because, by the Constitution, Congress is
expressly forbidden to suspend the privilege of this writ" (379), Crittenden
went on to argue that "[i]t is only by some confusion of ideas that such a conflict can be supposed to exist. It is not within the province or privilege of this
great writ to loose those whom the *law* has bound. That would be to put a writ
granted by the law in opposition to the law, to make one part of the law de-
structive of another" (380; emphasis original). Rather, "It is issued, upon proper
complaint, to make inquiry into the causes of commitment or imprisonment,
and its sole remedial power and purpose is to deliver the party from 'all
manner of *illegal* confinement'" (380; emphasis original). And further: "The
condition of one in custody as a fugitive slave is, under this law, so far as respects the writ of *habeas corpus*, precisely the same as that of all other prisoners under laws of the United States" (380).

Crittenden's recommendations would reverberate through Massachusetts
District Court Justice Peleg Sprague's charge to the jury in the 1851 trial of
James Scott, who was tried after assisting Shadrach Minkins, a Virginia slave
who had escaped his master in 1850 only to be arrested in Boston in 1851. In his
charge to the grand jury in March, Sprague had advised, "It is to be observed
that this statute subjects no person to arrest who was not before liable to be
seized and carried out of the State; for, ever since the adoption of the Constitution, these same persons have been liable to be taken and carried away by

those from whose service they had escaped."[34] In an extract published in the June 20 issue of the *Liberator*, Sprague similarly reminded jurors that

> [t]hose who, impressed only with the feelings of the present time, find it difficult to believe that our fathers in the North could have intended to render persons of color liable to be carried out of the State as slaves, without trial by jury, and with a hearing only before a magistrate, will find it useful to go back to the period when the Constitution was established. . . . Runaway negroes were taken back to their masters, generally, it is believed, by mere recaption without legal process, certainly without trial by jury, or formal, protracted proceedings before a court of record.[35]

The jurisprudence of Sprague and Crittenden notwithstanding, the abolitionist press continued to hammer home the point that the Fugitive Slave Law eroded basic civil rights. In April 1852, the *Essex County Freeman* declared, "If professional men-hunters can enter our territory, and run off free-born citizens—or those not free-born—to slavery, without a trial, and if every colored seaman, who happens to be landed at a Southern port, is liable to be seized and cast into prison, or sold at public auction, then we are indeed miserable cravens if we do not resist, and refuse to be thus kicked and cuffed about."[36] Moreover, a series of state courts and legislatures responded to the early events of 1850 by passing rulings and bills designed to contravene the Fugitive Slave Law. The Vermont General Assembly, for instance, passed on November 13, 1850, its "Act relating to the writ of *habeas corpus* to persons claimed as fugitive slaves, and the right of trial by jury," which directed that "[i]t shall be the duty of State's attorneys, within their respective counties, whenever any inhabitant of this State is arrested or claimed as a fugitive slave, on being informed thereof, diligently and faithfully to use all lawful means to protect, defend, and procure so as to be discharged, every such person so arrested or claimed as a fugitive slave" (Section 2) and, further, that "[t]he application of any State's attorney in writing to any one of the judges of the Supreme Court, or to any circuit judge . . . stating in substance the name of the prisoner and the persons detaining him, if known, and that the person arrested, claimed, or imprisoned, is arrested, claimed, or imprisoned as a fugitive slave, shall be sufficient authority to authorize the issuing of the writ of habeas corpus" (Section 3).[37] The Vermont bill insisted that accused fugitive slaves had the right to habeas corpus, in accordance with which the arresting party would be required both to establish the positive identity of the arrested and provide documented proof that the detained had indeed been at one time the slave of the accuser.

Crittenden and other supporters of the 1850 law may well have responded, thus far, that the Vermont bill added nothing to due process as defined by the law itself, since as Crittenden had advised the president, "The conditions of one in custody as a fugitive slave, under this law, so far as respects the writ of habeas corpus, is precisely the same as that for all other prisoners under laws of the United States." But the Vermont bill went further still in directing that "[t]he court to which such an appeal is taken, and any other court to which a writ of habeas corpus in behalf of such person claimed or arrested as a fugitive slave, is made returnable, may and shall, on application of either party to such proceeding, allow and direct a trial by jury, on all questions of fact in issue between the parties, in the matter aforesaid" (Section 6).[38] To be sure, a trial by jury on such questions of fact could not call into question the now-established rights of southerners to lay claim to fugitive slaves within free territory. But by insisting upon a locally convened trial, the Vermont bill attacked the strategy of extradition that formed the very basis of the Fugitive Slave Law.

In his 1850 Faneuil Hall address, Phillips had elaborated his own argument for refusing the extradition of fugitive slaves:

> *Where* a man finds stolen property, *there* he is to prove that it is his. That is common law. If I find a stolen horse in Marshfield, I am bound to prove *in Marshfield* that it is mine, and not leave the town with it until it is decided there by a jury of twelve men. [Applause.] But if an unfortunate colored man, claimed as a slave, should go to Marshfield, and he would be very unfortunate if he did, [laughter,] for of the few men who have been willing to consign their names to infamy by proclaiming their readiness to assist in a slave-hunt, certainly that of Daniel Webster should stand at the head [renewed laughter]; but if such an unfortunate should take refuge from a slave hunter there, he is not to have a jury trial of Massachusetts men. No! on the affidavit, paper testimony of any body, he is to be carried any number of thousand miles—carried off helpless. (51; emphasis original)

"This is not the Constitution," Phillips declared. "Bad as that is, it is nothing like this." Laying aside his own long-standing view of the Constitution as a pro-slavery compact, Phillips pointed out that according to the Constitution, "in all criminal cases, the right of trial by jury shall be preserved; in all civil cases, where the value is above twenty dollars, the right of trial shall be preserved." Therefore, Phillips, reasoned, "[w]hen a slave is arrested, it is either a criminal or a civil case; and the Constitution, therefore, requires a jury" (51). Rounding out his speech, Phillips remarked, "I had almost said, that jury trial was a law of nature,—certainly it is a law of the Saxon race; and the convenience of slavery must give way to that great jury trial which protects the liberties of the humblest race in our midst [Cheers]" (51).

Such lamentations over the denial of trial by jury and habeas corpus attended the very passage of the Fugitive Slave Law, which Phillips and Parker described repeatedly as an assault upon inviolate rights of Saxon inheritance, but events of May and June 1854 raised the controversy to a pitch just as Herbert was preparing to commence reserialization of his novel with the October 12 issue of the *National Era*. On May 24, Anthony Burns, a fugitive slave who had escaped his Virginia master by ship in 1853, was arrested in Boston and, after summary proceedings four days later, sent back to Virginia under armed guard on June 2. On the night of May 26, Parker addressed an angry throng at Faneuil Hall, beginning with the incendiary phrase "Fellow subjects of Virginia . . ." That morning, Thomas Wentworth Higginson had called for an armed assault on the courthouse, and indeed while Parker was giving his speech, audience members planted by Higginson exclaimed that such an assault was already under way, after which the Faneuil Hall crowd voted to storm the courthouse and liberate Burns by force.[39] Among the words preceding that turn were these, by which Parker once again called upon the endangered Saxon institutions of habeas corpus and trial by jury:

> Where are the rights of Massachusetts? A Fugitive Slave Law Commissioner has got them all in his pocket. Where is the trial by jury? Watson Freeman has it under his Marshal's staff. Where is the great right of personal replevin, which our fathers wrestled, several hundred years ago, from the tyrants who once lorded it over Great Britain? Judge Sprague trod it under his feet! Where is the sacred right of *habeas corpus*? Deputy Marshal Riley can crush it in his hands, and Boston does not say anything against it.[40]

The notion that not only Burns's rights, but also the rights of white Massachusetts citizens, descended from Saxon institutions wrested from tyrants several hundred years prior, was repeated by the Reverend Eden B. Foster, pastor of the John Street Congregational Church in Lowell, in a June 25 sermon entitled "The Rights of the Pulpit." What the Burns case had taught the people of Massachusetts, Foster argued, was that the Fugitive Slave Law "is not designed simply or mainly to hold the black race in subjection, but to place in bondage the white race of the North. It is a restriction on our Saxon blood, and Saxon will, and Saxon liberties. It is to restrain the education, conscience, and independence of our children. It is to limit our free speech, free thought, free worship, and free action."[41]

Antislavery politics not only configured northeastern apprehensions of ancient England, in other words. Abolitionist and sectional thought configured itself in relation to those apprehensions. Of those configurations, the repeated charge that the Fugitive Slave Law assailed Saxon rights of habeas corpus and the trial by jury became prominent, and in this light the Burns case cast a long shadow over U.S. congressional deliberations in June, which came to focus on habeas corpus and the right to trial by jury. On the twenty-second, Senator Julius Rockwell of Massachusetts presented a bill for the repeal of the Fugitive Slave Law. Four days later, Charles Sumner, in an impassioned argument that for weeks drew the contumely of virtually the entire southern section of the Senate, pointed out that "[i]n violation of the Constitution, [the Fugitive Slave Law] commits the great question of human freedom—than which none is more sacred in the law—not to a solemn trial, but to summary proceedings."

Moments later, he charged, "It authorizes judgment on *ex parte* evidence, by affidavits, without the sanction of cross-examination. It denies the writ of *habeas corpus*, ever known as the palladium of the citizen." Still later, he declared that the law "takes away that essential birth-right of the citizen, trial by jury, in a question of personal liberty and a suit at common law."[42] Rejoining Sumner, senator James Mason of Virginia echoed Crittenden in likening the fugitive slave to the arrested criminal, neither of whose recourse to habeas corpus could settle the charges upon which he or she was arrested:

> Sir, the proof establishes the legality of the arrest and detention, and is an answer to the writ of *habeas corpus;* and in this the fugitive slave law does not depart from the policy regulating the administration of all penal law. One arrested as a fugitive from justice is entitled, on his arrest, to a *habeas corpus*—for what? To determine whether he is committed the offense with which he was charged, at the place whence he escaped? Certainly not; but to determine only whether he was so charged in proper form of law to authorize his detention until a trial could be had: and proof that he was so charged is then, also, an answer to the *habeas corpus*, and he must be remanded without inquiring whether the charge is true or false.[43]

Habeas corpus, as Mason argued, affords the accused no more than a hearing to determine that charges have been made, that the arrested is indeed the designee of those charges, that the arrest itself has been carried out "in proper form of law."

But Mason was silent on the point behind Sumner's assertion that habeas corpus was rendered meaningless in the arrest of fugitive slaves, since the slave's state of rightlessness—codified most thoroughly two years later in the case of *Dred Scott*, but also indicated in other cases at the state level going back to *North Carolina v. Mann* (which held in 1829 that masters who killed their slaves could be tried only for manslaughter)[44]—effectively annulled the presumption of state nonauthority behind habeas corpus itself. The procedure that is habeas corpus had, since the Magna Carta, laid the burden of evidence upon the accuser who must justify the infringement of the accused's basic right to noninterference from the state. The court's role under habeas corpus is to presume that this right has been violated until the accuser produces compelling evidence to indicate that the accusation has been affixed to its proper designee. But as Phillips, Parker, and other abolitionist statesmen had argued since 1850, slaves—themselves without rights to be violated—cannot avail themselves of such court protection.

Firing back on June 28, Sumner ridiculed Mason while refusing to engage in the analogy between criminals and slaves:

> With imperious look, and in the style of Sir Forcible Feeble, that Senator has undertaken to call in question my statement that the fugitive slave bill

denied the writ of *habeas corpus*, and, in doing this, he has assumed a superiority for himself which, permit me to tell him now in this presence, nothing in him can sanction. . . . [A]s a Senator from Massachusetts, and as a man, I place myself at every point in comparison with that honorable assailant. And to his peremptory assertion that the fugitive slave bill does not deny the *habeas corpus*, I oppose my assertion, as peremptory as his own, that it does, and there I leave that question.

But Sumner also challenged Mason to answer the charge that the Fugitive Slave Law abrogated the right to trial by jury. "The Constitution," he reminded, "has secured the inestimable right of trial by jury in 'suits at common law,' where the value in controversy exceeds twenty dollars." Sumner insisted that "there can be no question that the claim for a fugitive slave is within this condition," and then challenged Mason "to show that a claim for a fugitive slave is not, according to the early precedents and writs, well known to the framers of the Constitution . . . as a *suit of common law*, to which, under the solemn guaranty of the Constitution, is attached the trial by jury, as an inseparable incident. Let the Senator undertake this if he can."[45]

Congressional debates over habeas corpus, jury trial, and the Fugitive Slave Law continued throughout the year, finally reaching a crescendo on February 23, 1855, when the Senate held a special session to deliberate a bill introduced by Isaac Toucey for the Judiciary Committee, "to protect officers and other persons acting under the authority of the United States" by referring all charges leveled against such federal agents to federal circuit court.[46] A number of the speeches given that day were published over the course of March in the *National Era*: on March 8, the newspaper included speeches by Sumner and William Seward, and the following week, the March 15 issue included a speech by newly elected Henry Wilson of Massachusetts. In it Wilson struck a more moderate tone than Sumner, explaining that "[i]f the Fugitive Slave Act were repealed, the Commonwealth of Massachusetts will fulfill her constitutional obligations; but she will do it in her own way, so as to protect fully the rights of every man within her jurisdiction," an assertion John Weller of California derided as he asked, "whether there is a Senator within the sound of my voice who believes . . . that if this subject were pretermitted to the State Legislatures, it would operate as a total denial of the right to slave-holders to go within some States and recapture their property?"[47] Sumner, speaking just before the question was called late in the night, referred once again to the Massachusetts bill for repeal of the Fugitive Slave Law, and described the present bill to protect federal officers as a usurpation of state and local jurisdiction, legislation that "lacks every essential element of law," and "an assumption by Congress of power not delegated it under the Constitution, and an infraction of rights secured to the States." Immediately after Sumner's speech, the bill was passed, 30 to 9.[48]

The *National Era's* extensive coverage of the Senate's February 23 debates juxtaposed excerpts of northern senators' speeches against the bill alongside the continuing saga of Herbert's Saxon serfs, which was now reaching a dé- nouement set within the twelfth-century legal system. The *Era's* placement of these speeches—which not only inveighed against the bill's provisions to pro- vide immunity from local and state prosecution for officers under the fugitive slave law operating in northern jurisdictions, but also repeated the broader charge that the law nullified constitutional guarantees of habeas corpus and trial by jury—orchestrated a dialogue between the events of the day and Her- bert's unfolding narrative. Sumner's speech, for instance, was published under the title "The Demands of Freedom" in the March 8 issue, where it shared its page with chapter 18 of *Sherwood Forest*, "The Arrest," which dramatized Ken- ric's misidentification and capture as Eadwulf. When Kenric demands of d'Oilly a legal writ authorizing his arrest, d'Oilly scoffs, "No, sirrah, I seize mine villeyn, of my own right, with mine own hand" (258).[49] "[Y]ou must seize me, to seize justly, by the sheriff; and I deny the villeynage, and claim trial," Kenric retorts, an assertion that predictably outrages d'Oilly. The chap- ter ends with Kenric's forcible removal to nearby Kendal, where (in the next chapter, published in the March 15 issue of the *Era*), d'Oilly is confronted by Yvo. The *Era's* placement of "The Arrest" next to Sumner's speech on the bill to extend immunity to slave hunters established a commerce between the events of the chapter and many of Sumner's assertions—for instance, Sum- ner's lamentation over "the number of free persons [the Fugitive Slave Law] has doomed to Slavery," as well his censure of "the brutal conduct of its offi- cers."[50] As if in enactment of Sumner's opening statement in the midnight speech that became "The Demands of Freedom"—"It is hardly an accidental conjunction which thus constantly brings Slavery and midnight together"— the placement of that speech and its insistence that "[b]ad as slavery is, it is not so bad as hunting slaves" next to d'Oilly's lawless removal of Kenric, under cover of night and in contravention of locally administered procedure, ampli- fied Sumner's insistence that the bill to protect federal officers, like the Fugi- tive Slave Law itself, made for an unconstitutional nullification of local and state authority, a usurpation of right by might.

The following week, chapter 19 of *Sherwood Forest* ("The Sheriff") appeared alongside Henry Wilson's speech insisting upon Massachusetts's willingness to prosecute the fugitive slave law "in her own way" without federal interfer- ence. Kenric, having been brutalized by d'Oilly's men, now awaits his removal to Waltheofstow when Yvo arrives on scene to halt the transportation through an assertion of Kenric's rights to due process. "There is some error here, Sir Foulke," Yvo insists. "That man, whom I see some one hath brutally mis- used, of which more anon, is not called Eadwulf at all, but Kenric. Nor is he your serf, fair sir, nor any man's serf at all, or villeyn, but a free Englishman, as any who stands on this floor" (*Wager* 266; *NE* 41). When d'Oilly repeats his insistence that Kenric is in fact Eadwulf, Yvo cuts off the debate by questioning d'Oilly's jurisdiction in Cumbria and initiating a formal call for trial. "There is some error here, Sir Foulke . . . but the law will decide it," Yvo repeats, before pointing out that d'Oilly, whose manor is situated on the other side of England, lacks the warrant to seize a Saxon fugitive in Cumbria. "And now, speaking of the law," he says, "Sir Baron, may I crave, by what right, or form of law, you have laid your hands on this man, within the jurisdiction of my manor, and under shadow of night? I say, by what warrant have you done this?" (*Wager* 266–67; *NE* 41).

Appearing in the *Era* on the same page as Senator Wilson's speech, Yvo's authoritative assertion of local rights of jurisdiction resonated not only with the reprinted exchange between Wilson and his skeptical southern colleagues, but also with Sumner's account from the week before of "outrages, plentiful as words, which enter into the existing Fugitive Slave Act, among which are the denial of trial by jury; the denial of the writ of *habeas corpus;* the authorization of judgment on *ex parte* evidence."[51] D'Oilly's response to Yvo's demand for a warrant, moreover, reveals him once again as an essentially lawless agent of force. "By the same right, and form, and warrant," he exclaims, "by which, wherever I find my stolen goods, there I seize them! By the best law of right; that is, the law of might" (267). D'Oilly's is an assertion of naked power to which Yvo responds, again, through reference to the demands of legal procedure: "[N]one can seize within this shire," he says, repeating Kenric, "but I, the sheriff of it."

> Or if you proceed by writ *de nativo habendo,* no one can serve that writ, within this shire, but I, the sheriff of it. What! When a man can not seize and sell an ox or an ass, that is claimed by another, without due process of law, shall he seize and take that which is the dearest thing any man hath, even as dear as the breath of his nostrils, his right to himself, his liberty, without any form at all? No, Sir Foulke, no! Our English law presumes every man free, till he be proved a slave; and no man, who claims freedom, can be deprived of freedom, no, not by my lord the King himself in counsel, except upon the verdict of an English jury. (*Wager* 267; *NE* 41)

Having invoked Wendell Phillips's 1850 contrast between the rights of a horse and of a slave, Yvo ends his speech by summoning his bailiff, who supplies the proper writ to initiate Kenric's trial as well as a bail bond—all of which, of course, reduces d'Oilly to "impotent fury" (271). The demands Yvo places upon d'Oilly transform *Wager of Battle* to a legal thriller, the narrative's economy of suspense now reorienting itself around the spectacle of court procedure, from the pomp of the king's judiciary to the satisfaction of vindicating argument. This is not to say that the novel enters into meet agreement with all details, for instance, of Charles Sumner's critique of either the Fugitive Slave Law or the bill to protect officers under that law. Still, as Herbert explains at the outset of the chapter "The Trial," "There is nothing in all the reign of that wise, moderate, and able prince . . . the Second Henry of England, so remarkable, or in his character so praiseworthy, as his efforts to establish a perfect system both of judiciary power and of justice throughout England" (272). Though administered by regal officials, this "perfect system," through which "justice was not for many centuries more equitably administered" (272), was in Herbert's account built upon utter respect for local jurisdictions and the authority of local officials. In the writ *de libertate probanda* for which Yvo has applied even prior to Kenric's arrest, Kenric is instructed to put his plea "before our justices, when they shall come into those parts, to wit, in our good city of Lancaster" the following month (269). In Lancaster, the local sheriff is directed to impanel a jury, which consequently consists of "twelve men being selected and sworn, six of whom were belted knights, two esquires of Norman birth, and four Saxon franklins . . . all lawful and free men, and sufficient to form a jury" (282). Herbert's emphasis throughout such passages falls upon a nationally formed system of justice that conducts itself locally, in courts near the site of arrest and empowering local citizens to form verdicts. Forced to make his case under such circumstances, d'Oilly is unable to veil the truth of Kenric's identity.

Nor is he able to control the effects of his own testimony upon the sensibilities of the jury. When one of d'Oilly's henchmen describes the pursuit of Eadwulf across the moors, Herbert tells us that

> the witness described, vividly and accurately, the pursuit of the fugitive with bloodhounds; his superhuman efforts to escape, both by speed of foot and by power of swimming; his wonderful endurance, and, at last, his vanishing, as it were, without leaving a single trace, either for sight or scent, in the midst of a bare moor. Great sympathy and excitement were manifested throughout the whole court, at this graphic narrative; and all eyes were turned, especially those of the fair sex, to the fine athletic person and noble features of Kenric, as he stood at the bar, alone of all that company, impassive and unmoved, with looks of pity and admiration. (288)

When d'Oilly's witness moves on to describe Eadwulf's escape across the sands of the Lune estuary, indeed, "the excitement in the vast assembly knew no bounds. There were wild cries and sobs, and the vast multitude rocked and heaved to and fro, and several women swooned, and were carried out of the courthouse insensible, and seemingly lifeless. It was many minutes before order could be restored" (289).

The rule of might d'Oilly acclaims as he apprehends Kenric, that exercise of sheer extralegal power through which he seizes Kenric by his own hand, in the end ushers the lord's demise. After Kenric's exoneration in court, Yvo brings an indictment of d'Oilly for the murder of Philip, an accusation d'Oilly chooses to fend off not through legal deliberation but through the medieval institution of trial by combat. In the ensuing wager of battle, d'Oilly is killed by Yvo's second, Sir Aradas, and with his demise Herbert ends the threat he poses not only to Kenric but also to Eadwulf, who after receiving a king's pardon for his crimes rejoins Kenric and his family to resume life in the northern regions of Cumbria. And so, whether Herbert or his editors at the *National Era* intended the resonance, d'Oilly is prosecuted—executed, in fact—by the very legal process he initiates in his illegal capture of Kenric; as a result of this narrative turn, he becomes an example of the slave hunter from distant regions who is trapped within the snares arising as a result of his seizure of an allegedly fugitive slave outside of his home jurisdiction, the very eventuality that the February bill to protect federal officers had sought to prevent. Herbert thus not only commits his narrative to a reversal of the ethos behind that bill—in apparent insistence upon the necessary vulnerability of slave hunters to prosecution for their crimes—but also to his larger affirmation of the trial by jury as an institution for the slave as well as the citizen, and the mechanism best equipped to transform the one into the other. It was, Herbert tells us in the final sentence of both *Wager of Battle* and *Sherwood Forest*, "the grand force of that holiest Saxon institution, Trial by Jury, that raised Kenric from a Saxon serf to be an English freeman" (336), which in the context of 1850s America is another way of proclaiming a society of laws—whether whose statutes descend from the Magna Carta, English Common Law, or the U.S. Constitution—inimical to a nation of slavery.

Picturing America

1. Lay of the Land

Liberated from slavery, his free Saxon heart flaring with the "sacred spark of liberty," Henry Herbert's eponymous Saxon, Kenric, exults in an English landscape serenading his passage from the serfdom of the East Anglian lowlands to the freedom of the Cumbrian heights. For Herbert and the *National Era*, Kenric incarnates an imagined English past, yoked into synchronicity with other incarnations of a felt American present. A similar kind of functional anachronism pervades the drama of Child's insurrecting plantation in "The Black Saxons," as well as those parts of *English Traits* celebrating the liberty-loving Saxon who provides the most democratizing energies Emerson discerns within the political and social community of the United States. When, in his preface to his 1867 collection *War Poetry of the South*, William Gilmore Simms stated that the verse of his anthology "[b]elongs to the national literature, and will hereafter be regarded as constituting a proper part of it, just as legitimately to be recognized by the nation as are the rival ballads of the cavaliers and roundheads, by the English, in the great civil war of their country," he too realigned American and English historical vectors—as did, in a related way, the *Charleston Mercury* when it published in 1861 an anonymous sonnet entitled "The Irrepressible Conflict," which spoke of the war with the northern states as an "ancient conflict with the foreign foe!"[1] Though distanced by centuries and leagues, the Saxon and Norman figures conjured by Herbert, Douglass, Child, Emerson, Fitzhugh, and many others writing prior to the war nevertheless provided devices for retheorizing the contemporary in terms of a constructed English past. Beneath both the biological alignments forming the subject matter of chapter 1 and the historical analogy pervading the literary and intellectual histories examined in chapter 2, ancient sites of English lineage provide the genome by which the political entanglements of the antebellum might be mapped, reconsidered, and potentially maneuvered.

But at that juncture of *Wager of Battle* to which I allude again, Herbert also calls attention to an exhilarating experience of the English landscape surrounding his liberated Saxon serf. Indeed, even for Kenric's new kinsman, Sir Yvo de Taillebois, it is "the very wildness and solitude of the locality, as much as the exquisite charm of the loveliest scenery in England, to which, strange to say, he was fully alive," which is to say that under the influence of such natural splendor, even the Norman lord feels the flush of egalitarian sympathies.[2] Pursuing the axiom that connects an aesthetic preference for English landscape to a politics of liberation, my next chapters turn to an English model of natural gorgeousness in order to explore further how U.S. artists and intellectuals of the antebellum period reimagined their environs—and through those, their sectional controversies—in terms suggested by English space. Whereas the first two chapters have detailed sectionalist invocations of England within historical frames of reference—bygone realities to which other, present circumstances may be anchored—the next two turn to English environments whose relations with history were less fixed. These environments were aesthetic achievements, "natural" spaces that in fact comprised an exemplar of carefully constructed, practically virtual experience. The historical dimensions of such spaces are conflicted, in that the aesthetics they engendered—which I consider under the category of the picturesque, a rendition of English romanticism that has in recent years garnered much attention from literary investigators—were both immediate and nostalgic, invested in the moment of perception even while rooted in a retrospective because wistful set of preferences and values. The picturesque is of interest for my purposes because within the picturesque mode American thinkers found a series of opportunities not only to rethink the appearance of their environments and to reconsider their effects upon human sensibilities, but also to reimagine the economic and political horizons of the human beings who populated such places. All of these undertakings took instruction from English predecessors, and many carried ramifications for how Americans understood the circumstances underpinning the sectional crisis.

The next two chapters work toward an understanding of how American investments in the English picturesque—which is to say particular readings of the aesthetic, which in turn imply particular uses to which it might be put—speak to the conflict over slavery that forms the ultimate referent of all sectional struggle in antebellum America. To begin, my interest in this chapter is to examine an antebellum pattern of engagement with the picturesque as it took shape in the northeastern United States, and, as I trace the terms of that engagement, it will also be helpful to situate Emerson in relation to its unfolding. Emerson provides a meter of a larger northeastern investment in picturesque ways of seeing, in one sense, because those ways of seeing aligned what

Emerson calls the "axis of vision" informing his extremely influential 1836 essay *Nature*. But even as it speaks a terminology of the picturesque, *Nature* registers Emerson's anxieties over a broader U.S. capitulation to English landscape aesthetics. That the picturesque exerted such force upon the essay that launched Emerson's career—and a work that would provide such ballast for transcendentalist thought across the North Atlantic prior to the Civil War—is of interest here in its own right as a matter of intellectual history. But tracing such transmissions of influence also advances a more nuanced understanding of the sectional mind in the United States, because in its emphatic phenomenology of the grand sweep and its prioritization of broad impressions of spatial continuity over natural variety—in short, inasmuch as it offered a powerful set of tropes concerning the composition of unified landscapes—the picturesque would also resonate at other, cisatlantic registers as U.S. lands became rhetorically, politically, and eventually literally, divided.

2. Finding the America of America

Emerson makes for a fine entrée into U.S. conversation about English landscape precisely because his assessment of that conversation was so conflicted, and to plum the depth of that conflictedness one could do worse than to turn to his own response to the English landscape itself. Unfortunately, Emerson was far less effusive, especially during his first trip to England in 1833, on the subject of English topography than many other U.S. visitors, but during his second visit of 1847–48, he was more willing to compliment. In *English Traits*, he muses over the beauty of the English countryside: "England," as he says there, "is a garden. Under an ash-colored sky, the fields have been combed and rolled till they appear to have been finished with a pencil instead of a plough." The English land is a production of art for Emerson, who dotes upon a nation where "[n]othing is left as it was made," where "[r]ivers, hills, valleys, the sea itself feel the hand of a master." Recapitulating the Saxonist and racialist discourse he both develops and interrogates elsewhere in *English Traits*, Emerson supposes that in England, "[t]he long habituation of a powerful and ingenious race has turned every rood of land to its best use, has found all the capabilities, the arable soil, the quarriable rock, the highways, the byways, the ford, the navigable waters, so that England is a huge phalanstery, where all that man wants is provided within the precinct." The result of centuries of cultivation by the "ingenious race," whose handiwork Emerson now beholds from the vantage of the locomotive, is to have transformed a nation to a vast panorama laid out, as it were, for the gratification of the eye: "Cushioned and comforted in every manner, the traveler rides as on a cannon-ball, high and low, over rivers and towns, through mountains, in tunnels of three or four miles, at near twice the speed of our trains; and reads quietly the Times newspaper, which, by its immense correspondence and reporting, seems to have machinized the rest of the world for his occasion."[3] A picturesque tourist who now traverses the breadth of England in cushy, high-tech conveyance, Emerson cannot help but concede to England the terms America often reserves for its own assertions of cultural superiority: technological preeminence, ecological sublimity.

Emerson's description of the English landscape here is also an account of the special enthrallment England exacted from him during his second visit, and for other Americans throughout the era. Bearing the impress of aesthetics that had framed English experiences of landscape since the middle of the eighteenth century, it also diverges from Emerson's more guarded response to Europe during his first trip abroad in 1833. Beholding "[a]ll of England" as "a garden" hints at Emerson's eventual adaptation of picturesque ways of looking at landscape, as does his supposition that the "combed and rolled" vistas of the English countryside "appear to have been finished by the pencil rather than the plough." Imagining an England finished by the pencil, sketched as it were by "the hand of a master" who, having "turned every rood of land to its best use . . . [finding] all the capabilities," leaves "[n]othing . . . left as it was made," Emerson in one sense embraces a discourse of improvement initiated by John Locke, who famously asserts, in his *Two Treatises on Government* (1689), "Land that is left wholly to Nature, that hath no Improvement of Pasturage, Tillage, or Planting, is called, as indeed it is, *Waste*" (even as Locke designated America as just such an unimproved wasteland: "I ask, whether in the wild Woods, and uncultivated Waste of *America*, left to Nature and without any Improvement, Tillage or Husbandry, a thousand Acres yield the needy and wretched Inhabitants as many Conveniences of Life, as ten Acres of equally fertile Land do in *Devonshire*, where they are well cultivated?").[4] But in regarding the improved English countryside as an analog of a pencil sketch or written composition, Emerson more precisely referenced a tradition of large-scale improvement initiated by the great landscape architect Lancelot "Capability" Brown but more widely associated, in Emerson's day, with the generation of romantic landscape architects who succeeded him, who imagined their work in terms suggested by painting, and who most often used the word "picturesque" to describe their aesthetic aims.[5]

The Reverend William Gilpin, whose 1768 *Essay on Prints* provided a theoretical basis for the picturesque aesthetic in romantic landscape architecture, explained in his 1792 *Three Essays on Picturesque Beauty* that "[t]he picturesque eye, it is true, finds its *chief* objects in nature; but it delights also in the images of art. . . . *A painter's nature* is whatever he *imitates;* whether the object be what is commonly called natural, or artificial."[6] Painters and sketch artists, Gilpin believed, should strive to represent not the aesthetically imperfect forms nature actually took, but those intended for it by timeless standards of picturesque beauty. Too often real nature lacked the composed presentation artistic rendering might otherwise install, and so it fell to the picturesque artist

to enrich the real through expert intervention. Most often for Gilpin, such interference consisted in accentuating asymmetry over balance, dynamism over
calm, undulation over uniformity, variety over monotony, "rough" over
"smooth." For instance, "An extended plain is a simple object. It is the continuation only of one uniform idea. But the mere *simplicity* of a plain produces no
beauty. Break the surface of it, as you did your pleasure-ground; add trees,
rocks, and declivities; that is, give it *roughness*, and you give it also *variety*.
Thus by inriching the *parts* of a united *whole* with *roughness*, you obtain the
combined idea of *simplicity*, and *variety; from whence results the picturesque*."[7]
Near the outset of *Three Essays*, Gilpin turned his aesthetics of the rough upon
the gardens laid earlier in the century by landscapers such as Brown, criticiz-
ing their overall impression of regularity and finish:

> Again, why does an elegant piece of garden-ground make no figure on
> canvas? The shape is pleasing; the combination of the objects, harmonious;
> and the winding of the walk in the very line of beauty. All this is true; but the
> *smoothness* of the whole, tho right, and as it should be in nature, offends in
> picture. Turn the lawn into a piece of broken ground: plant rugged oaks
> instead of flowering shrubs: break the edges of the walk: give it the rudeness
> of a road: mark it with wheel-tracks; and scatter around a few stones, and
> brushwood; in a word, instead of making the whole *smooth*, make it *rough*;
> and you make it also *picturesque*. All the other ingredients of beauty it al-
> ready possessed.[8]

The artificiality of the formal lawn provided Gilpin with a foil for his own
ideas, a staid convention against which the more dynamic qualities of the picturesque could not but appear in ebullient relief. He declaims elsewhere in
Three Essays: "How flat, and insipid is often the garden-scene! how puerile and
absurd! the banks of the river how smooth, and parallel! the lawn, and its
boundaries, how unlike nature!"[9] Gilpin's specifications concerning picturesque composition, along with his depiction of the artist—not as mimetic
duplicator of the real, but rather an improver who reshaped nature in accordance with artistic principles—exerted a tremendous influence upon the
romantic landscape architects who succeeded Capability Brown. One of these,
the rural improver Uvedale Price, who authored *Essays on the Picturesque* in
1794, wrote there that "there is a wide difference between looking at nature
merely with a view to making pictures, and looking at pictures with a view to
the improvement of our ideas in nature: the former often does contract the
taste when pursued too closely; the latter I believe as generally refuses and
enlarges it."[10] Price formalized Gilpin's ideas on the picturesque, coining his
own term "picturesqueness" in 1794, and arguing in his essay's second edition
in 1796 that the picturesque—far from some mediation of Burke's classifica-
tions of the sublime and the beautiful, constituted its own emotional and
psychological category, "not only as distinct as those [qualities] which make

them sublime or beautiful, but are equally extended to all our sensations, by whatever organs they are received."[11] Like Gilpin, Price privileged roughness over smoothness in nature and in garden design, proclaiming, "I am therefore persuaded, that the two opposite qualities of roughness, and of sudden variation, joined to that of irregularity, are the most efficient causes of the picturesque."[12] In this sense Price's ideas resonated with those of Humphry Repton, generally regarded as the last great landscape architect of the eighteenth century and who, in over four hundred "Red Books" in which he proposed sometimes radical transformations of manors and estates, reconceived those spaces as a series of views composed of both "borrowed" landscapes (in which distant objects reconfigured the environment along replotted lines of sight) and more proximate presentations of trees, plantings, trellises, and follies, arranged so as to lure the gaze and incite curiosity.

Though the very phrase "picturesque school," as it sometimes circulates, can exaggerate the state of agreement among a group of landscape theorists who often elaborated divergent views, the pastoral, rustic, and rough qualities Gilpin and Price described would form an aesthetic recognizable as essentially picturesque, certainly by the time Emerson visited England, by appreciators of landscape across the North Atlantic.[13] And indeed, two decades prior to his admiration of the English countryside and its drawn-out capabilities, Emerson had worried over the likelihood that European ways of beholding would commandeer his apprehension of Europe. During his first passage across the Atlantic aboard the *Jasper* in 1833, Emerson braced himself for the European landscape—communicated to Americans through visual and written representations of Europe whose westward transmission his own journey buffeted—simultaneously opening himself to its splendor while attempting to control its influence. Nearing the Strait of Gibraltar, Emerson recounts that the dawn-illumined clouds over the Atlantic "shone with light that shines on Europe, Afric, and the Nile, and I opened my spirit's ear to their most ancient hymn. What, they said to me, goest thou so far to seek? You now feel in gazing at our fleecy arch of light the motions that express themselves in arts. You get no nearer the principle in Europe. It animates man. It is the America of America."[14] In some ways the journal entry anticipates the complaint about "the superstition of Travelling" Emerson would air in "Self-Reliance," where he says that "the wise man stays at home, and when his necessities, his duties, on any occasion call him from his house, or into foreign lands, he is at home still," since "[h]e who travels to be amused . . . travels away from himself" (*CW* 2: 46). In middle passage in 1833, Emerson imagines the ocean itself deriding his impulse to see the Old World, to "count it much, the three or four bubbles of foam that preceded your own on the Sea of Time." Assuring him that "ye need not go so far to seek at all if it were not within you," the Atlantic yet bids Emerson "welcome and hail! So sang in my ear the silver-grey mists, and the winds and the sea said Amen" (*J* 3: 6).

What are the natural splendors of Europe that express themselves in arts, Emerson asks even prior to seeing these splendors for himself, if not also the America of America? In his effort to domesticate the "fleecy arch of light," bending over his oceanic passage—this same sunlight shining on Europe and the Nile and that would only hours hence illumine Provincetown, Boston, Concord—Emerson draws westward the great "motions that express themselves in arts," "the principle" toward which he can get no nearer in Europe. Bracing himself for the impact of the Continent, insisting in a way that he will be underwhelmed, Emerson attempts at least to lessen Europe's effect upon him. European civilization becomes, in his anticipation, "the mighty Lilliput or anthill of [his] genealogy," and visiting becomes a finally harmless sally: "if, instructed as [he has] been, [he] must still . . . count it much," it is yet hardly "worth your enthusiasm" (J 3: 6). As "Self-Reliance" might suggest, the voyage to the Old World is a folly, an effort to "follow the Past and the Distant" (CW 47). The wise man will find that on the Continent, "he is home still."

None of which is to gainsay the fact that during the 1833 voyage, Emerson occasionally found himself captivated, especially in Italy, with various European landscapes. The seaside village of Locanda he found "the most picturesque of places," while Sicily itself struck him for its "green fields, and trees in bloom, and thick villages the turns in the road showed" (J 3: 56, 55). He called Monselice "the most picturesque town I have seen in Italy . . . [with] an old ruin of a castle upon the hill . . . [commanding] a beautiful and extraordinary view" (J 3: 128). Italy became for Emerson "a country of beauty" (J 3: 140). Still, refusing to give himself over entirely, in Naples he complained, "It is so easy, almost so inevitable, to be overawed . . . that . . . it is hard to keep one's judgment upright, and be pleased only after your own way." The ancient reputations of places like Vesuvius and Procida overwhelm whatever impression they make in the moment, such that "we are ready to surrender at discretion and not stickle for our private opinion against what seems the human race." Indeed, in calling Locenda and Monselice "picturesque," Emerson surrendered his own perceptions to the ways of looking prescribed by a prior generation of European aesthetes; he beheld such locales, however momentarily, in the ways Europe recommended. And so, regathering the resolution he had formed aboard the *Jasper*, Emerson asks, "Who cares? Here's for plain old Adam, the simple, genuine self against the whole world. Need is, you assert yourself, or you will find yourself overborne by the most paltry things" (J 3: 62).

Emerson's apprehensions about being overawed by Europe recall him to the very mode I have set *English Traits* against, a posture of anxiety and resistance that seeks to assert the worth of American culture against European, and specifically English, prepossession and worth. It is a mode Robert Weisbuch reveals lurking within an account given by Henry James, Jr., decades after he and Emerson had spent an afternoon together in the galleries of the Louvre, where Emerson had struck James for his apparent indifference to European art. Questioning James's verdict, Weisbuch suggests that "[j]ust possibly Emerson's opacity to art objects at the Louvre and Vatican does not mark a limit but a determined resistance," a "fully sophisticated cultural strategy" by means of which to deny high European culture the thrall it might otherwise exact.[15] In a similar way, Emerson often appears standoffish with regard to European scenery. Perhaps one effect of his resolution not to find himself overborne by paltry things, to remain the plain American Adam throughout his sojourn in the Old World, Emerson's descriptions of European landscape during the first voyage of 1833 are largely devoid of the sweeping picturesque panoramas that to a much greater extent permeate the narrative of the second journey to England documented in *English Traits*. Like picturesque Italy, the English countryside afforded Emerson some thrilling moments in 1833. But just as often as he relays his absorption in the scenery of Europe, Emerson configures European natural ecology as the analog of America, as if bearing out his earlier supposition that what he would find in Europe was no more grand than what he knew from home. Making the Strait of Gibraltar and admiring the Spanish farmhouses visible to the port, he asked, "Is not a hut in America a point that concentrates as much life and sentiment as a hut in Europe or on the ragged side of Mount Atlas?" (*J* 3: 22) Even the Sierra Nevada of Spain, he wrote, "remind us of New England" (*J* 3: 23). After his arrival in England, he noted, "I marked that the botany of England and America is alike. The clematis, the mints, the goldenrods, the gerardias, the wild geranium, the wild parsley, and twenty more better known to my eye than to my ear, I saw and recognized them all." Later in the same entry he remarks, "We see throughout Europe the counterparts of the Americans" (*J* 3: 175–76).

The next chapter will explore the political implications such elisions carried for southern plantations and the people who oversaw and worked them. But a broad capitulation to English landscape aesthetics was also underway in Emerson's New England of the 1830s, '40s, and '50s, and this context of cultural deference would certainly shape Emerson's considerations over what happens when we think about nature. *Nature* emerged in part out of Emerson's optativeness about America's potential for envisioning the natural world in an unmediated fashion, and this strain in Emerson's thinking had everything to do with his sense that many Americans had become used to viewing nature, as it were, though English eyes. Moreover, the terms of America's arrest in English theories of the picturesque shifted as the political and geographical United States fractured, and so in this sense it is striking that in Emerson's filtration, picturesque ways of looking became instrumental for dispelling a world broken, and in heaps—suited, rather, for apprehending a world of continuity and connectedness, a landscape of unity.

3. Picturesque Nature in the Antebellum Northeast

Emerson's concerns over his own capacity to see Europe as an American—
along with his attendant impulse to behold European landscapes in comparison with American "counterparts"—were formed within a North Atlantic
culture that had embraced English landscape aesthetics. By 1833 many of
Emerson's countrymen, especially in the Northeast, had accepted English
picturesque aesthetics as *the* most apt frame of reference for the appreciation
and improvement of U.S. landscapes. The aesthetic coordinates of the picturesque, moreover, had configured the language of landscape appreciation in
New England by the time Emerson embarked on his first Atlantic crossing
and would continue to exert significant cultural influence through Emerson's
second voyage and the publication of *English Traits*—that is, through virtually
the entire antebellum period.

For example, the 1831 dedication of Mount Auburn Cemetery in Cambridge (which Emerson had attended with his brother Charles),[16] was reported
to the public in language that channeled the lexis of the English picturesque
school. A volume published soon after the event presented Judge Joseph
Story's dedication along with a lengthy introduction describing the proceedings in picturesque terminology. The view from Mount Auburn itself afforded
views of "[c]ountry seats and cottages seen in various directions, and especially those on the elevated land at Watertown, add[ing] much to the picturesque effect of the scene";[17] the winding avenues of the cemetery, for that
matter, allowed for "the greatest economy of the land, combining at the same
time the picturesque effect of landscape gardening" (29). Describing a proposed tower at the top of Mount Auburn, the anonymous author predicts,
"From the foot of this monument will be seen in detail the features of the
landscape, as they are successively presented through the different vistas
which have been opened among the trees; while from its summit, a magnificent and unbroken panorama, embracing one of the most delightful tracts in
New-England, will be spread out beneath the eye" (28). This last, imagined
description of a view from a tower not yet erected speaks in textbook picturesque, envisioning a series of borrowed landscapes forming an "unbroken
panorama" "opened among the trees," the bowers of which would hence
frame that group of prospects in the manner of the landscape paintings of
Claude Lorrain, whose arboreal framing effects had represented the height of
achievement for many of the English picturesque school. Story's dedication
regaled with the series of distant views the cemetery offered. The city of Boston
to the east, for instance, now appeared as noiseless and still as in a painting:
"In the distance, the city—at once the object of our admiration and our love—
rears its proud eminences, its glittering spires, its lofty towers, its graceful
mansions, its curling smoke, its crowded haunts of business and pleasure,
which speak to the eye, and yet leave a noiseless loneliness on the ear" (17).[18]

Turning his glance, Story admired the "cultivated farm, the neat cottage, the village church, the sparkling lake, the rich valley, and the distant hills . . . before us through opening vistas; and we breathe amidst the fresh and varied labors of man" (18).

Such deployments of the picturesque lexicon were part of a larger Anglicization of the American landscape already underway by the time of the Mount Auburn dedication. As John Conron has documented, the four decades prior to the Civil War saw the publication in the United States of 145 drawing instruction books, most of which transmitted picturesque principles of perspective and composition, and a series of prominent journals—the *Ladies Magazine of Literature*, *Graham's American Monthly Magazine of Literature and Art*, and *Fashion and Fine Art* among them—devoted special issues to the subject of the picturesque.[19] As early as 1793, the *New-York Magazine; or, Literary Repository* had reprinted Gilpin's essay "On Picturesque Travel," and during the first half of the century a series of American tour books guided by picturesque principles came into print, including Henry Tudor's *Narrative of a Tour in North America* (1834), Caroline Gilman's *The Poetry of Travelling in the United States* (1838), Theodore Dwight's *Summer Tours; or, Notes of a Traveler Through Some of the Middle and Northern States* (1847), and *The Home Book of the Picturesque; or American Scenery, Art, and Literature* (1852). Such publications both incited and serviced a widespread appetite for picturesque appreciation and sightseeing. William Combe's *The Tour of the Doctor Syntax in Search of the Picturesque* (1812), a book-length verse satire on the rage of picturesque touring, begins with its title character's ploy to gain wealth and prestige by devising and publishing his own picturesque tour:

> I'll make a TOUR—and then I'll WRITE IT.
> You well know what my pen can do,
> And I'll employ my pencil too:—
> I'll ride and *write*, and *sketch* and *print*,
> And thus create a real mint;
> I'll *prose* it here, I'll *verse* it there,
> And *picturesque* it ev'ry where:
> I'll do what all have done before;
> I think I shall—and somewhat more.[20]

The English market upon which Syntax imagines himself capitalizing mirrored an American turn toward English landscapes implicitly contesting, for instance, Thomas Jefferson's insistence upon both the difference and preference of North American landscapes from the landscapes of Europe in *Notes on the State of Virginia* (1781–83). There, Jefferson emphasized the sublimity of places like Natural Bridge, Falling Spring, and the caves near Cumberland Mountain in order to settle, down to the last squirrel, whether "nature has enlisted herself as a Cis- or Trans-Atlantic partisan?"[21] Jefferson's postrevolutionary project in

Notes had been to assert the superiority of American spaces or, barring that, at least to differentiate their fruits, fauna, and other capabilities from those of Europe. But for most antebellum Americans writing about landscape, the most worthwhile North American views were those remindful of Gainsborough or Turner, just as the greatest gardens were those providing similar intellectual transport to England. So, for instance, while living in Birmingham, Washington Irving would extol the English for their skill in gardening, insisting that "[t]he taste of the English in the cultivation of land, and in what is called landscape gardening, is unrivalled." Turning toward English rural life, he described the picturesque talents of unprofessional enthusiasts as a form of high art from which Americans might take instruction, explaining that "what most delights me is the creative talent with which the English decorate the unostentatious abodes of middle life," where "[t]he rudest habitation, the most unpromising and scanty portion of land, in the hands of an Englishman of taste, becomes a little paradise." Continuing, Irving rhapsodizes:

> With a nicely discriminating eye, he seizes at once upon its capabilities, and pictures in his mind the future landscape. The sterile spot grows into loveliness under his hand; and yet the operations of art which produce the effect are scarcely to be perceived. The cherishing and training of some trees; the cautious pruning of others; the nice distribution of flowers and plants of tender and graceful foliage; the introduction of a green slope of velvet turf; the partial opening to a peep of blue distance, or silver gleam of water;—all these are managed with a delicate tact, a pervading yet quiet assiduity, like the magic touchings with which a painter finishes up a favorite picture.[22]

For Irving, as for Gilpin, the particular loveliness of such English environs makes it possible to imagine them as works of two-dimensional art. Voicing the sway such impressions exerted upon American apprehensions of landscape, James Fenimore Cooper praised the scenery near Cooperstown, New York, not long after his tour of England in 1828, by likening it to an improved English countryside.

> Our landscapes have much the same effect of English park scenery, too, aided by the isolated and graceful woods that belong to every farm, and the negligent accidents of clearing, of which the celebrated art of landscape gardening is merely an imitation. . . . I can recall a portion of the road between Cooperstown and Utica, that comes almost up to the level of what would be thought fine rural scenery even in England, surpassing it in outline and foliage, and perhaps falling as much short of it, by the want of country houses and picturesque dwellings, bridges, churches, and other similar objects.[23]

Even among northeasterners not so closely affiliated with England as Irving and Cooper, a similar impulse to view domestic landscapes through the lens of the English picturesque pervaded the decades to follow. Other commentators have noted the extent to which American painting during the early century comprised what Peter Hugill calls a "capitulation to English values" by replicating the romantic landscapes that so influenced theorists like Gilpin, Price, and Repton.[24] In the areas of landscape design and architecture, perhaps the most influential advocate of the picturesque aesthetic in the United States prior to the Civil War was Andrew Jackson Downing, who as editor of the *Horticulturalist* magazine from 1846 until his death in 1852, and as author of a series of influential pattern books, convinced a generation of wealthy Americans to adopt English picturesque aesthetics in the design of their own residences and grounds. Downing met and impressed Frederick Law Olmsted, who had already designed Mount Auburn before going on to execute Downing's call for a major park in New York City. In the fourth edition of *The Architecture of Country Houses*, Downing called the picturesque style the birthright of the Anglo-Saxon race and hence the proper mode for North America, since "[i]t is quite natural that we, largely descended from this Anglo-Saxon stock, when we have fortunes to spend, should fondly delude ourselves with the idea of realizing this old and pleasing idyl of beautiful country life."[25] A decade earlier, in his *Treatise on the Theory and Practice of Landscape Gardening, Adapted to North America* (1841), Downing had culled from Claude Lorrain, Salvator Rosa, Gilpin, Price, and Repton the vocabulary of picturesque beauty through which he would advocate for landscape improvement in the United States. Indeed, in the sixth edition of this text (1859), Downing's posthumous editor, Henry Winthrop Sargent, included two appendices naming scores of American estates and parks as successful adopters of Downing's Anglo-American picturesque style, while also including a detailed overview of what would become Olmsted's Central Park.

Downing's influence upon American taste, both through the *Horticulturist* and his pattern books, was to encourage what was already a burgeoning predilection for the rustic and the cottagey, and a reimagining of rural space imbuing it with the charm of the picturesque English hovel. Many of the illustrations of Downing's *Cottage Residences* (1842; figure 3.1) instantiate this reimagining, presenting the sorts of "cottage villas" Downing helped popularize, usually nestled harmoniously in Constablesque environs. But in a broader sense, the coordination of American rural structures and countryside with an English picturesque imagination encompasses the era, ranging from Irving's presentation of Rip Van Winkle's upstate New York village—with its public house, gnarled oaks, and curls of smoke from cottages appreciated at a distance—to visual representations such as an engraving used as the frontispiece for *Brook Farm: The Amusing and Memorable of American Country Life*, a reminiscence of a happy valley in upstate New York (not the Massachusetts utopian community) published in London in 1859 (figure 3.2).[26] The frontispiece for *Brook Farm* depicts an estate nuzzled by gentle hills and curvaceous country roads, its semi-dilapidated fences complemented by a partially blasted

DESIGN V.

A COTTAGE VILLA, IN THE BRACKETED MODE.

Fig. 36.

Fig. 37.

FIGURE 3.1 *Illustration from Andrew Jackson Downing, Cottage Residences: or, A Series of Designs for the Rural Cottages and Cottage Villas and Their Gardens and Grounds Adapted to North America (New York and London: Wiley and Putnam, 1842), 99.*

BROOK FARM.

FIGURE 3.2 *Frontispiece to Brook Farm: The Amusing and Memorable of Country Life (London: Wertheim, Macintosh, and Hunt, 1859).*

tree in the foreground. It is a place of labor and production, but not of industrial fervor, a dichotomy indicated by the freely ranging hens and pigs meandering about the functional but ramshackle gate. Even if the real Brook Farm endured a smallpox epidemic, numerous starvation periods, and what Orestes Brownson called a "horrible" atmosphere before the main phalanstery burned in 1846, this imaginary space, conjured later in the anonymous publication, inscribes an idealizing mythology through this picturesque representation.

Indeed, the aesthetic left its imprint on Thoreau's *Walden* (1854), the frontispiece of which, for the first printing, was drawn by Sophia Thoreau (figure 3.3). Looking at this representation of Thoreau's hut at Walden, one might find the image less unabashedly "Englishy" than, for instance, the image of Brook Farm from 1859, or for that matter the highly picturesque rendering of Uncle Tom's cabin in the frontispiece to the 1852 edition of Stowe's novel (figure 3.4). Even if the spruce trees are drawn at divergent axes, pointing slightly askew so as to disrupt the linearity and parallelism they might otherwise bring to the sketch, the hut itself reestablishes that symmetry, picking up their vertical lines. Other elements, as Gilpin might say, make the hut and its setting more categorically "rough" and therefore picturesque: the worn path to Thoreau's door, the more knotty and irregular deciduous trees forming the backdrop. But even if certain elements of the image accord only imperfectly with the requirements delineated in England by theorists like Gilpin and Price and popularized in America by architects such as Downing, what is overwhelmingly picturesque about this

WALDEN;

OR,

LIFE IN THE WOODS.

By HENRY D. THOREAU,

AUTHOR OF "A WEEK ON THE CONCORD AND MERRIMACK RIVERS."

I do not propose to write an ode to dejection, but to brag as lustily as chanticleer in the
morning, standing on his roost, if only to wake my neighbors up. — Page 92.

BOSTON:

TICKNOR AND FIELDS.

M DCCC LIV.

FIGURE 3.3 *Frontispiece to Henry David Thoreau, Walden (Boston, Ticknor & Fields, 1854).*

FIGURE 3.4 *Frontispiece to Harriet Beecher Stowe, Uncle Tom's Cabin (Boston: John P. Jewett, 1852).*

image is not so much the presentation as the choice of its subject matter; its focus upon Thoreau's modest house as the centerpiece of *Walden*, that is to say, reveals an exceedingly picturesque state of mind.

One might say that this frontispiece directs our very reception of *Walden*: after all, Henry Thoreau's title points us toward what is seen *from* the hut, not to the hut itself, which in some sense Thoreau regards only as the means by which he establishes his proximity to nature. Walden is in this sense the true subject of *Walden*.[27] But Sophia Thoreau's frontispiece is a reinscription of her brother's book, one that addresses the thematics of *Walden* not to the unmediated transcendentalist's nature depicted in chapters like "Higher Laws," "Sounds," or "Brute Neighbors," but back toward the house, which now becomes the focus of the experiment in confronting the essential facts of life. Indeed the frontispiece reveals the extent to which Thoreau's plea for simplicity speaks to a popular aesthetic typified, for instance, in *Villages and Farm Cottages: The Requirements of American Village Homes* (1856), an instruction book in picturesque principles of house and landscape design. "The true admirer of nature," the authors contend, will avoid "ambitious display" in home design, since "[t]he majesty which is around and above him, will awe him into meekness, and his modest habitation, nestling among the cliffs, will look as if seeking their protection."[28] With Sophia Thoreau's illustration sounding a similar keynote, Henry's Thoreau's sojourn in the woods and encounter with the real of nature becomes, in some sense, a cultural journey toward a popularly aestheticized rendition of rustic country living.

What did Americans like Irving, Cooper, Downing, and Olmsted find in the picturesque to call for such embrace? Though picturesque theory, especially as written by its English proponents, can sometimes sound rule-bound in its delineations of "roughness" or—to cite a most widely mocked prescription— its insistence upon how many objects make for a felicitous grouping (three), the point of the picturesque is to flood the senses with inspiration. In delineating a painterly nature available not only at the extremes of experience described by Burke, but well within the everyday range of aesthetic encounter— not reserved for wealthy tourists or Alpine shepherds only but, at least hypothetically, constantly available on the edges of experience familiar to most English people (at least, familiar to more of them before the migrations to urban centers that marked Gilpin's era and that may well orient the nostalgic bent of his work)—Gilpin had relocated and broadened the sources of high sensibility. For this reason Gilpin instructed the picturesque traveler in the proper vantages through which to peer upon scenes of natural beauty, cautioning against a myopic focus upon details that otherwise detract from the pleasing prospect. Since, Gilpin explained, "it is not only the *form*, and the *composition* of the objects in the landscape, which the picturesque eye examines," what the picturesque beholder seeks is the vantage that "connects them with the atmosphere, and seeks for all those various effects, which are produced from the vast, and wonderful storehouse of nature. Nor is there in travelling a greater pleasure, than when a scene of grandeur bursts unexpectedly upon the eye, accompanied with some accidental circumstance of the atmosphere, which harmonizes it, and gives it double value."[29] For Gilpin, sweeping panoramas instilled the viewer with "religious awe," provoking a state of reverence "having a moral tendency."[30] And it is perhaps due to this emphasis upon the currents of affect and wonder to which the picturesque promised access that the aesthetic achieved such cultural dominance in the United States—not exclusively, for instance, for what Kris Fresonke compellingly describes as its compatibility with projects of geographical conquest.[31] An 1844 treatise by Warren Burton entitled *The Scenery-Shower, with Word-Paintings of the Beautiful, the Picturesque, and the Grand in Nature*, reveals the extent to which such promise had captured the minds of New England appreciators of landscape, who found in their own region's scenery example and confirmation of the ideas expounded by Gilpin and Price.

In the first pages of his book, Burton describes his conversion of two boys into picturesque tourists of the Massachusetts countryside near Roxbury:

> We contrived to get them into our own current of entertainment, which was scenery-seeing, and they took to it marvelously, entirely forgetting their loaf and their literature. If we recollect aright at this distance of time, there was near by a tree of singular appearance. They had before observed it as curious; and now, with our own interest excited, they descanted on the subject with surprising volubility. They were now ready to follow the pointing of our finger or the guidance of our footsteps anywhere. We showed them a narrow field, with a grey fence at one end and a cliff at the other, if we remember, and on each side a grove, walling it up with thickset trunks all regularly round, and overtowered by interlapping foliage. We made them gaze at the spectacle till they thought it beautiful, and seeming almost like a very picture from a book. We then went down to a brook that stole into view from a bridge-shadow and flowed beside a dusty road, and we gazed down upon its ripples and the stones and pebbles that roughed the bed beneath. They seemed interested in the sight. At any rate, they looked, and looking was a discipline that would lead into pleasure. We came back and ranged below a high cliff overtopped by trees. We tried to make them feel the picturesqueness, although they may not have understood the word by which we now express the idea. We are certain they caught the desirable emotions. . . . There was withal a kindled and still kindling love for scenery; we know there was, and in consequence of our success we truly wished that there was such an establishment as a Scenery School, and that we were appointed Professor of the charming science of the Picturesque.[32]

The picturesque was worth professing, for Burton, because it offered a means to tap nature's inspirational potential. The upshot of the itinerary through which

Burton puts the children is not only to render them pliable, receptive students who are willing "to follow the pointing of our finger or the guidance of our footsteps anywhere"; more important, it causes them to feel "desirable emotions," "a kindled and still kindling love." Though Burton describes picturesque observation as a form of discipline, the point is not finally to produce observers of nature who experience that discipline self-consciously. As Kenneth John Myers demonstrates, the real achievement of the picturesque was not simply to make admiration of the landscape intellectually laborious but also to produce observers who are forgetful of their effort, who remain cognizant only of the desirable emotions to which Burton refers.[33] Hence the central tension of Burton's account, in which the aim is make the children feel something as if spontaneously, of their own uncoerced volition—for such is the paradox of compelling anyone to "gaze at the spectacle till they thought it beautiful," of enforcing "a discipline that would lead into pleasure."

Nor were the fundamental promises of the picturesque typically dismissed by more subtle minds than Burton's. Over the course of the early 1850s, Thoreau made a concerted study of Gilpin, praising him as a perspicacious appreciator of nature's charms. In early April 1852, while in the midst of revising *Walden*, he remarked, "Gilpin's 'Forest Scenery' is a pleasing book, so moderate, temperate, graceful, roomy, like a gladed wood; not condensed; with a certain religion in its manners and respect for all the good of the past, rare in more recent books. . . . Some of the cool wind of the copses converted into grammatical and graceful sentences, without heat. Not one of those humors come to a head which some modern books are, but some of the natural surface of a healthy mind."[34] Though eventually Thoreau would come to criticize Gilpin for observing nature too exclusively through a painter's eye, he would nevertheless quote from Gilpin's works in *Walden* (hailing him there as "so admirable in all that relates to landscapes, and usually so correct"),[35] *Cape Cod*, and *The Maine Woods*. Later, he borrowed from Harvard an edition of Price's *Essays on the Picturesque*, portions of which he cited approvingly in his journal (for instance, echoing Price's delight in the "midsummer shoot . . . that gives relief to the eye, after the sameness of color" of the spring).[36] Like many other Americans who themselves had undertaken none of this reading, Thoreau—whose patterns of ecological observation have been more recently examined for their arduous processes of abstraction and inference[37]—found in picturesque nature a language resonant with his own sense for the varied labors of natural beholding.

4. A World Broken and in Heaps

Writing in his journal in 1837, Emerson commended a painterly *and* laborious way of looking at nature. "Go out to walk with a painter," he suggested, "and you shall see for the first time groups, colors, clouds, and keepings, and shall have the pleasure of discovering resources in a hitherto barren ground, of finding as good as new a sense in such skill to use an old one" (*J* 4: 321). In the 1836 *Nature*, he proclaimed that "nature is a discipline"; though "[e]very property of matter is a school for the understanding," the instructive potentials of nature could be tapped only through arduousness: "Our dealing with sensible objects," he wrote, "is a constant exercise in the necessary lessons of difference, of likeness, of order, of being and seeming, of progressive arrangement" (*CW* 1: 23, 24). Moreover, *Nature* calls upon a rhetoric of improvement resonant with—if not identifiable as—a discourse of landscape transformation. In some sense Emerson registers his own Virgilian bent as he asserts the potential for a rejuvenated and "original relation to the universe" through a pastoral metaphor: "There is more wool and flax in the fields" (*CW* 1: 7). But he is also drawn in *Nature* to other figures of speech according to which the syncretic powers of the poet resemble some landscape-altering agency: The poet, he says, "unfixes the land and sea, makes them revolve around the axis of his primary thought, and disposes them anew" (*CW* 1: 31); while at another moment he describes the poet "animating nature like a creator" (*CW* 1: 33).

One reason for Emerson's attraction to picturesque aesthetics lay in its promise of ecstatic (the preferred English lexicon tended toward "delightful" or "charming") contact with the incipient force of nature, ubiquitous not in the overpowering way of the Burkean sublime, but in the insistent energy with which picturesque nature crumbled walls, twisted trees, produced ruins, and harmonized both natural and manufactured forms. (That Emerson was attuned to such picturesque imagery as he considered an inexorable transcendence immanent in degenerative processes is equally clear in the 1841 "Circles": "I am God in nature," he says there. "I am a weed by the wall" [CW 1: 182].) Another point of intersection concerned Emerson's repeated emphasis upon the integrative powers of human perception. Why, according to him, was the eye the best of all artists? Through the production of perspective, which by definition orients beheld reality around fixed vanishing points, the eye "integrates every mass of objects of what character soever, into a well and shaded globe, so that where the particular objects are mean and unaffecting, the landscape which they compose, is round and symmetrical" (*CW* 1: 12).

This motif according to which the eye of the naturalist binds together the contingent parts of surface scenery, forming of those elements a new continuity revelatory of an underlying order and pattern, in turn forms its own binding principle for Emerson's essay, cropping up at signal moments throughout the argument. Earlier, in the chapter entitled "Nature," Emerson speaks of

> the integrity of impression made by manifold natural objects. It is this which distinguishes the stick of timber of the wood-cutter, from the tree of the poet. The charming landscape which I saw this morning, is indubitably made up of some twenty or thirty farms. Miller owns this field, Locke that,

and Manning the woodland beyond. But none of them owns the landscape. There is a property in the horizon which no man has but he whose eye can integrate all the parts, that is, the poet. (*CW* 1: 9)

Then the assertion that few adults actually see nature, followed by the qualification that most of us, at best, see superficially. The metaphor of an otherwise noncontiguous landscape that, discerned from the proper angle, assumes a kind of coherence and continuity, would appear again in "Self-Reliance" (1841), where Emerson would deploy it as a trope for the consistency of individual character emerging across a history of capricious, whimsical, self-reliant behavior. "I suppose no man can violate his nature," he would there argue. "All the sallies of his will are rounded in by the law of his being as the inequalities of the Andes and Himmaleh are insignificant in the curve of the sphere" (*CW* 2: 34). The hobgoblin of foolish minds it may be, consistency is only discernible at distance, just as the contiguity of landscape is only apparent from afar. Indeed, Emerson's vehicle here may have come from Gilpin, who wrote in his 1798 *Observations on the Western Part of England*, "If a comprehensive eye, placed at a distance from the surface of the earth, were capable of viewing a whole hemisphere together, all its inequalities, great as we make them . . . would be compressed, like the view before us; and the whole would appear perfectly smooth. To us, a bowling green is a level plain; but a minute insect finds it full of inequalities."[38] We know nothing rightly, Emerson would say in the 1844 "Nature," "for want of perspective" (*CW* 3: 105).

If the integration of otherwise divided lands became for Emerson the sine qua non of transcendental beholding—"Nothing is quite beautiful alone," he would say in the 1836 *Nature*: "nothing but is beautiful in the whole" (*CW* 1: 17)— picturesque theory provided its own phenomenology of seamlessness, in which principles of continuity bind what may otherwise appear as a juxtaposition of discrete geographies. In order to attain the perspective from which landscape can excite emotions, Gilpin urged the picturesque traveler to gain what he called a "comprehensive view" of natural forms, beholding them not as isolated entities but as part of a larger sweep. "But as we have less frequent opportunities of being thus gratified," he regretted, "we are more commonly employed in analyzing the *parts of scenes;* which may be exquisitely beautiful, tho unable to produce a whole."[39] Beheld as discrete elements, the variety of forms within the prospect tends to detract from the scene's picturesque quality, for Gilpin; a focus upon minutiae prevents the beholder from partaking in the picturesque experience and hence enjoining the "religious awe" such syncretically absorbed scenes transmit.

Similarly, Price warned, "There is . . . no small difficulty in uniting breadth, with the detail, the splendid variety, and marked character of nature."[40] This was because "where the separate objects are set down, as it were, article by article, and where the confusion of lights so perplexes the eye . . . one might suppose the artist had looked at them through a multiplying glass."[41] In paint-ing, such "violations of this principle of breadth and harmony . . . are, perhaps, more frequent, and more disgustingly offensive than those of any other."[42] As with Gilpin, variety was for Price to be harmonized through felicitous combi-nation, since "[v]ariety, of which the true end is to relieve the eye, not to per-plex it, does not consist in the diversity of separate objects, but in that of their effects when combined together; in diversity of composition, and of charac-ter."[43] Though Repton, for his part, would acknowledge that "[t]he mind requires a continuity, though not a sameness; and . . . is pleased with succes-sion and variety," he similarly argued that the refined observer "is offended by sudden contrast, which destroys the unity of composition."[44]

Because the mind is offended by sudden contrasts, picturesque improve-ment reorganized nature in order to prevent its lapse into banal "variety," a form of aesthetic failure Price found "disgustingly offensive" and which thus provided the improver license for radical intervention. Certainly Emerson's descriptions of the poet in *Nature* almost continually deploy the trope of un-fixing the land; like an improver drawing out capabilities, the Emersonian poet is almost constantly "disposing" the landscape at his whim, "animating nature like a creator, with his own thoughts" (*CW* 1: 33). But at the same time, a picturesque emphasis upon achieving the perspective from which variety dissolves into "unity"—and a unity, no less, providing access to a form of what Gilpin called "religious awe"—dovetails with Emerson's interest in the inte-grative eye and its capacity to instill a broader connectedness. "[N]ature is already, in its forms and tendencies, describing its own design" (*CW* 1: 7), he wrote. Intended to capitalize upon a similar connectedness, Repton's Red Books were informed by intricate trigonometries plotting the limits of visual perception along what Repton continuously referred to as the "axis of vision." Perfecting our visual experience of landscape, Repton reasoned, was largely a matter of manipulating angles, of plotting with care the trajectories along which we apprehend objects in both their wholeness and their harmony with other objects.[45]

Speaking in a language resonant with Repton's, Emerson envisions a dys-functional gaze whose worst effect is to impoverish nature by divesting its wholeness: "The ruin or the blank, that we see when we look at nature, is in our own eye. The axis of vision is not coincident with the axis of things, and so they appear not transparent but opake. The reason why the world lacks unity, and lies broken and in heaps, is, because man is disunited with himself" (*CW* 1: 43). It is not the picturesque ruin—some folly in the distance—but rather the ruin of the eye and of the I that deprives us of what Emerson calls the world's "unity." For Emerson, the stakes of this ruination were extraordinarily high—not confined to some aesthete's appreciation of the rough and the smooth, but rather, by the time he began writing *Nature* in earnest, involving the dispersal of an otherwise essential oneness: the world appears disunited, he posits, because we are so. Hence the statement he makes earlier in *Nature*: "When I behold a rich landscape, it is less to my purpose to recite correctly the order and superposition of the strata, then to know why all thought of multitude is lost in a tranquil sense of unity" (*CW* 1: 40).

Hence, for that matter, the maneuver he makes in this passage from the 1844 "Nature," which begins as if in new variation upon the theme of the integrative eye, but which ends by elaborating broadened stakes enjoined by "us": "Things are so strictly related, that according to the skill of the eye, from any one object the parts and properties of any other may be predicted. If we had eyes to see it, a bit of stone from the city wall would certify us of the necessity that man must exist, as readily as the city. That identity makes us all one, and reduces to nothing great intervals on our customary scale" (*CW* 3: 106). The passage begins by once again envisioning an act of envisioning, a glance that at once "relates" and "predicts" . . . what? Certainly it is relation that makes possible prediction, in the sense that bits of a larger continuity allow some observers ("according to the skill of the eye") to discern wider patterns. A fragment of the stone wall (crumbling, as it were, in the manner of the stonework to which Gilpin had advised picturesque artists to apply the hammer rather than the chisel—the better to achieve an appearance of rustic decay) relays metonymically the whole of which it is still in some sense a part.[46] But the final sentence shifts focus back toward "us"—we are all of us "all one," Emerson now explains; a transformation has taken place that reverses the processes of ruination he described eight years earlier, when he connected a disunified landscape to the beholder's internal disunification. Here a redeemed point of view reduces to nothing great intervals, making us all one.

What I am suggesting about Emerson's comportment toward the picturesque approaches from a different angle what other investigators have contended about his visit to the Jardin des Plantes in 1833, where he reconditioned what had been to that point intimations of an abiding connectedness in nature, moving now toward a scientifically engaged account of natural unity.[47] At the Jardin, and amid the Cabinets of Natural History, Emerson discerned in diversity "strange sympathies" linking only superficially disparate natural forms, and that would surely have everything to do with his eventual rejection of polygenetic racial thought as well as his view of England as a successful fusion of racial types (*J* 3: 163).[48] But the picturesque gaze Americans appropriated from English theorists also engendered a continuum between phenomenologically and politically divided lands. One 1857 reviewer of *Village and Farm Cottages*, for instance, would declare "English treatises" on landscape art "essentially aristocratic" while declaring "works on landscape-gardening that have issued from the English press [. . .] hurtful, by affecting the mind of the reader with an ambition to imitate the unattainable grandeur of foreign models." A more republican landscape aesthetic, the reviewer explains, will instill a greater degree of cohesion and social unity in the United States.

"Our people should be governed by a republican feeling, and not endeavor to distinguish their own grounds from those around them," the reviewer insists, "but should strive . . . to make their grounds harmonize with all adjacent scenery."[49] A landscape aesthetic drawn in accordance with a republican ethos is a more unified landscape, one indicative of a nation composed of "all classes of the people" existing "in mutual understanding."[50]

Such discourses assumed a more literal resonance during congressional deliberation over the Compromise Bill of 1850, which William Seward denounced in his declaration that "Slavery and Freedom are conflicting systems brought together by the union of the States, not neutralized nor even harmonized."[51] In contrast, supporters of the bill—most notably Henry Clay and Daniel Webster—tended to emphasize the oneness out of many which the Constitution had formed and the compromise would cement. One political editorialist, surveying the Senate speeches of Clay, John Calhoun, Seward, and Webster regarding the bill, described a politics formulated in disregard of plausibility, something like a landscape architect's imposition of extravagant design onto an unobliging landscape:

> There, unimpeded by the difficulties of the every-day world beneath him, of hills to be leveled and streams to be bridged, he draws, in free air, his straight lines, and his angles and curves of geometrical accuracy. But unhappily he takes no care to fit the aerial plan to the inequalities of the terrestrial landscape; and the rivers run, and the mountains stand, in most contumacious disregard of the continuity and philosophic beauty of his plans. To give rotundity to his symmetrical outlines, he had ignored the existence of such obstacles, and expects them when thus dismissed to vanish; but they do not, nor are they like so to do.[52]

A politics of fancy, oblivious to the ground and its actual capabilities, defines opponents on either side of the Compromise Bill who are unable to articulate a program in accommodation of political reality, but the federal union thus endangered is not simply akin to a contumacious landscape; it of course *is* such a landscape, "in the enlargement of its territories, and in the gathering of new States into the bonds of national unity,"[53] just as the Constitution itself "is not a mere league and confederacy of separate sovereignties," but rather an infusion "binding them into one dissoluble whole."[54]

The unbinding of that whole conditioned the forms of spectacle U.S. beholders of landscape found in battlefield daguerreotypy, photographs contextualized within a more general sense of a loss of environment. Hawthorne would express that sense of loss in the *Atlantic Monthly* as he opined, "Even in an aesthetic point of view, the war has done a great deal of enduring mischief, by causing the devastation of great tracts of woodland scenery, in which this part of Virginia would appear to have been very rich." "Fifty years will not repair this desolation," he predicted, prior to noting his own blank response to the landscape of the liberated Harper's Ferry. "A beautiful landscape is a luxury, and luxuries are thrown away amid discomfort," Hawthorne would comment there: "I cannot remember that any very rapturous emotions were awakened by the scenery."[55] Similarly, one *Harper's Weekly* writer, describing Matthew Brady's Antietam daguerreotypes in 1862, discerns a picturesque sweep now violated by the carnage: "Here and there are beautiful stretches of pastoral scenery, disfigured by the evidences of strife, either in the form of broken caissons, dead horses, or piles of human corpses." The *New York Times* lamented not only the loss of men but of landscape: "[T]he ground whereupon they lie is torn by shot and shell, the grass is trampled down by the tread of hot, hurrying feet, and little rivulets that can scarcely be of water are trickling across the earth like tears over a mother's face."[56]

In many lithographic representations of battlefields that appeared alongside reportage in periodicals such as *Harper's Weekly* or *Frank Leslie's Illustrated Monthly*, we see a rendering that may leave twenty-first-century observers bemused at what appears as a relatively ordered, even bloodless, representation of battle. Even when intended to depict the harrowing fray of armed conflict, illustrations such as the Currier and Ives lithographs *The Battle of Williamsburg, VA., May 5th 1862* (1862; figure 3.5) or *The Gallant*

FIGURE 3.5 *Currier & Ives, The Battle of Williamsburg, Va. May 5th 1862, 1862. Lithograph, 29.4 × 40.4 cm. Library of Congress, Prints & Photographs Division, LC-DIG-pga-00615.*

Charge of the Fifty Fourth Massachusetts (Colored) Regiment (1863) seem antiseptic to us, a visual equivalent of Tennyson's charge of the light brigade, because in our collective mind's eye the human cost of the conflict has already been fixed by Brady, Alexander Gardner, Timothy O'Sullivan, and other daguerreotypists who undertook the first systematic photographic documentation of human beings killed in war. We know now that the bodies were manipulated, that Gardner often arranged the corpses in order to accentuate what he thought of as their moral impact, or that he photographed the same groups of corpses from different angles before captioning them as variously southern or northern, traitorous reapers of a bitter harvest or glorious if fallen defenders of Union (figure 3.6).[57] But such touching up and improvement of the scenery one finds is, of course, a part of the picturesque as well, and in any case the effects of these corpses rarely prove obeisant to Gardner's variously improvised visual polemics. "Even the corpse," as Emerson had written in *Nature*, "hath its own beauty" (*CW* 1: 13). In populating a disunified bellum

FIGURE 3.6 *Alexander Gardner, A Harvest of Death, Gettysburg, Pennsylvania, negative July 1863, print ca. 1865. Albumen photographic print. Library of Congress, Prints & Photographs Division, Civil War Photographs, LC-DIG-ppmsca-12557.*

landscape even as they depopulate it, the bodies do not merely transmit the platitudinous semiotics by which Gardner attempted to manage their effects so much as they signal the limits of artistic control over human responsiveness to any plot of ground.

All of which might bring us back to Jefferson's intriguing way of imagining his purpose, in *Notes on the State of Virginia*, as that of revealing whether "nature has enlisted herself as a Cis- or Trans-Atlantic partisan." In *Notes*, Jefferson asserts supremacy for North American nature, bearing witness to the utter sublimity of Natural Bridge, the majesty of the Alleghenies, the greater numbers and heights of the very trees of Virginia. And so it seems striking that by the 1830s, so many Americans had reversed the terms of that invidious transatlantic comparison, now imagining North American space to be at its most exalted when rendered at its most English. More striking, perhaps, is that for Jefferson, that cisatlantic, unified national space is encompassed in Virginia itself—Virginia, in Jefferson's ante-antebellum moment, is capable of representing the entire United States, a synecdoche for the national whole, a politically impossible semiosis by the time so many Americans began looking at America, as it were, along the axes of vision suggested in the picturesque. And so the next chapter takes up that southern space as it appeared during the later era, when it could only represent itself, and when its inhabitants, as in places such as New England or upstate New York, were more disposed to view their topographies as well as their politics from the vantages of English lands.

John Pendleton Kennedy's Plantation of the Picturesque

1. Working the Land

Aligning its axis of vision with the axis of things, Emerson's 1836 *Nature* theorizes a syncretic experience through which otherwise atomized landscapes unify, and in this way circuits a picturesque phenomenology into its transcendentalist's vision of nature. Emerson's first major essay regales the reader with a sensory experience imminent in apprehensions of vast space. But at the same time, *Nature* breaches the panoramic through close consideration of natural phenomena, offering a reverie of the proximate. Out of the many, the one—the essay both claims picturesque expanse as the domain of its musings and promotes an experience of nature in propinquity, a consideration of the close through which the naturalist may discern "occult relations" connecting all of creation.

In a related way, picturesque theory privileged the distant vantage from which discrete spaces merge into a singular aesthetic impression—orienting all around a singular axis of vision—even as it valuated discrete objects composing the landscape, objects whose positioning within the prospect plotted the direction of the picturesque tourist's gaze. English picturesque thought itemized those scenic objects within varying scales of aesthetic value that assessed any element's potential for heightening the charm of a given view. Perhaps most famously, and as Jane Austen would mock in *Pride and Prejudice* (1813) and *Mansfield Park* (1814), groupings of three (for instance, trees or bushes) were considered more picturesque than pairs.[1] Ruins tended to imbue picturesque scenery with melancholy, signifying an Ozymandian collapse into natural decay and a lapse from former grandeur. Prospects framed by bowers of trees replicated the framing effects of Lorrain's canvasses, described by several picturesque theorists as a zenith of artistic effect. All such elements were of course dependent for their picturesque value upon precise positioning and treatment. As were, for that matter, human beings.

The human figures appearing in English picturesque landscape painting introduced to these works a form of pastoral interest picturesque theorists treated almost invariably as another form of aesthetic detail, something akin to a ruined abbey or grouping of bushes. But the rustic types sometimes included in these works—farmers, shepherds, rural workers—presented problems for picturesque theorists like Gilpin, who regarded obviously cultivated land as potentially unpicturesque unless balanced against "wild" nature. In his 1798 *Observations on the Western Part of England*, Gilpin complained that on the whole, England had failed to realize her picturesque potential because of overfarming. "*Picturesque beauty*," he insisted, "is a phrase but little understood. We precisely mean by it that kind of beauty which *would look well in a picture*. Neither grounds laid out by art, nor improved by agriculture, are of this kind." The Isle of Wight, Gilpin insisted, was in fact "a large garden, or rather a field, which in every part has been disfigured by the spade, the coulter, and the harrow. It abounds much more in tillage than in pasturage; and of all species of cultivation, corn-lands are the most unpicturesque. The regularity of corn-fields disgusts; and the color of corn, especially near harvest, is out of tune with everything else."[2]

Farming diminished the picturesque impact of English landscape, for Gilpin, but the inclusion of farmers themselves was a different matter. In his 1772 *Observations, on Several Parts of England*, Gilpin had elaborated the aesthetic rewards of representing workers who performed no work. Even if, "[i]n a moral view, the industrious mechanic is a more pleasing object, than the loitering peasant," Gilpin went on to explain that "in a picturesque light, it is otherwise. The arts of industry are rejected; and even idleness, if I may so speak, adds dignity to a character. Thus the lazy cowherd resting on his pole; or the peasant lolling on a rock, may be allowed in the grandest scenes; while the laborious mechanic, with the implements of labour, would be repulsed."[3] This, Gilpin explained, is because figures "are of a negative nature, neither adding to the grandeur of the idea, nor taking from it. They merely and simply *adorn* a scene" (45; emphasis original). In one sense Gilpin nods to a work ethic tying industry to stolid morality; but his aesthetics of controlled decrepitude erase all evidence of productivity from his landscapes, drawing him to representations equating industry with idleness.

Three years prior to Gilpin's remarks in *Observations*, the Lancashire industrialist Richard Arkwright had patented his water frame, a device for mechanizing the production of high-quality yarns for the warps of cotton textiles, and in 1775, he patented his improved carding engine, which separated individual cotton fibers prior to the spinning process. In 1771, Arkwright and his partners Jedediah Strutt and Samuel Need had opened the first mechanized cotton mill at Cromford, in the northern district of Derbyshire, and after the expiration of Arkwright's patent in 1785, such mills would spread across the North of England. Such developments in industrial technology, especially in connection with the processing of cotton from the U.S. South, were evacuating the landscapes picturesque aesthetes such as Gilpin idealized and theorized. The rustics they imagined were no longer at work in those landscapes—instead, they were entering the mills and moving to urban centers. An economic process was under way that outdated even shepherds themselves, since the mechanized spinning of cotton—as well as the developing textile markets among the very populations producing the raw materials for cotton textiles in the American South, where there was little use for woolen fabrics—effectively led to the replacement of wool by woven cotton as Britain's most valuable export.

In later chapters I will delve further into some of the ramifications of this shift within transatlantic imaginings of England during the antebellum period, but the point for the moment is to note that the picturesque was—perhaps especially in its English rendition—a nostalgic semiotic that fantasized a rural laboring existence by and large falling away from English experience. The rustic past showcased in the picturesque was being ushered away by developments in agriculture and nutrition, for example, that would double the population of England from five million in 1760 (when the country finally reattained the population levels of the early fourteenth century, prior to the bubonic plague) to ten million in 1800. Poor people were living longer, having larger families, migrating to urban centers, and in turn earning relatively higher wages allowing them to purchase certain imports as well as manufactured goods—which is to say that a self-perpetuating process of industrialization was under way that is utterly foreclosed in the imagery of the picturesque. The images preoccupying painters like Constable and theorists like Gilpin were seized upon in denial of economic and social trends. From the very beginning, they functioned as fantasies of worked and inhabited lands.

Even more than Gilpin, Price saw indispensable aesthetic value in rustic types, leading him into reveries over pastoral wanderers as well as dormant artifacts of industry and production. In his *Essays on the Picturesque*, Price maintained, "In our own species, objects merely picturesque are to be found among the wandering tribes of gypsies and beggars; who in all the qualities which give them that character, bear a close analogy to the wild forester and the worn-out cart-horse, and again to old mills, hovels, and other inanimate objects of the same kind."[4] Price's habit of referring to picturesque human beings as "objects" carried into his praise for contemporaneous painters whose work captured what he saw as the visual charm of the impoverished. "Whoever has looked with delight at Gainsborough's representations of cottages and their inhabitants," he supposed, "at Greuze's interesting pictures; at the various groups and effects of the Dutch masters, will certainly feel from that recollection, an additional delight in viewing similar objects and characters in

nature." Gainsborough's achievements in aestheticizing rustics were instructive to Price, who knew the painter personally. Recollecting his country jaunts
near Bath with Gainsborough, Price recalled that "when we came to cottage or
village scenes, to groups of children, or to any objects of that kind which struck
his fancy, I have often remarked in his countenance an expression of particular
gentleness and complacency." Impoverished children, according to Price, elic-
ited Gainsborough's sympathies (to which Price then points, further, as an
indication of Gainsborough's "natural philanthropy," a "kindness and interest" not surpassed by "the most affectionate parent"); but these children
remain, at least for Price, "objects" to strike our "fancy."[5]

Destitute human beings were laden with a moral symbology in picturesque
theory, but at the same time they circulated within an essentially conservative
semiotics of poverty. Gilpin's aversion for landscapes that had been transformed by economic industry of any kind, along with his interest in the imagery of ruination, translates in Price to an interest in the aesthetic potentials of
the rural poor, but the impoverished are for Price never more than objects to
be distantly grouped, as it were, like trees, rocks, ruins, or other elements of
picturesque composition. As Malcolm Andrews points out in his history of
picturesque art in England, "Gainsborough's cottage subjects and Goldsmith's
Deserted Village (1770) typify these new tastes in the representation of the rural
poor. 'Sensibility,' 'soft' primitivism, the rise of evangelicalism—these and
other pressures manipulated the images of the rural poor and their environment, and endowed them with complex moral and political associations." But
for Andrews, "The trouble is that the Picturesque enterprise in its later stages,
with its almost exclusive emphasis on visual appreciation, entailed a suppression of the spectator's moral response to those very subjects which it could least
hope to divest of moral significance—the ruin, the hovel and rural poverty."[6]

We are not dealing, in picturesque fantasy, exactly with Wordsworth's
ruined cottage, for while properly within the picturesque vantage, we never
progress *into* the hovel in order to bear witness to what actual poverty entails
for individuals. This is a point hinted by Gary Lee Harrison, who points out
that the picturesque "'view from the top' was a familiar topos in eighteenth-
century loco descriptive poetry and landscape painting" even as he argues that
"[t]his 'prospect of Britain' . . . involved a generalization of the social and to-
pological landscape below and a kind of self-aggrandizement of the spectator."[7] For Harrison, the picturesque desensitized the spectator by installing a
distance between his or her perspective and the dwellings of the poor even as
it capitalized upon the latter's imagined aesthetic impact, and in this way
comprised a euphemistic response to the problem of the rural poor.[8] (Similarly, John Barrell argues that in English picturesque painting from the late
eighteenth to early nineteenth centuries, "the poor of England were, or were
capable of being, as happy as the swains of Arcadia" and that such representations aimed at neutralizing the moral pressures extreme poverty generated.)[9]

Like Edmund Burke, who "politicizes the aesthetic stance of the privileged spectator as he considers the 'elevated ground' from which the natural aristocrat oversees his . . . world," the picturesque viewer's "self-aggrandizing" stance involves (in Harrison's quotation of Joshua Reynolds' third *Discourse*) "being able to get above all singular forms, local customs, particularities, and details of every kind."[10]

The picturesque was fashioned out of such impulses to aestheticize the political and social margins, to transform poverty into rusticity, to reconfigure actual misery and its sources as a display of pastoral repose. Like the imaginary Saxons and Normans who populated the medievalism of Victorian histories as well as partisan fantasies of English genealogy in the antebellum North and South, the rustic laborer helped English intellectuals configure a political and social present in salient ways. Like many English spectators who valued such images for their implicitly euphemistic commentary upon problems related to the poor and the overworked, U.S. picturesque tourists and appreciators of landscape in the South channeled the aesthetic toward their own concerns over disenfranchised labor, freighting the picturesque, ultimately, as a commentary on the nature and efficacy of U.S. slavery.

2. From a Distance and On High

In her work on the pastoralism of the American farm in nineteenth-century painting, Sarah Burns demonstrates that the rural spaces depicted by northern landscape artists during the antebellum period often lionized free labor and free land over land worked by slaves. Indeed, as Burns shows, northern aesthetes often codified their critique of the slave system through imagery of desolated plantations, spaces in which slaves groaned under the whip and where potentially productive fields went fallow.[11]

But the corollary of such sectionally driven representations appeared among southern depictions of the plantation, where the convention of the picturesque provided images of rural labor suited to the project of idealizing social economies of human bondage. As in England, a sanguine view of labor and impoverishment attended the U.S. embrace of the English picturesque during the antebellum period, but rather than attempting to pursue that connection as it would pertain broadly to the sectional conflict—which became among other things a rhetorical contest pitting free labor against chattel slavery—in this chapter I will draw out such implications of the English picturesque for laborers, toiling in the distance, within the literary tradition of the slave-holding states. In tarrying with a formative text of southern plantation fiction—John Pendleton Kennedy's *Swallow Barn*, itself a signal work within the broader history of American engagements with the picturesque—I do not imply that northern deliberations over landscape and labor are any less fraught or euphemistic. My maneuver here is to explore the extent to which the picturesque's capacity for generating sanguine contexts for laboring others was clear to southern authors whose appropriation of picturesque aesthetics announced more complex implications for toiling slaves, who often played the role of the rustic human objects Price admired so much in the work of Gainsborough. Such an elaborate conceptual, visual, and ideological apparatus as the picturesque was well suited to a proto-national culture on the verge of building a decades-long discourse drawing plantation slavery into invidious comparison with other labor economies.

As Angela Miller points out in her work on southern landscape painting during the nineteenth century, prewar landscape paintings of southern subjects are far less ubiquitous than their northeastern counterparts.[12] But as was the case for northeastern painters of Luminism and the Hudson River school, in the South the picturesque gained purchase among a series of artists who would take instruction from English writers of picturesque theory and from English examples of picturesque art. From the 1790s onward, under the influence of William Gilpin and other formulators of the school, painters such as Thomas Coram (1756–1811), Francis Guy (1760–1820), John Rogers Vinton (1801–47), and Thomas Addison Richards (1820–1900) represented southern subjects through established English styles. For instance, in canvases such as those that make up his series *Views of Mulberry* (1800), Coram treated various views of southern landscapes, often including plantations, in accordance with the rules of composition described by Gilpin, some of whose watercolors Coram had copied during the 1790s (figure 4.1). Guy, who was a native of the Lake District, won a series of commissions to paint southern plantations over the course of the first decade of the century, resulting in works such as his series on the thousand-acre Baltimore plantation of Harry Dorset Gough, Perry Hall (named after Gough's father's family castle in Staffordshire). Guy's representations of Perry Hall reveal his deeply picturesque commitments, rendering the activity of the plantation as a pastoral landscape of broad sweeps, panoramic views, and distant laborers (figure 4.2).

Coram and Guy were among many other artists working in the South to instill the region's visual language, as it were, with the terms developed by English picturesque theorists. A collection of aquatint prints of paintings by British artists compiled by Joshua Shaw under the title *Picturesque Views of American Scenery* (1820–21) focused primarily upon southern locales—Washington's sepulcher at Mount Vernon, "Oyster Cove" along the York River in Virginia, the Falls of St. Anthony on the Mississippi—although none of these works depicted plantations.[13] As Rebecca Sokolitz sums up, "With its varied formal vocabulary, the picturesque style adapted seamlessly to plantation views as an identifiable part of America's burgeoning national culture of scenic and landscape art and literature at the turn of the nineteenth century. Artists such as Coram, Fraser, and Guy meticulously documented prominent

Ruins of Wilton Castle

FIGURE 4.1 *Thomas Coram, Ruins of Wilton Castle, from Sketches Taken from W. Gilpin's Observations on the River Wye and Several Parts of South Wales, 1791. Oil, watercolor, pencil and ink on paper, 9⅛ × 6¾ in. Courtesy of the Gibbes Museum of Art.*

southern plantations as English estates, relying on elements of the picturesque aesthetic when it suited."[14]

Such visual appropriations of the picturesque were complemented by two generations of writers who consciously deployed the lexicon of Gilpin and Price while extolling the delights of southern lands. In 1853 Thomas Addison Richards (who had emigrated from England at age eleven and went on to write panegyrics to the landscapes of the upper South) would boast in *Harper's Monthly* that the Southland was more rigorously arranged than the North by picturesque aesthetic principles including "variety." For instance, while the Alleghenies in the North form a monotonous "stately and unbroken line, like saddened exiles, whose stern mood is ever the same, and whose cold features are never varied with a smile," in the South the same mountain range suddenly ascends into a riot of tectonic forms. "All is Alpine variety," Richards boasts, "intricacy and surprise." The South, in a most direct sense, makes the Alleghenies rough. From their heights, "panoramic views command vast assemblages of ridge and precipice, varied in every characteristic—the large in proportion to the small, the barren in contrast with the wooded, the formal and the eccentric, the horizontal and the perpendicular." Indeed, Richards explains, the inhabitants of the South understand the beauty of their environs in such self-consciously picturesque terms as to understand "the existence of this

FIGURE 4.2 *Francis Guy, Perry Hall, Slave Quarters with Field Hands at Work, ca. 1805.*
Oil on canvas, 22 × 30 in. Courtesy of the Maryland Historical Society, 1986.33.

variety, so essential an element of the picturesque" as a form of property to safeguard, "so completely felt by the poor peasant who refused to sell, though to provide for his necessities, one of his three cows, upon the sole ground that they would not group well."[15]

Indeed, a similar configuration of the picturesque as a sectional wedge would emerge during the Civil War itself, as with Frank Alfriend's warning in 1863 that "[w]e must not allow our beautiful and picturesque villages to become immense manufacturing marts, breeding an overwhelming laboring population, with all its ignorance, vice and demoralizing influences" charac- terizing northern cities. Such an eventuality, Alfriend advises, would amount to a sacrifice "of the refinement, cultivation, and morality which characterizes all *sparsely* settled agricultural and pastoral countries."[16] Similar written renditions of southern picturesque space circulated throughout southern lit- erary productions through the same decades as in the Northeast: for instance, William Gilmore Simms's 1846 poem "The Ruins"—which uses that stock pic- turesque trope to represent and chastise an unfaithful lover—as well as his contribution to the 1852 volume *The Pro-Slavery Argument* published in Charleston and anthologizing the work of several prominent apologists. Re- sponding to Harriet Martineau's indictments of U.S. slavery, Simms likens what he regards as patently variable scales of human temperament to the varieties of picturesque landscape: "[G]raduated endowments," he insists, "which enable one to fly, while another creeps; one to dilate in grandeur, while another trembles in insignificance," also install in creation natural hierarchies that in turn underpin social orders. Such variations, in fact, contribute to the world what Simms describes as its loveliness. "Whether we survey the globe which we in-habit," he suggests, "the sky which canopies, the seas which surround us, or the systems which give us light and loveliness, we are perpetually called upon to admire that infinite variety. . . . The stars are lovely in their inequalities; the hills, the trees, the rivers and the sea; and it is from their very inequalities that their harmonics arise. Were it otherwise, the eye would be pained by the monotony of the prospect everywhere."[17] While Emerson's engagement with the pictur-esque had led him to formulate a connectedness out of diversity that yet af-firmed the flux of creation, Simms—while attentive to a "harmonics" setting the terms of relation between the objects of variety—nevertheless found in a sort of picturesque roughness the correlative of ascending racial orders.

But as with any picturesque scene, the point of variety is to arrange within a harmonious composition. Though Richards would quip about southern farmers organizing their livestock into picturesque triads, the accounts he, Simms, and others would generate of the particular and picturesque gorgeous-ness of the South entailed a euphemistic treatment of slavery. Indeed many of Richards's canvases—for instance, *River Plantation* (figure 4.3)—relay a sedgy

FIGURE 4.3 *Thomas Addison Richards, River Plantation, 1855–1860. Oil on canvas, 20¼ × 30 in. Morris Museum of Art, Augusta, Georgia.*

landscape composed through picturesque principles of distancing, wherein slaves and their masters populate a middle distance harmonizing all figures as part of a pleasant if only dimly perceived gathering. In *River Plantation*, a black child sits with a triad of ponies, waiting upon two other figures strolling in the shade of a live oak covered in Spanish moss. All here is calm and hush; a settled if not beneficent tenor infuses the scene. The painting implies another sense in which the southern landscape is more picturesque than the northern, insofar as the coerced labor of the slave represented here amounts to a form of leisure, even recreation.

Kennedy's *Swallow Barn*, initially published in 1832 but then revised for a second release in 1851, serves as another instance in the southern picturesque trajectory that renders the plantation as a scenic space, with the slaves who populate this space as picturesque objects. In this way *Swallow Barn* provides an example of the picturesque in its capacity to address distinct ideological objectives in the South, but it also points to Kennedy's elision of picturesque distance, a closure of expanse tending to undercut the book's otherwise steadfast political agenda. In some ways, it is tempting to view *Swallow Barn* as an instance of southern picturesque narrative partaking of the distancing effects Price so valued in Gainsborough's landscapes and that also appear in Guy's representations of plantation life in the Chesapeake Valley, and Richards's representations of slaves and masters in Georgia. Viewed from this angle, *Swallow Barn* might appear to instill picturesque distance in order to sentimentalize and rationalize the economy of forced labor forming the backdrop for Kennedy's sketches of charming southern life. In fact, *Swallow Barn* does pursue such an agenda. But Kennedy also mitigates the distancing effects of the picturesque, producing perspectives that complicate the apparent ideological mission of his book.

Indeed, Kennedy—writing in 1832 under the persona of his narrator, Mark Littleton—dedicates the book by inscribing himself into a dichotomy of labor and idyll. Addressing the work to former U.S. attorney general William Wirt, Littleton asks his friend to "[a]ccept, therefore, this first-fruit of the labours (I ought rather to say, of the idleness) of your trusty friend."[18] So idleness as well as labor can bear fruits—or at least, in Kennedy's estimation, produce art— and in keeping with this Gilpinesque paradox Littleton moves on to introduce *Swallow Barn* as a production of visual impressions only loosely confederated. The work is not a novel, he explains, however much he would have liked it to have been. Rather, it conveys "in detached pictures" an impression "of time and place." From the first moments, Littleton describes his writing in terms of visual art: he has undertaken "to portray . . . impressions . . . [of] scenery" (*SB* 1832, vii); he has simply "describe[d] what he saw" (*SB* 1832, vii); he has provided us with "sketches" (*SB* 1832, vii); he has simply played the part of "attentive observer" (*SB* 1832, viii). Not a novel, he explains, but rather "a rivulet of story wandering through a broad meadow of episode" (*SB* 1832, vii), more of a Constable or Gainsborough canvas in words than a plot-driven story line, a picturesque idyll relatively ungoverned by narrative. Harriet Martineau, writing about *Swallow Barn* in her 1837 *Society in America*, both praised the impartiality entailed in similar literary reportage and intimated its limits. "The best productions of American literature are, in my opinion, the tales and sketches in which the habits and manners of the people of the country are delineated, with exactness, with impartiality of temper, and without much regard for the picturesque," she suggested. "Such are the tales by the author of Swallow Barn; where, however, there is the addition of a good deal of humour, and a subtraction of some of the truth."[19]

Nor is Kennedy's visual, painterly, and topographical way of thinking about his own project some passing metaphor for Littleton, who calls upon language that might appear in Gilpin or Price as he characterizes his own "book of episodes" with its "occasional digression[s] into plot" (*SB* 1832, viii). A fair evaluation of *Swallow Barn*, he imagines, will acknowledge that none of its "pictures are exaggerated or false in their proportions"; but because Littleton has "not striven to produce effect" through such exaggerations, he must acknowledge the possibility of having failed to achieve high drama in his execution of these "pictures." "I may be open to the charge of having made them flat and insipid," he admits (*SB* 1832, viii–ix). The phrase "flat and insipid" was used frequently by Gilpin to characterize a range of poorly conceived landscapes, ostensible productions of art that finally disfigure the scene. The picturesque tourist, he insisted, "is frequently disgusted . . . when art aims more at beauty, than she ought. How flat, and insipid is often the garden-scene! how puerile, and absurd! the banks of the river how smooth, and parallel! the lawn, and its boundaries, how unlike nature!"[20] Overly "smooth" landscapes are like a mirror "in an unreflecting state," Gilpin explains elsewhere: "insipid."[21] Excessively refining landscapes evacuates them of their grandeur, which is why "The more refined our taste grows from the *study of nature*, the more insipid are the *works of art*."[22] And, indeed, in his 1772 *Observations, Relative Chiefly to Picturesque Beauty*, Gilpin considered the relative virtues of written description over drawn or painted nature, admitting that writing can "add form to a castle; and [tip its] shattered battlements with light." But for all of these powers, "all that words can express, or even the pencil describe, are gross, insipid substitutes of the living scene."[23]

Just such an apprehension of the potential for writing to render nature "insipid" structures Littleton's apologia for *Swallow Barn*. Whether, through his refusal to "exaggerate" "proportions," Littleton has produced a "flat and insipid" series of sketches or rather a rivulet of story wandering through broad meadows of episode, he has at last endeavored to relay an unembellished "true narrative," both in its representation of landscapes and of people. "The country and the people are at least truly described," he explains. "If my book be too much in the mirthful mood," he supposes, "it is because the ordinary actions of men, in their household intercourse, have naturally a humorous or mirthful character." Since the mode of country life *Swallow Barn* depicts is naturally "grotesque, peculiar and amusing," "it only requires an attentive observer to make an agreeable book by describing them" (*SB* 1832, viii). For his part, Gilpin went so far as to say that few artistic efforts actually pleased anyone, since "the idea of the original is so strong, that the copy must be very pure, if it do not disgust."[24] In both *Swallow Barn* and *Three Essays on Picturesque Beauty*, artists who (as Littleton describes himself) "profess a design to amuse" (*SB* 1832, ix) most effectively furnish (as Gilpin would say) such "sources of pleasure and amusement"[25] when they are at their most passive, providing an unembroidered rendering of either human or topographical nature. No wonder, in the end, Kennedy decided he was not writing a novel.

Kennedy's professions of a verisimilitude verging upon authorial absence are complicated, however, by his relentlessly stylized picturesque presentations in *Swallow Barn*—which is why Martineau suggested that *Swallow Barn* could not stand with those truly "impartial" books written "without much regard to the picturesque," and that Kennedy's work operated through a "subtraction of some of the truth"—and I want to continue on in this chapter to explore the ramifications of grafting that picturesque style of narration with an apologia for the plantation economy of the upper South during the 1830s. But even an initial consideration of the book's relationship with picturesque thought raises the problem of Kennedy's handling of his own picturesque landscapes, for this facet of *Swallow Barn* changes much between its first edition in 1832 and its revised version in 1851. Indeed, it is as if the history separating these two publication dates—among other things, a polarizing national political history that might render quaintly nostalgic the fresh-faced tone of the northerner's journey into the Old Dominion—reinscribes an altered landscape.

Kennedy's presentation of certain landscapes remains constant through both editions. Take, for instance, Littleton's description of his tour down the James River, a Virgilian pastoral domain where elements merge, where there are no hardened boundaries, where the wild and the domesticated listlessly converge:

I gazed upon the receding headlands far sternward, and then upon the sedgy banks where the cattle were standing leg-deep in the water to get rid of the flies: and ever and anon, as well followed the sinuosities of the river, some sweeping eminence came into view, and on the crown thereof was seen a plain, many-windowed edifice of brick, with low wings, old, ample and stately, looking over its wide and sun-burnt domain in solitary silence: and there were the piney promontories, into whose shade we sometimes glided so close that one might almost have jumped on shore, where the wave struck the beach with a sullen plash: and there were the decayed fences jutting beyond the bank into the water, as if they had come down the hill too fast to stop themselves. All these things struck my fancy, as peculiar to the region. (*SB* 1832, 5; 1851, 16)

Littleton's description is the very picture of pastoral idyll, of nature seemingly in the process of repossessing a realm only borrowed by human beings. Such aestheticization of a collapse or return to the natural informed the English picturesque theorists' partiality to ruins and other crumbling structures, as with Uvedale Price's swooning descriptions of "the process by which time, the great author of such changes, converts a beautiful object into a picturesque one" while forces of erosion "loosen the stones," "tumble in irregular masses," and germinate "wild plants and creepers, that crawl over, and shoot among the fallen ruins."[26]

Just such an attraction to the aesthetic effects of decayed structures also shapes Littleton's description of his passing views of the ruins of Jamestown:

> You would have laughed to see into what a state of lady-like rapture I had worked myself, in my eagerness to get a peep at James Town, with all my effervescence of romance kindled up by the renown of the unmatchable Smith. The steward of the boat pointed out when we had nearly passed it— and lo! there it was—an old steeple, a barren fallow, some melancholy heifers, a blasted pine, and, on its top, a desolate hawk's nest. What a splendid field for the fancy! What a carte blanche for a painter! With how many things might this little spot be filled! (*SB* 1832, 5–6; 1851, 16–17)[27]

The 1851 edition of *Swallow Barn* included illustrations by David Hunter Strother, the southern-born, European-trained artist whose work appeared frequently in *Harper's*, including a rendition of the ruins of Jamestown striking for its adherence to picturesque codes. Strother's Jamestown appears not unlike J. M. W. Turner's Tintern Abbey, a stately decay enshrouded in ivy, framed by overgrowth, and generally worthy of inclusion in one of Gilpin's sketchbooks or Price's *Essay on the Picturesque* (see figures 4.4 and 4.5).

Still, passages like this from the book's introductory epistle remain only slightly altered from 1832 to 1851. Our opening views of Virginia in both versions render that country as an essentially English picturesque space, as indeed Littleton's first glimpses of Swallow Barn itself characterizes the plantation as a sort of pastoral or medieval village. "The road was smooth, and canopied with dark foliage, and, as the last blush of twilight faded away, we swept rapidly round the head of a swamp, where a thousand frogs were celebrating their vespers, and soon after reached the gate of the court-yard," Littleton tells us. "Lights were glimmering through different apertures, and several stacks of chimneys were visible above the horizon; the whole mass being magnified into the dimensions of a great castle" (*SB* 1832, 12–13; 1851, 22–23). Seemingly determined to place Virginia in its most English light (as when he describes Littleton's guide, Scipio, "an old free negro, formerly a

FIGURE 4.4 *David Hunter Strother, illustration of Jamestown in John Pendleton Kennedy, Swallow Barn, rev. ed. (New York: George P. Putnam, 1851), 17.*

retainer in some of the feudal establishments of the low country" [*SB* 1832, 11; 1851, 21]), Kennedy suspends his opening epistle within a constellation of picturesque codes—the pastoral idyll of the James River, the stately decay of Jamestown, the imagined castles and feudal vassals heralding Littleton's approach to Swallow Barn—most of which remains in place through the 1851 edition of the book.

But with the first chapter of the 1851 edition, Kennedy repositioned his picturesque gaze in significant ways. For instance, the very first sentences of chapter 1 in the 1832 text present the main mansion of Swallow Barn itself in this way: "Swallow Barn is an aristocratical old edifice, that squats, like a brooding hen, on the southern bank of the James River. It is quietly seated, with its vassal out-buildings, in a kind of shady pocket or nook, formed by a sweep of the stream, on a gentle acclivity thinly sprinkled with oaks, whose magnificent branches afford habitation and defense to an antique colony of owls" (*SB* 1832, 19). In the 1851 version, Kennedy alters the description: "Swallow Barn is an aristocratical old edifice which sits, like a brooding hen, on the southern bank of the James River. It looks down upon a shady pocket or nook, formed by an indentation of the shore, from a gentle acclivity thinly sprinkled

FIGURE 4.5 *J. M. W. Turner, The Chancel and Crossing of Tintern Abbey, Looking Towards the East Window, 1794. Pencil and watercolor on paper, 358 × 255 mm. © Trustees of the British Museum.*

with oaks whose magnificent branches afford habitation to sundry friendly colonies of squirrels and woodpeckers" (*SB* 1851, 27).

Aside from the metamorphoses that transform owls to squirrels and woodpeckers, and a squatting hen to a sitting one, Swallow Barn is in the 1851 rendition situated at a higher topographical point, now "look[ing] down" upon a picturesque bend in the James River. This shift in emphasis and position is important, for it partakes of what John Conron has described as "the psychological power to look down on things, as if they were spread at one's feet," that conditions the picturesque from Claude Lorrain's canvases to Humphrey Repton's redesigned estates.[28] By the 1850s, Conron notes, American painters of the Hudson River school were composing their works along increasingly elevated lines of sight or axes of vision. In one way, these perspectives allowed painters such as Asher Durand or Thomas Cole to foreground effects of light that were simply different when perceived among ground-level objects. But in another sense, such perspectives tend to domesticate wilderness, exalt the perspective of the viewer, and subordinate that which is under view.[29]

Such perspective upon those who populate the landscape seems to inform another significant set of revisions Kennedy undertook in the first chapter of *Swallow Barn*. In his 1832 edition, Kennedy presents a view of a nearby brook, and the slaves who work on its shores, in this way:

> At a short distance from the mansion a brook glides at a snail's pace towards the river, holding its course through a wilderness of alder and laurel, and forming little islets covered with a damp moss. Across this stream is thrown a rough bridge, and not far below, an aged sycamore twists its complex roots about a spring, at the point of confluence of which and the brook, a squadron of ducks have a cruising ground, where they may be seen at any time of the day turning up their tails to the skies, like unfortunate gun boats driven by the head in a gale. Immediately on the margin, at this spot, the family linen is usually spread out by some sturdy negro women, who chant shrill ditties over their wash tubs, and keep up a spirited attack, both of tongue and hand, upon sundry little besmirched and bow-legged blacks, that are continually making somersets on the grass, or mischievously waddling across the clothes laid out to bleach. (*SB* 1832, 22–23)

The "rough bridge" skirting the stream and the twisted roots of the sycamore—one recalls both Gilpin's relentless advocacy of the "rough" over the "smooth" as well as Price's decided recommendations for gnarled trees rather than straight[30]—are among the most obviously picturesque elements in the sketch, and in his second edition Kennedy, apparently concerned that readers might miss his homage here, would underline it more explicitly. For that matter, the present-tense narration to which Kennedy resorts at his most visual moments increases the immediacy of the presentation, the sense that one is really looking at a sort of painting.

But in 1851 he also took steps to re-present the scene as more clearly apropos of visual art—to appropriate Gilpin's 1768 definition of the picturesque, as "that peculiar kind of beauty, which is agreeable in a picture."[31] Here is the same passage as rewritten for the 1851 edition of *Swallow Barn*:

> A few hundred yards from the mansion, a brook glides at a snail's pace towards the river, holding its course through a wilderness of laurel and alder, and creeping around islets covered with green moss. Across this stream is thrown a rough bridge, which it would delight a painter to see; and not far below it an aged sycamore twists its roots into a grotesque framework to the pure mirror of a spring, which wells up its cool waters from a bed of gravel and runs gurgling to the brook. There it aids in furnishing a cruising ground to a squadron of ducks who, in defiance of all nautical propriety, are incessantly turning up their sterns to the skies. On the grass which skirts the margin of the spring, I observe the family linen is usually spread out by some three or four negro-women, who chant shrill music over their wash-tubs,

and seem to live in ceaseless warfare with sundry little besmirched and bow-legged blacks, who are never tired of making somersets, and mischievously pushing each other on the clothes laid down to dry. (*SB* 1851, 29)

Kennedy's multiple shifts in presentation here serve to intensify the pictur-esque underpinnings of the scene, but these amplifications accompany other subtle shifts in his way of handling the slaves who inhabit the margins of this visually arresting moment. First, Kennedy now informs his reader that the rough bridge, which he first erected in 1832, would delight a painter. More-over, the gnarled roots of the sycamore now constitute a "framework" to the spring (before, they were simply twisted "about" it), which Kennedy now de-scribes as a "pure mirror" reflecting the scene to come. In other words, the reader of *Swallow Barn* is at this moment effectively examining a picturesque painting, framed by those twisted roots, and the content of that painting ap-pears in the sentences to follow: we see a squadron of cruising ducks, but more absorbingly, a group of slaves to whom Kennedy had already likened those ducks in the first edition (since there the slave children are "waddling" across their mothers' washing laid out to dry). And *this* scene of pastoral levity is es-sentially the same but for certain adjustments. Whereas before, the slave children "are continually making somersets," now they "never tire" of this activity—a change in phrasing that accentuates the novel's depiction of the plantation as a space conditioned by mutual consent between overseer and slave. If there is "warfare" in this scene, it is far from the sort of war against natural rights, and for that matter democracy and divinity, many northern commentators were already ascribing to southern slaveholders—and still fur-ther from the kind of race war Nat Turner would enjoin as Kennedy prepared his first edition of *Swallow Barn* for publication in the late summer of 1831. The conservative semiotics of the picturesque gaze—traditionally serving to an-aesthetize the ethical responsiveness of otherwise sympathetic viewers to what would otherwise constitute obvious horrors of deprivation and poverty—are here arrayed in apology for the system of human chattel itself, but only in the form of a passing glance at a pastoral idyll. Mark Littleton, after all, has not come southward in order to editorialize or otherwise deliver indictment upon his southern cousins, or so he frequently informs us. Instead, he has come to observe, to view, to present "true pictures" of this picturesque tour of the Old Dominion.

3. Distance and Closure in the Plantation Mode

Swallow Barn aligns its aesthetics with its political trajectory as an account of southern slavery, and for this reason the book is explicit about its investments in the picturesque as a mode for apprehending not only landscape but also the

human beings who populate it. Most of the book consists of a series of character sketches that frequently call upon specifically picturesque language, even if
with satirical purpose. Of Prudence Meriwether, whose brother Frank presides over Swallow Barn, Kennedy explains, "There is a dash of the picturesque in the character of this lady. Towards sunset she is apt to stray forth
amongst the old oaks, and to gather small bouquets of wild flowers, in the
pursuit of which she contrives to get into very pretty attitudes; or she falls into
raptures at the shifting tints of the clouds on the western sky, and produces
quite a striking pictorial effect by the skillful choice of a position which shows
her figure in strong relief against the evening sky" (SB 1851, 48). Carey, the
slave who operates Frank's livery, is possessed of "a picturesque effect" owing
to his "German forage-cap of light cloth . . . rather conceitedly drawn over his
dark, laughing eye" (SB 1851, 51). Moreover, Kennedy draws picturesque characters like Prudence and Carey into the larger sweep of Swallow Barn, which
places human beings as elements of scenery whose wider scope is worthy of a
Gilpin essay or Gainsborough canvas.

Littleton's descriptions of the regions surrounding Swallow Barn regale the
reader with the charms of the land while also situating a remote perspective.
In his description of the Brakes, the nearest estate to Swallow Barn, Littleton
retains the distance afforded by the elevated situation of the latter estate, composing all elements of the scene within his lofty, panoramic perspective: "The
principle feature in this region is an extensive range of low lands, reaching
back from the river, and bounded by distant forest, from the heart of which
tower, above the mass of foliage, a number of naked branches of decayed trees,
that are distinctly visible from this remote perspective. These lowlands are
checkered by numberless gullies or minute water-courses, whose direction is
marked out to the eye by thickets of briers and brambles" (SB 1851, 76). The
main house of the Brakes can by "bound" by the nearby forest only when
viewed from the "remote perspective" Ned occupies, that which also causes
him to imagine that the herbaceous growth on the banks of creeks exist in
order to mark "out to the eye" the course of the waterways, not simply because
the moist soil along those waterways provides a more rich manure for plant
life. All of nature, at this moment for Littleton, orients itself around vectors
extending from the porch at Swallow Barn, though he is also able to imagine
other, equally remote perspectives upon the estate. "Seen from the river," he
reports, "the buildings stand partly in the shade of a range of immense Lom-
bardy poplars, which retreat down the hill in the opposite direction until the
line diminishes from the view. Negro huts are scattered in that profusion
which belongs to a Virginia plantation" (SB 1851, 77).

The visual language of Kennedy's narrative oscillates between this sort of
picturesque distance and the proximity afforded by later excursions into the
landscape. The picturesque experience of the South that so delights Littleton
situates itself in the view from away and on high, the elevated vantage from

which radiates the axes of vision plotted by Humphry Repton and that coordinates the perspective of so much picturesque landscaping and painting. In Littleton's estimation, this sort of distance and the elevated detachment it promotes inform the ethos of the Virginia planter, whose ancestry consists of "sober and thinking English[men]" whose descendants now "live apart from one another" (SB 1851, 70). Virginia planters, Littleton explains, "are surrounded by their bondsmen and dependents; and the customary intercourse of society familiarizes their minds to the relation of high and low degrees" (SB 1851, 71). Littleton considers this disconnectedness among planters one of the "traces of the feudal system" discernable in Virginia plantation life, where "[t]he solitary elevation of a country gentleman, well to do in the world, begets some magnificent notions" (SB 1851, 35). Frank Meriwether, the patriarch of Swallow Barn, is an acme of the model, whose demise he predicts and opines. In one way, Frank embodies what Littleton describes as the Virginia country squire, isolated from his peers and presiding over "bondsmen and dependents" until "[h]e becomes as infallible as the Pope; gradually acquires a habit of making long speeches; is apt to be impatient of contradiction, and is always very touchy on the point of honor." The effect of Frank's "solitary elevation" is to shape him as a kind of sovereign who subjects his dependents to a near-constant stream of allegedly didactic commentary.

But Kennedy also sketches Frank in ways to deflate his image of detached regality, since Frank is largely unaware that beyond the bounds of the (often literally) captive audience of Swallow Barn, his powers of erudition would be treated with less deference. "Meriwether's sayings, about Swallow Barn, import absolute verity," as Littleton reports. "But I have discovered that they are not so current out of his jurisdiction. Indeed, every now and then, we have had quite obstinate discussions when some of the neighboring potentates, who stand in the same sphere with Frank, come to the house; for these worthies have opinions of their own, and nothing can be more dogged than the conflict between them" (SB 1851, 35).

Even so, as Littleton tells us, the solitary elevation of a country gentleman begets some magnificent notions. One of Frank's concerns those forms of distance limiting "intercourse" among members of the planting class, and which Frank imagines now to be threatened by the progress of the age. One of the theses to which he subjects his dependents concerns the steamboat, which Frank admits is "destined to produce valuable results," but which also threatens an "annihilation of space" that, Frank proclaims, "is not to be desired," since "our protection against the evils of consolidation consists in the very obstacles to our intercourse" (SB 1851, 72–73). For Frank, the sovereignty of Virginian civilization is shored up in obstacles to unrestrained intercourse; the society of the planting class, whose aristocratic standing depends upon the feudal disconnection Littleton notes, is imperiled by the closure of distance the steam engine announces. Indeed, for Frank, this elision of space betokens other ramifications concerning Virginia's standing within the federal Union, as he later warns a group of pupils assembled in a nearby schoolroom "to keep a lynx-eyed gaze upon that serpentine ambition which would convert the government at Washington into Aaron's rod, to swallow up the independence of their native state" (*SB* 1851, 74–75).

Frank's ideas on aristocratic detachment align well with the picturesque distance arranging most of Kennedy's depictions of Swallow Barn as visual compositions, and in this way, also, with the distance separating the spectator from the rustic and which typifies the picturesque mode. We see this distance, for instance, in Mark Littleton's description of the Brakes, viewed from on high at Swallow Barn, a bucolic panorama beautified by "Negro huts . . . scattered about over the landscape in that profusion that belongs to a Virginia plantation," just as we see it in the picturesque framing of the slave family washing laundry on the banks of the spring well below the main house. And so in this way Frank's thesis on distance and advisedly restrained intercourse provides a commentary on *Swallow Barn*'s visual ordering of the plantation and its environs. Just as placid relations between landed peers call for a cordial detachment, so do the sights of the plantation compose with greater felicity when viewed from afar.

But even as Frank holds forth on the importance of aristocratic aloofness and disconnection, his position is undercut by the fact that he is constantly breaching the distance that would otherwise separate him from not only his "dependents" but also his "bondsmen." Even as a country gentleman who typifies what Kennedy presents as a certain James River Valley personality, Frank is in practice unmindful of the "relation of high and low degrees" supposedly safeguarded in the restraint of "intercourse." Usually unable to provoke long-inured family members who endure his polemics in silence, Frank seeks out audiences among other populations at Swallow Barn: frequently, in fact, his slaves. Of Carey, the "pragmatical old negro" who runs Frank's livery, Littleton tells us, "He and Frank hold grave and momentous consultations upon the affairs of the stable, in such a sagacious strain of equal debate, that it would puzzle a spectator to tell which was the leading member in the council" (*SB* 1851, 36). In fact, Frank's authority over Carey becomes practically indiscernible as a result of their egalitarian "intercourse," since "Carey thinks he knows a great deal more upon the subject than his master, and their frequent intercourse has begot a familiarity in the old negro which is almost fatal to Meriwether's supremacy" (*SB* 1851, 36–37). In theory, then, Frank is correct that the restraint of intercourse is crucial to the social arrangement of his milieu, the "relation of high and low degrees" vouchsafed in Virginian sovereignty. But in his day-to-day relations, even with his slaves, Frank is unwilling to swear off such intercourse.

The closure of social distance between master and slave is a part of the way *Swallow Barn* attempts to sentimentalize slavery, since for instance Carey's infractions of hierarchy go unpunished by Frank, who typically "gets a little nettled by Carey's doggedness, but generally turns it off with a laugh" (*SB* 1851, 37). But a closure of distance also qualifies *Swallow Barn*'s commitment to hierarchies of high and low degrees. Though Kennedy did not regard *Swallow Barn* as a novel, its many sketches and episodes are at least loosely situated along two narrative arcs. One of these concerns the courtship of Frank's brother-in-law, Ned Hazard, and Bel Tracy, whose father, Isaac, presides over the Brakes. Ned's failure to woo Bel, paradoxically, owes to his genial demeanor—though Ned treats Bel with deference and affection, in other words, the effect has been to instill between them a rapport of kinship rather than of romance. Bel's cousin Harvey, who supports Ned's bid for Bel, explains the paradox when he points out that "Ned is falling rapidly into that privileged intimacy that is fatal to the pretensions of a lover. This jesting, careless friendship will lodge him, in a short time, high and dry upon a shoal in her regard, where he will become a permanent and picturesque landmark. He will acquire the enviable distinction of a brother, as she begins to call him already, and he will be certain to be invited to her wedding" (*SB* 1851, 237). By likening Ned to a picturesque landmark, a kind of folly in the distance, Harvey critiques the kind of intercourse Ned has pursued with Bel, a "jesting, careless" type of intercourse "fatal" to his romantic aims (in the same way, we might say, that the kind of intercourse taking place between Frank Meriwether and Carey is "almost fatal" to the former's "supremacy"). Ned resists the open expressions of ardor Harvey recommends because he regards that courtly mode with irony. Yet by dealing with Bel outside that convention, he has installed in its place an unromantic familiarity. It may be that his dealings with Bel have up until this point constituted a more genuine rapport than Ned associates with more swooning affections, but, as Harvey notes, pursued as a matter of course they will result in a sibling-like regard rather than the consummation Ned desires. This distance, for Harvey, is akin to a picturesque distance, wherein Ned will become for Bel a pleasing "landmark," permanently if fondly remote.

So the antidote, Ned discovers, is a transformation of their "jesting, careless" rapport through a gesture that redirects the trajectory of their relationship. As it turns out, Ned's recovery of Bel's escaped pet hawk does the trick. One could point out that hawking itself carries a certain Tennysonian connotation, and furthermore that Kennedy couches the venture in metaphors of bondage, wherein the hawk itself becomes a fugitive slave to be hunted, and Bel, in a reversal of the usual gendered courtly economy, becomes Ned's "slave for life," so enthralled is she with his noblesse (*SB* 1851, 372). But a more important point concerns the unrestrained "intercourse" Frank Meriwether regards as lethal to the intersubjective distance he takes as foundational to Virginia planter society. In the courtly drama of Bel and Ned—the outcome of which will certainly reconfigure the social distance between the two plantations in the event that Bel and Ned marry—a certain kind of intercourse (the jesting, friendly kind) has made another kind of intercourse improbable. The redirection of that intercourse toward the more romantic sort that will unify the plantations and satisfy Bel's wish for a courtly suitor involves an errand into the wilderness, the recovery of Bel's fugitive hawk, which as it turns out is finally captured near a slave's cabin. This dynamic—wherein some form of social distance is happily compressed through a journey into the landscape previously viewed from afar—becomes a kind of formula in *Swallow Barn*, where excursions into the middle ground of the picturesque landscape repeatedly serve to obviate social distance, eventually with results that have clear ramifications for the plantation system.

To wit, the second of *Swallow Barn*'s narrative arcs enacts a similar breaching of distance and excursion into the middle ground. This second plot curve concerns Isaac's lifelong obsession with the boundary line between the Brakes and Swallow Barn, which was in the prior century negotiated around a mill pond long since evaporated. What remains of the site of the mill is located in Apple-pie branch, a desolate swamp separating the two estates described by Frank's amused attorney, Philly Wart, as a "fine garden of wankpins and snake-collards!" (*SB* 1851, 200). Isaac's interest in the land remains unaccountable, since Apple-pie branch, as Philly declares, "is as worthless as the Pomptinæ Paludes . . . [and] should be relinquished by unanimous consent to the skunks and the muskrats!" (*SB* 1851, 200). But since Isaac, armed with family letters from the prior century, insists that the precise boundary between the two estates should be redrawn, Philly proposes a resolution to the dispute through a "trial by view," for which both parties first assemble on a promontory overlooking the disputed area only to then descend into the swamp in order to examine the location of the former boundary.

The journey into the swamp is predictably droll, but it also invests that space with the semiotics of murky natural boundaries: not only the legal boundary between the two estates, and not only the legal boundaries between whites and blacks, we might further suppose, but also the social boundaries *Swallow Barn* recognizes as the structural foundation of Virginian cavalier culture, the distance Frank Meriwether holds up as the sine qua non of plantation aristocracy but which he also frequently violates through his intercourse with both neighbors and slaves. Eventually, the two parties determine a new boundary line through recourse to an arcane and comically Latinate clause of Virginia statute, but Kennedy's real point here seems to be that a potentially rancorous dispute between neighbors is settled through pleasant "intercourse"—the companionable rapport between Meriwether and Isaac, who at one point tells Frank that the suit "has been conducted with so much courtesy, from beginning to end, that I had almost flattered myself with the hope, I should have had the luxury of it for the rest of my life" (*SB* 1851, 196).

Perhaps because of their semiotic value in a text concerned with shifting boundaries, there are as many swamps per square acre in *Swallow Barn* as in southern literature itself, and in the chapter immediately following the settlement of Isaac's suit, Kennedy takes his reader into Goblin Swamp, adjacent to Apple-pie branch and through which Ned Hazard leads Littleton as the two journey homeward from the Brakes.[32] Like Apple-pie branch, Goblin swamp appears initially as a desolate "forsaken region," Littleton tells us, but as Hazard and Littleton approach a ruin in the marshes, Kennedy describes a suddenly evanescent landscape:

> When we arrived at this spot the sun was just peering, with his enlarged disk, though the upper branches of the trees, in the western horizon. The clouds were gorgeous with the golden and purple tints that give magnificence to our summer evenings; and the waning light, falling on the volume of the forest around us, communicated a richer gloom to its shades, and magnified the gigantic branches of some blasted oaks on the border of the plain, as they were relieved against the clear sky. Long and distorted shadows fell from every weed, bush, and tree, and contributed, with the forlorn aspect of the landscape, to impress us with an undefined and solemn sensation, that for a moment threw us into silence. Flights of crows traversed the air above our heads, and sang out their discordant vespers, as they plied their way to a distant roost; the fish-hawk had perched upon the highest branch of the tallest oak, and at intervals was seen to stretch forth his wing and ruffle his feathers, as if adjusting his position for the night. All animated objects that inhabited this region seemed to be busy with individual cares; and the nocturnal preparations for rest or prey resounded from every quarter. (*SB* 1851, 251)[33]

It is a vivid moment in terms of the visual and picturesque currency in which *Swallow Barn* trades. Ned's and Littleton's journey into Goblin Swamp restages the prior journey into Apple-Pie branch, but coming after the amicable resolution of the boundary dispute over that locale, it fulfills different aesthetic ends bound up with Littleton's presentation of the swamp in an aspect of stunning beauty. Kennedy's description here is not, however, at home with the picturesque mode predominating the rest of *Swallow Barn*. Himself a kind of picturesque tourist up until this point, Littleton departs from that mode by venturing into the prospect, abandoning the view from on high that defines the picturesque. What Ned and Littleton find in Goblin swamp amounts to a kind of ecstasy with the varieties of nature, so discerning is the passage of the "magnified" components of the scene, where "every weed, bush, and tree" stand out in singularity, where "[a]ll animated objects that inhabited this region" appear in relief, accentuated in "waning light." Rather than the syncretism of the grand sweep characterizing the aesthetic experience upon which the picturesque capitalizes, and whose achievement requires remoteness of perspective, here *Swallow Barn* breaches that distance in order to present an extremely proximate, phenomenologically complex landscape whose beauty rivals, perhaps surpasses, any other in the book.

This is not the final moment during which *Swallow Barn* abandons the elevated perspective of the picturesque by moving into the prospect itself, thus violating the optical principles of picturesque beholding. Perhaps the most strikingly picturesque presentation of *Swallow Barn* occurs near the end of the book, as Mark Littleton describes his approach, with Frank Meriwether, toward the slaves' quarters of the estate. In the initial stages of Littleton's description, the quarters appear through the dilated retina of picturesque presentation, wherein the rustic quarters of the slaves serve mainly to heighten the aesthetic rewards of the view:

> These hovels, with their appurtenances, formed an exceedingly picturesque landscape. They were scattered, without order, over the slope of a gentle hill; and many of them were embowered under old and majestic trees. The rudeness of their construction rather enhanced the attractiveness of the scene. Some few were built after the fashion of the better sort of cottages; but age had stamped its heavy traces upon their exterior: the green moss had gathered upon the roofs, and the coarse weatherboarding had broken, here and there, into chinks. (*SB* 1851, 449)

Littleton's presentation of the rustic dwellings of the slaves initiates his journey toward their cabins, and at this first point in his narration of that approach the rustic charm of the scene reduplicates a stock treatment of impoverished pastorals whose presentation as aesthetic objects promotes the self-aggrandizing experience of the picturesque spectator. The slaves of the quarter afford for Littleton the kind of aesthetic pleasure Price valued in Gainsborough's paintings, a form of delight that entails, to quote Andrews, a similar suppression of moral response. Indeed, as Littleton moves further into the quarters, his assessment of the slaves' situation seems in keeping with the conservative sentimentality proper to such picturesque treatments of marginal others. Examining the doors and hinges of the cabins, the clay filling the interstices of their log construction, and the chimneys "communicating a droll expression" over the roofs, Littleton concludes, initially, that though "the inmates of these dwellings were furnished according to a very primitive notion of comfort," "there was no want of what, in all countries, would be considered a reasonable supply of luxuries" (*SB* 1851, 450). Through some process of reification, impoverishment becomes a lack of want, which in turn becomes "a reasonable supply of luxuries," and as Littleton moves further into the quarter to encounter the slaves themselves, he presents them as pastoral types relaxing in "lazy, listless" repose:

> Nothing more attracted my observation than the swarms of little negroes that basked on the sunny side of these cabins, and congregated to gaze at us as we surveyed their haunts. They were nearly all in that costume of the golden age which I have heretofore described; and showed their slim shanks and long

heels in all varieties of their grotesque natures. Their predominate love of sunshine, and their lazy, listless postures, and apparent content to be silently looking abroad, might well afford a comparison to a set of terrapins luxuriating in the genial warmth of summer, on the logs of a mill-pond. (*SB* 1851, 450–51)

As with Littleton's description of the "besmirched and bow-legged blacks" who playfully trample their mothers' washing much earlier, this description of chattel slavery as a form of rustic idyll serves to maintain Littleton's epistemological remove even as he gains literal proximity. The slaves he now encounters appear as if as stylized rustics, as sentimentally framed as the earlier children and their mothers are literally framed by the twisted roots of a picturesque sycamore.

As Andrews and Harrison point out, the picturesque generates a moral symbology around rural impoverishment not only by maintaining visual distance from the poor but in depicting their poverty as consistent with their postures of relaxation. The poor, in picturesque landscape, are poor because of their lack of industry, but rather than opining the causality it invents, the picturesque elevates rural poverty as a charming return to the primitive and the carefree. In *Swallow Barn*—as in the nostalgic plantation fiction that would flourish during reconstruction—the "lazy, listless" repose of Frank Meriwether's slaves serves initially to provide a rationale for the larger system of chattel slavery, in this case converting Littleton into a reluctant supporter of the institution. Since Frank, as Littleton explains, "is a kind and considerate master," and since the slaves in the quarter are surrounded by an abundance of provisions (some of which, we are told, they are permitted to sell to Frank), it becomes difficult for Littleton to locate here an evil to denounce. "I had come here a stranger, in great degree, to the negro character," Littleton explains, "knowing but little of the domestic history of these people, their duties, habits or temper, and somewhat disposed, indeed, from prepossessions, to look upon them as severely dealt with, and expecting to have my sympathies excited toward them as objects of commiseration" (*SB* 1851, 452). But now, Littleton explains, "The contrast between my preconceptions of their condition and the reality which I have witnessed, has brought me to a most agreeable surprise. I will not say that, in a high state of cultivation and of such self-dependence as they might possibly attain in a separate national existence, they might not become a more respectable people; but I am quite sure that they never could have become a happier people than I find them here" (*SB* 1851, 452–53).

There is little about this sentimental presentation of slavery to distinguish this passage of *Swallow Barn* from many other literary rationalizations composed until the Civil War and indeed well afterward; even Littleton professes uncertainty as to whether the deficient "moral constitution" of the slaves around him are a justification for slavery or a result of it, though he supposes that "[i]n the present stage of his existence," the slave is, "in his moral constitution, a dependent upon the white race," on whose "guidance and direction" all slaves depend (*SB* 1851, 453). In any case, Littleton resolves that immediate emancipation would be "the most cruel of all projects" since it would deprive these rustics of both that guidance and the resulting, carefree life of plenty (*SB* 1851, 454). So far as it goes, this logic should certainly have been familiar to Kennedy and his southern audience by the time of the novel's second release in 1851. But *Swallow Barn* does not allow Littleton the last word on this point, and nor does it present his point of view as the final effect of his and Frank's journey into the "exceedingly picturesque landscape" of the quarter.

When Littleton shares his newly formulated views with Frank, Meriwether's lengthy response indicates a much more conflicted view on the matter. "I believe," he says, "there are but few men who may not be persuaded that [slaves] suffer some wrong in the organization of society—for society has many wrongs, both accidental and contrived, in its structure" (*SB* 1851, 455). Extreme poverty, Frank acknowledges, provides such an example of structural oppression, since "[s]ociety can have no honest excuse for starving a human being." And so "[i]ngenuous men," he explains, are "likely . . . to find, in this question of slavery, a theme for highest excitement. . . . For slavery, as an original question, is wholly without justification or defense. It is theoretically and morally wrong" (*SB* 1851, 455).

Frank's sudden denunciation of the system of slavery as wholly without justification or defense opens a rupture in the panegyric Littleton had up until this moment formulated in spite of his "prepossessions," his former bias against the system. But if, in some sense, the moral signification of the quarter is finally not under the control of the picturesque gaze to which Littleton submits it, neither is the ideological impact of Frank's excursus under the complete control of Kennedy, who seems ambivalent about what it entails to describe slavery as "theoretically and morally wrong." Frank's speech opens questions it then attempts to close: while slavery is "wholly without justification or defense," he then stipulates that those who call for immediate emancipation can be only "fanatical and one-sided thinkers" (*SB* 1851, 455). But though it sounds, at first, as if Frank might be able to regard slavery as a theoretical and moral wrong and yet still agree with Littleton that as an extant circumstance it cannot be alleviated through a general emancipation, it turns out that such emancipation is indeed what Frank forecasts:

> When the time comes, as I apprehend it will come,—and all the sooner, if it be not delayed by these efforts to arouse something like a vindictive feeling between the disputants on both sides—in which the roots of slavery will begin to lose their hold in our soil; and when we shall have the means for providing these people a proper asylum, I shall be glad to see the State devote her thoughts to that enterprise, and, if I am alive, will cheerfully and gratefully assist with it. (*SB* 1851, 456)

Frank now advocates, and says he would like to help hasten, an end to slavery in Virginia.

He doesn't stop there. From his forecast of a future when slavery will loosen its hold "in our soil," Frank launches into a critique of slavery as an inefficient economic system wherein "[t]he evil is generally felt on the side of the master," since "[l]ess work is exacted of them than voluntary laborers choose to perform" (*SB* 1851, 457). As before, Frank's remarks oscillate between penetrating critique and textbook apologia: one of the reasons slavery makes for an inefficient economic model, he says, is that slaveholders in Virginia "are, in the main, men of kind and humane tempers" whose slaves enjoy more "comforts" than those of "the rural population of other countries" (*SB* 1851, 457). Moreover, Frank supposes that free labor can result in more severe overseers, since he "suspect[s] it is invariably characteristic of those who are in the habit of severely tasking themselves, that they are inclined to regulate their demands upon others by their own standard" (*SB* 1851, 457).

But this doubling backward notwithstanding, Frank's analysis of slavery as not only morally indefensible but also economically unsustainable amounts to a damning scrutiny much less resonant with the pro-slavery Virginian discourses of his era than with contemporaneous abolitionist discourses of the North. Going on, Frank informs Littleton,

> You gentlemen of the North greatly misapprehend us, if you suppose that we are in love with this slave institution—or that, for the most part, we even deem it profitable to us. There are those among us, it is true, some persons who are inclined to be fanatical on this side of the question, and who bring themselves to adopt some bold dogmas tending to these extreme views. . . . But at present, I am sure, the Southern sentiment on this question is temperate and wise, and that we neither regard slavery as a good, nor account it, except in some favourable conditions, as profitable. (*SB* 1851, 458)

None of which is to say that Frank is less committed, at this final juncture of *Swallow Barn*, to the feudal distance upon which he imagines Virginian planting society to be founded. In fact, toward the end of his polemic, Frank imagines that prior to a general emancipation, it may be possible to establish a quasi-aristocracy of slaves, possessed of their own estates and dependents. Perhaps, Frank proposes, Virginia might "establish by law, an upper or privileged class of slave—selecting them from the most deserving, above the age of forty-five years. These I would endue with something of a feudal character. They should be entitled to hold small tracts of land under their masters, rendering it for a certain rent, payable either in personal service or money" (*SB* 1851, 459–60). The scheme Frank imagines—a "dream" he acknowledges as "not yet fully matured"—would certainly accentuate Frank's sense of his own feudal elevation, and yet at the same time his idea of elevating his slaves as quasi-lords of pseudo-estates seems also to destabilize that system, tampering as it does with the "relation of high and low degrees" to which, in Littleton's prior description, "customary intercourse of society" "familiarizes" the mind of the Virginia planter. When Littleton points out that Frank, for instance, may have difficulty compelling Carey to abandon the livery for his own estate, Meriwether laughs, exclaiming "Faith! I shall be without a feudatory to begin with," an estimation that indicates, perhaps beyond Frank's intention, a potential fall from dominance for the slave-holding aristocracy (*SB* 1851, 460).

All this has an effect on Littleton, who still again revises his outlook on slavery, now regarding Africans in America as "truly a class of people to whom justice has seldom been done, and who possess many points of character well calculated to win them a kind and amiable judgment from the world." Abandoning his former optimism over the life of carefree plenty enjoyed by slaves, he now decides that "[t]hey are a neglected race, who seem to have been excluded from the pale of human sympathy, from mistaken opinions of their quality, no less than from the unpretending lowliness of their position" (*SB* 1851, 470). To be sure, Littleton attempts to retain access to the mystique of the rustic charms of the Old Dominion, and that includes some part of the perspective afforded when one regards slavery, as it were, through the Claude glass of picturesque distortion and distance. "To me," he sums up, "they have always appeared as a people of agreeable peculiarities, and not without much of the picturesque in the development of their habits and feelings" (*SB* 1851, 470–71). And yet it is more or less impossible to regain a distant prospect already abandoned, to recover the farsighted mirage once one has endeavored to encounter reality up close. Perhaps Kennedy was right to say that *Swallow Barn* is not really a novel, since the twin plots of the book, both concerning the renegotiation of boundaries separating two families, wind up a bit too thin to consolidate Kennedy's many sketches into one narrative trajectory. But the larger arc of the book, which takes Mark Littleton and Kennedy's reader beyond the view from on high to a close encounter with those who work the middle ground, also describes a traversal from picturesque and English ways of seeing—a species of what Emerson thought of as the "paltry things" threatening the sovereignty of his own American axis of vision—to a more clearsighted apprehension of the objects and people residing in the distance.

{ 5 }

Embodied Eloquence, the Sumner Assault, and the Transatlantic Cable

1. Knock-Down Arguments

Not long after South Carolina congressman Preston Brooks caned within an inch of his life Massachusetts senator Charles Sumner on the floor of the U.S. Senate, the future U.S. attorney Richard Dana, Jr., wrote a letter to the recuperating Sumner, describing the political effect of the assault using a rhetoric of electricity. "When Brooks brought his cane in contact with your head," he declared, "he completed the circuit of electricity to 30 millions!"[1] One wonders how Sumner could have responded to Dana's enthusiasm. Notwithstanding its inconvenience to Sumner's head, Dana's metaphor celebrates the polarization of thirty million Americans, now inflamed by a criminal assault in the U.S. Senate; but sectional polarization was the handicap under which the Senate labored in 1856, not the result it was striving to hasten. Then perhaps Dana's trope—through which one form of battery takes on the characteristics of another—couldn't comfort the felled senator, but it certainly enjoins an impulse to describe the public mood in terms of electrical charge, a rhetoric reaching back to the Federal period but which underwent reconfiguration with the laying of the transatlantic telegraphic cable connecting the United States with Britain, finally successful in 1858.[2]

It can only be coincidental that the cane Brooks brought into contact with Sumner's head was made of gutta-percha, the same sap-derived resin that was used to insulate the transatlantic cable, appropriations for which were impending in Congress even as Brooks stalked Sumner into the Senate chamber. However fluky this detail of the event, it is conspicuous how often the gutta-percha construction of Brooks's cane was mentioned in the press as the incident was reported, as if to suggest that Dana was in broad company seeing Brooks's cane as a sort of conductor or transistor, communicating a circuit of electricity to millions. The *Washington Star* observed that Brooks had "struck

Mr. S. with rapid and repeated blows about the head with a gutta percha cane," while the *New York Observer* reported, "With a gutta percha cane [Brooks] then commenced a violent assault."[3] Readers of the *Brooklyn Circular* were told that Brooks's "cane was of gutta percha," as were readers of the *National Era, Littell's Living Age,* and the London *Times.*[4] Acting in the wake of such accounts, citizens' groups in the South not only presented Brooks with scores of gutta-percha canes to replace that which he had shattered over Sumner's head, but also seized upon the substance itself as a semiotic relay between assault and debate, adopting resolutions such as that passed by acclamation in Martin's Depot, South Carolina: "If Northern fanatics will persist in meddling with our private institutions, we deem it expedient that Southern members should reply to them by the use of *gutta-percha.*"[5] In the weeks following the assault, Harriet Beecher Stowe revised her manuscript for *Dred* (1856), now including in its narrative two beatings delivered by slaveholders wielding gutta-percha canes, while an October, 1857 *New York Times* editorial derided "the Southern Order of Gutta Percha"—a phrase repeated in the *National Era* and echoed in the *Liberator*, which scorned the false Christianity of the slave power as a form of "gutta percha religion."[6]

If gutta-percha stood out from other details of the Sumner assault, this may be because of the material's renown in 1856, when the substance was widely hailed as one of the exotic materials that made submarine telegraphic transmissions possible.[7] Writing for *Graham's Magazine* during the fall prior to the assault, William Dowe marveled over the superior insulating qualities of gutta-percha: "Nature . . . had something better than hemp and tar for the use of telegraph cables; as if she had foreseen the difficulty" of encasing copper wire at oceanic depths. Echoing Emerson's statement from his 1856 address "Works and Days," that "[n]o sooner is the electric telegraph devised, than gutta-percha, the very material it requires, is found," Dowe continued, "This was gutta-percha. . . . None recognized the real value of that vegetable excrement till men wanted to run lightning trains at the bottom of the sea."[8]

In addition to gutta-percha's much-publicized application for transoceanic telegraphy, its use in the construction of tubing for the amplification of the human voice was also widely noted, as in an 1853 *New York Daily Times* column associating its capacity, "[b]eneath the waves of the English channel," to "bring London and Paris within the limits of the watch-tick" to its "especial qualities for the transmission of sound." Gutta-percha, the writer noted, "conveys the voice to the ear of the deaf, enables it to speak to the engineer through the roar of a railway train, carries domestic messages to different parts of the house, opens the closed ears of a congregation to the words of the minister, and faithfully transmits the slightest whisper to the miner in the lowest depths."[9]

Indeed, over the course of the decade, gutta-percha-wrapped cable became the metonym not only of telegraphy itself, but of a broadening electrical eloquence, flashing across ocean depths to link entire civilizations. Brooks's beating of Sumner both deepened and complicated such associations as journalists, commentators, and citizens appropriated gutta-percha as the symbol of both the assault and the national dissolution it portended. In the South, gutta-percha became a rallying point for resistance against northern encroachment, an emblem of fire-eating Brooks and his gallant defense of southern institutions. In such representations, gutta-percha's prior associations with advanced telecommunications technology dovetailed with a broad tendency in the slave states to figure Brooks as not simply a warrior-cavalier (though he was certainly hailed as that), but as a rhetorician, a statesman, a communicator. In contrast to northerners who saw the attack as an assault upon free expression (for which reason, as James Dawes explains, "the battery was continually depicted by Yankee congressmen in a series of tightly coupled binaries: 'words . . . violence,' 'speech . . . blows,' 'ruthless attack . . . liberty of speech'"[10]), southerners came to regard Brooks's cane as the conductor of some set of messages. During the aftermath of the assault, a chamber of commerce in Virginia and a citizen's group in Charleston presented Brooks with two separate canes emblazoned with the words "Hit Him Again," while other canes bore inscriptions figuring Brooks as a crack debater, as with the cane engraved "Use Knock-Down Arguments."[11] Such descriptions of the assault as a form of statesmanship were repeated not only at Martin's Depot but also in Clinton, South Carolina, where supporters adopted the resolution "[t]hat in using arguments stronger than words, [Brooks] has convinced our Northern brethren of the true spirit of Southern chivalry and has expressed the undivided sentiments of his constituency."[12]

In this way, Brooks and his cane were connected with other discursive circuits, activated during the second half of the 1850s, linking eloquence to electrical communications technology. Two years later, in the 1858 version of his lecture "Eloquence" (published as the lead essay in the September issue of the *Atlantic Monthly*—that following the first successful transatlantic telegraphic transmission on August 16), Emerson would describe successful oration as a controlled electrical event, an effect of "sympathy . . . which fills . . . the orator as a jar in a battery is charged with the whole electricity of the battery."[13] Earlier in the essay, Emerson speaks of the persuasive power of eloquence through his assertion that mellifluous words make listeners "good receivers and conductors" who channel the current of eloquent rhetoric (*E* 385). In both instances from "Eloquence," Emerson recapitulates long-standing associations between the rhetorical and the electrical, according to which persuasive rhetoric "charges" its audience members inasmuch as it renders them receptive or sympathetic. But the same year Brooks smote Sumner with his gutta-percha cane, as the prospect of transatlantic telecommunication preoccupied journalists writing for daily editions across the North Atlantic, Emerson had divested his metaphor of its original gist, the sympathetic accord between speaker and listener mused over in "Eloquence," even as he enlarged his battery to oceanic proportions. "Perhaps," Emerson speculated in the 1856 *English Traits*, "the Atlantic serves as a galvanic battery to distribute acids at one pole, and alkalies at the other. So England tends to accumulate her liberals in America, and her conservatives at London" (*CW* 5: 28).[14] In 1856, electricity—or more specifically, the process of galvanization, whereby metals are hardened through the introduction of electrical current—offers Emerson a metaphor not for sympathetic identification but political estrangement, in this case the polarization of the "liberal" United States from "conservative" England.

Emerson's trope of a giant galvanic battery spanning the Atlantic reads as if addressed to a culture caught in throes of wonderment over the possibility of transatlantic telegraphic communication, but his conjecture here—that the effect of an electrical circuit connecting the Old World to the New is, paradoxically, to set two nations at variance with each other—resists then-dominant public discourses over the probable effects of transatlantic telegraphy. Late in *English Traits*, Emerson would echo more common sentiments about telegraphy, whose effect would be to promote understanding and diplomacy between nations. "The telegraph," he wrote, "is a limp-band that will hold the Fenris-wolf of war. For now, that a telegraph-line runs through France and England, every message it transmits will make stronger by one thread, the band which war will have to cut" (*CW* 5: 91). But in his 1858 rendition of "Eloquence," Emerson interrupts his many depictions of eloquent speech as a harmonizing current with other descriptions of a malfunctioning eloquence whose effect is precisely to galvanize. Near the outset of the essay, Emerson chides the "patty-pan ebullition" of the quick-tempered interlocutor who "is brought to the boiling point by the excitement of conversation in the parlor" or who "requires the additional caloric of a multitude, and a public debate" (*E* 385). Irascible listeners and speakers, Emerson explains, are possessed of a "two-inch enthusiasm," too shallow for "the grandeur of absolute ideas" (*E* 385). These opening remarks chiding the speaker too readily whipped into "hot indignation" also appear, slightly modified, in Emerson's lecture notes on "Eloquence" dated 1847, from which we may reasonably assume he drew his earlier deliveries of the lecture during his English tour of that year.

But pages later in the *Atlantic* version of 1858, Emerson's treatment of the visceral passions of eloquent speakers shifts as it narrows to a cisatlantic and sectional focus. "The resistance to slavery in this country," Emerson states, "has been a fruitful nursery of orators" (*E* 396). Abolition, Emerson now explains, has not only honed the rhetorical skills of northeastern orators whose words are now charged with what Emerson calls "the exponent of all that is grand and immortal in the mind" (*E* 397); the fervency of the cause itself lends New England speakers what Emerson calls "aboriginal strength," making of the speaker "some tough oak-stick of a man who is not to be silenced or insulted or intimidated by a mob, because he is more mob than they,—one who mobs the mob" (*E* 396). Continuing, Emerson imagines the abolitionist orator "fit to meet the bar-room wits and bullies; he is a wit and a bully himself, and something more. . . . His hard head went through in childhood the drill of Calvinism, with text and mortification, so that he stands in the New England assembly a purer bit of New England than any. . . . He has learned his lessons in a bitter school" (*E* 396). For Emerson, the eloquence of the New England abolitionist imbues him with the fortitude to face down the threat of violence—to endure, with his "hard head," the attacks of "bullies."

This depiction of New England eloquence as a form of "unassailable" "aboriginal strength" appears nowhere in the 1847 manuscripts for "Eloquence." As an addition to the essay apparently written for the 1858 *Atlantic Monthly* rendition—during the period when Brooks's assault on Sumner was very much upon the New England mind—the passage charges eloquent speech with a pugilistic force overlapping with Emerson's similarly pugnacious tone in "The Assault on Mr. Sumner," delivered in Concord a few days after the assault. "The whole state of South Carolina," he then hazarded, "does not now offer one or any number of persons who are to be weighed for a moment in the scale with such a person as the meanest of them all has now struck down. . . . It is only when they cannot answer your reasons, that they wish to knock you down."[15]

This is not to suggest that "Eloquence" acquired its agonistic themes only in the wake of the Sumner assault, though Emerson did accentuate the motif for the *Atlantic* version of 1858. The manuscript dated 1847 includes a title page upon which Emerson placed, apparently as an epigram for the lecture, the quatrain he would only later publish, in the 1867 *May-Day*, under the title "Orator": "He who has no hands/Perforce must use his tongue/Foxes are so cunning/Because they are not strong."[16] The poem works to embody eloquence, transforming it from an abstraction to an organ, a "cunning" "tongue" that may be substituted for "strong" "hands." Thus, eloquent speech is the projection of the mind but also an expression of the body, an acme of presence and corporeality. By 1858 such substitutions seemed to Emerson, as for other northeastern liberals, subject to the tyranny of southern demagogues and ruffians. Indeed, others aside from Emerson viewed Sumner as an example of northeastern eloquence so vexing to the slave power as to agitate southerners into violence. John L. Magee's lithograph of the Sumner assault, "Southern Chivalry—Argument Versus Club's [*sic*]" (1856)—a visual depiction that more than any other fixed the event in the public mind—juxtaposes Brooks's cane against Sumner's pen, the tool of his statesmanship now raised in defense, and in this way presented visually the opposition offered in the lithograph's title (figure 5.1).

The assault on Sumner, then, occurred within a technologically conditioned semiotic space pregnant with associations between eloquence and violence. In fact, Sumner's two-day speech on the unfolding insurrections in

SOUTHERN CHIVALRY — ARGUMENT versus CLUB'S.

FIGURE 5.1 *John L. Magee, Southern Chivalry—Argument Versus Club's, 1856. Lithograph, 9-¼ × 16 in.; 23.495 × 40.64 cm. Division of Home and Community Life, National Museum of American History, Smithsonian Institution, Harry T. Peters lithography collection.*

Kansas—a spoken performance that formed the pretense for Brooks's attack on the senator since, Brooks maintained, Sumner had used the speech to assail the personal honor of Brooks's uncle, South Carolina senator Andrew Butler—was itself a part of a long-standing antagonism between Sumner and Butler that often turned on each statesman's accusation that the other was either overly or insufficiently eloquent. In the speech on Kansas, Sumner had ridiculed Butler as having "with incoherent phrases discharged the loose expectoration of his speech"; Butler, Sumner scoffed, was a man who "cannot ope his mouth but out there flies a blunder," a blurter who was "always profuse in words," a propagator of pro-slavery demagoguery who "lies howling" in Congress.[17] For his part, Butler had often ridiculed Sumner for an excessive eloquence. During the 33rd Congress of 1854, Butler had commented of Sumner that "if he wished to write poetry, he [might] get a negro to sit for him" (*CGA* 33: 1: 234). Later Butler extended the trope, suggesting that Sumner's rhetoric "may furnish materials for what I understand is a very popular novel—Uncle Tom's Cabin. I have no doubt they might do this, but I put it to the gentleman, *are his remarks true?*" (*CGA* 33: 1: 236; emphasis original). For Butler in 1854, Sumner's rhetorical gifts applied a veneer to his deceit, though he allowed that, through his oratorical skills, Sumner "dealt some hard licks" (*CGA* 33: 1: 236).

The prehistory of the assault on Sumner, in other words, was imbued with controversies over eloquence: the lack of eloquence Sumner had mocked in Butler as well as the purple eloquence Butler had ridiculed in Sumner. Moreover, in characterizing Sumner's speech-making abilities as themselves a form of spoken assault—a series of "hard licks" dealt out by the Massachusetts senator—Butler anticipated Emerson's characterization of the New England abolitionist orator as the rhetorical pugilist, an embodied verbal combatant. It was a point Butler honed after the assault in a two-day speech to the Senate in which he defended Brooks, maintaining that Sumner "is unfit for the war of debate. He has no business to gather the glories of the Senate Chamber and fight with orators, unless he is prepared to maintain the position of an honorable combatant. Though his friends have invested him with the dress of Achilles and offered him his armor, he has shown that he is only able to fight with the weapons of Thersites, and deserved what that brawler received from the hands of the gallant Ulysses" (*CGA* 34: 1: 625–26).

In some ways, the verbal jousting between Sumner and Butler (and for that matter the Emersonian depiction of the abolitionist speaker whose "aboriginal strength" makes of him "a wit and a bully") was of a piece with what Robert Connors documents as the agonistic tradition in antebellum deliberative oratory, wherein extemporaneous speech functioned as the orator's personal display of talent. Instruction in rhetoric, until about 1860, emphasized spoken debates, "fortnightly rhetoricals" and other agonistic practices in which rhetors stood ready to "pick up a challenge, answer a point, refute a position, come up with a turn of phrase, and in general protect their vitals from one another and from the master."[18] Written speeches and other carefully crafted oratorical displays held a subordinate place within such a system of deliberative, public eloquence, though as Connors demonstrates, the advent of coeducation would significantly enhance the role of writing in the American rhetorical curriculum. Magee's lithograph of the Sumner assault includes a detail that may hint that Sumner had been guilty of violating this priority of the spoken over the written: at the lower right-hand corner of the illustration appears Sumner's written speech on Kansas, which Sumner would later stand accused of having circulated prior to its delivery in the Senate—a point I will dwell upon later. But if this agonistic tradition in American rhetoric (like abolition, and for that matter ordinary irascibility, as Emerson suggests in his 1858 rendition of "Eloquence") had the effect of embodying eloquence, linking words directly to the bodies from which they issue, the effect of telegraphy was precisely the opposite. Commentary after commentary, written during the early 1850s on both sides of the Atlantic, developed the motif according to which telegraphic communication disjoined the voice from the body.

Popular treatments of the assault as a form of violent (tele)communication in this way mark a moment of epistemological crisis within a constellation whose coordinates—eloquence and violence, oratory and embodiment, telegraphy and disembodiment—were being recharted in U.S. culture in 1856. In the remainder of this chapter, my treatment of the Sumner assault will place that event further into the context of such considerations, drawing out the stakes at play in the epistemological crisis to which I allude. After tracing some of the ways in which the motif of the disembodied voice developed within public jubilation over the prospect of transatlantic telegraphy, I will turn to congressional discourse on both the transatlantic cable and the Sumner assault in order to suggest that the disembodiment of the human voice suggested by telegraphy was in some ways that to which Brooks's caning of Sumner responded—or rather, a problem the event came to engage. More specifically, I will work toward the argument that the transatlantic mode of telegraphy Brooks's gutta-percha cane represented called up a cisatlantic contest over transatlantic connection that would play out in Congress almost immediately after Brooks's exculpation for the assault. The assault on Charles Sumner, I suggest, in which a defender of the plantation system struck down an abolitionist speaker, using for the assault a fragment of the era's most salient symbol for international diplomacy and peace, brings into relief the ways in which sectional tensions between North and South were exacerbated by the prospect of transatlantic telecommunication with England.

2. Disembodied Voices

In conjuring his giant galvanic battery spanning the Atlantic and serving to polarize rather than unite England and America, Emerson not only gainsaid the delight *English Traits* expresses for the peace-giving potentials of international telegraphy; he also departed from the generally enthusiastic tones pervading public discourse on transatlantic telegraphy throughout the 1850s.[19] By and large, the laying of the transatlantic cable occasioned outpourings of optimism over a future free from international strife, beginning with giddy coverage, in the English press, of the laying of telegraphic cable across the English Channel in 1850. In one 1850 illustration from London's *Punch*, for instance, a personified "Peace" and "Good-will" float ghostlike along the submarine cable now cutting a path through the detritus of centuries of war between England and France, ushering in a new age of diplomacy and understanding (figure 5.2).[20]

With the first successful transatlantic transmissions between Queen Victoria and President Buchanan, English commentators reiterated the equation between telegraphy and diplomacy, predicting a stabilization of relations between the two countries. In the first message transmitted over the cable, Queen Victoria hoped that "the cable, which now connects Great Britain and the United States, will prove an additional link between the two nations, whose friendship is founded upon their common interests and reciprocal esteem," and in his response President Buchanan declared the telegraph "a triumph more useful to mankind than was ever won on a field of battle." The telegraph, he announced, would "prove to be a bond of perpetual peace."[21] The London press shared President Buchanan's hopes. One commentator in the *Englishwoman's Review* called the laying of the cable a "great work, so pregnant with

EFFECT OF THE SUBMARINE TELEGRAPH; OR, PEACE AND GOOD-WILL
BETWEEN ENGLAND AND FRANCE.

FIGURE 5.2 *"Effect of the Submarine Telegraph; Or, Peace and Good-Will Between England and France," Punch (September 14, 1850): 119.*

consequences for civilization,"[22] while an earlier writer in *John Bull and Britannia* mused that "the telegraphic cable may repose in peaceful solitudes as far removed from the turmoil of the surface waves as the vital peace-giving stream it is destined to carry will ultimately sever from blood and strife the race of our common cousinship."[23] In the *Times* (London), one writer asked, "What have Old Englander and New Englanders got to keep them asunder except those leagues of ocean which are now annihilated?"[24] while in another image, once again from *Punch*, the transatlantic cable entangles and confounds "Despotism" to the mutual delight of Yankee Jonathan and British John Bull (see figure 5.3).

American public discourse over the transatlantic telegraph followed a mostly similar line. Frederick Townsend's 1855 volume *Ghostly Colloquies*, which narrated a series of hypothetical conversations between eminent figures from western history, had Christopher Columbus extolling the virtues of the telegraph to Cadmus of Thebes.[25] In an August 1858 speech given in celebration of Queen Victoria's and President Buchanan's transmissions, Henry Ward Beecher declared that "it is the separation of nations, as of individuals, that works the most mischief. . . . Bringing people together is the way to disperse world of unkind feeling," since "[b]ringing the nations of the earth, thus as they are, together, will contribute to hasten the day of universal brotherhood."[26] Like the commentator for *John Bull and Britannia* who finds a kind

FIGURE 5.3   *"The Atlantic Telegraph—A Bad Look Out for Despotism," Punch (August 21, 1858): 79.*

of sublimity in the thought of the cable "repos[ing] in peaceful solitudes," leagues beneath the "turmoil of the waves," Beecher imagines soundless transmissions traveling beneath the Atlantic with a kind of transfixed wonder: "Markets will come up, and fortunes will be made, and the silent wire will carry the news to us. Fortunes will go down, and the silent road will bear the message; and thus, without voice to speak, it will communicate thunders and noise and earthquake. But all these things will go through the sea, and by a silent travel, though quicker than thought. . . . To me the functions of that wire seem sublime."[27]

Beecher's portrayal of the oceanic telegraph as a "silent road" "without voice to speak" indexes one way in which the underwater telegraph captured the public imagination through a discourse emphasizing the distancing of the voice from the body, a motif also captured in the themes of disembodiment, of ghosts and spiritualism, written large in works such as *Ghostly Colloquies* or *Punch*'s visual depiction of "Peace" and "Goodwill." A widespread misapprehension permeates many commentaries over the operation of telegraphic technology, an example of which is hinted at, for instance, in Beecher's statement about the "silent wire" that nevertheless "speaks" under the Atlantic. Though information about Morse code circulated throughout 1850s reporting on telegraphy, many writers on the subject lapse into a depiction of the technology as if it operated not through the transmission of modulated baud rates of electrical pulse (the "dots and dashes" comprising Morse code), but rather through the transportation of human voices.

A most vivid example of this notion is found in Christopher Cranch's piece "An Evening with the Telegraph Wires," published in the *Atlantic* in September 1858—the same issue, directly following Buchanan's and Victoria's inaugural transmissions, that also contained Emerson's "Eloquence." Cranch's first-person narrator, giving himself over to a state of transcendental reverie during his evening constitutional, on an impulse climbs a tree and hears the hum of a telegraph wire passing through the branches above. Noticing the live wire spurs the narrator into a description of the State of New York as a giant guitar strung with telegraph cables, a notion resonating with Emerson's description, from the essay on eloquence printed only pages earlier, of public oration itself as a kind of musical performance ("Of all the musical instruments on which men play," Emerson explains, "a popular assembly is that which has the greatest compass and variety, and out of which . . . the most wondrous effects can be drawn").[28] Drawn into a heightened state of sensitivity earlier that evening, he tells us, at the hands of a mesmerist, Cranch's narrator proceeds into a more global state of meditation: "I could fancy I saw the Roman Campagna and the wondrous dome of St. Peter's, as when first beheld on the horizon ten years before."[29] The telegraphic network, he realizes, is an intercontinental umbilicus, and so awash in visions of the Old World, thoughts that then swing pendulum-like back to "the memories . . . of days . . . passed in my own native land," Cranch's speaker is suddenly moved to grasp the cable.

This transnational telegraphic system is at some points in Cranch's piece a massive musical instrument of some kind; at other moments, a global nervous system, and into this magnetically charged network Cranch's narrator now connects himself as he seizes to the vibrating iron string. "The jerks instantly were experienced in my elbow," he tells us, "and it was not long before certain short sentences were conveyed, magnetically, to my brain" (*ETW* 491). Over the rest of the story, Cranch's narrator suffers a kind of information overload, or rather, a flood of sympathies released by the ever-accelerating flow of news: marriages, divorces, the deaths of children, financial collapse. "And then," the narrator tells us, "my thoughts wandered across the Atlantic, and I remembered those long rows of telegraphic wires in France, ruled against the tops of high barrier-walls, and looking against the sky like immense music-lines" (*ETW* 491). The story ends in a flight of speculation, forwarding Cranch's hypothesis that electromagnetic impulses may be impressible upon the brain—perhaps, the narrator supposes, the human nervous system may be made to interact cybernetically with electrical technology. Such possibilities raise the possibility of a new era of human peace and goodwill made possible through telepathically swift telecommunication. "It gives one a great idea of human communion," Cranch explains, "this power of sending these spark-messages thousands of miles in a second. . . . All mankind are one" (*ETW* 494).

Americanist cultural historians have noted the intense optimism accompanying deployments of telegraphic cable since Samuel Morse's transmission from Washington to Baltimore in 1844.[30] The sheer preponderance of such accolades should not suggest, however, that the public response to transatlantic telegraphy was univocally positive. Some North Atlantic commentators, indeed, viewed the telegraph's potential to instill greater connection among formerly distant societies as cause for alarm. Englanders both old and new registered concern at the potential of telegraphic networks to bind non-slaveholding societies to the southern plantation system through an increasingly globalized economy. A poem published in *Punch* on August 14, 1858, entitled "The Anglo-Saxon Twins: Connected by Atlantic Telegraph," reiterated popular assessments of international telegraphy as the harbinger of peace, destined to promote diplomacy and sympathetic connection between the United States and England. The poem's speaker boasts, "Accomplished is the mighty job,/In spite of wind and weather;/JONATHAN, we now shall throb/With sympathy together."[31] Pulled into "close communion" through the telegraphic link, the two nations now stand against despotism and for "the cause of Freedom," since the telegraph guarantees that "Free utterance of opinions,/shall live in the United States,/And British QUEEN'S dominions." These predictions become a kind of vacant bravado, however, once the poem's speaker turns to the economic machinations served by the cable: "Now every squabble we have had/Is pretty nigh forgotten,/So let us set to work like mad,/And deal in corn and cotton." Telegraphic diplomacy becomes cotton diplomacy; the rhetoric according to which the telegraph confounds despotism and promotes liberty is now undercut by *Punch*'s acknowledgment of the economic agenda driving the transatlantic telegraphic project, one effect of which is to bring the cotton plantations of the American South closer to the textile mills of Lancashire. The poem thus asks its reader to consider the probable effect of the transatlantic cable drawing England into closer rapport with U.S. slavery. "Two thousand miles beneath the sea,/If you're inclined as I am," the speaker rhymes, now directly addressing its North American reader, "That wire will draw close you and me/As those famed twins of Siam."[32]

An earlier anonymous poem from England, published in the *Liberator* in January 1853, similarly juxtaposes the telegraph as a signal of peace and liberty against the recognition that in telegraphically communing with the United States, England will enjoin an economy built upon slave labor. "The Song of the Telegraph" presents another telegraphically disembodied voice, audible to sailors who, "Journeying over some lone morass,/Where the endless wires of the telegraphs pass,/[. . .] have stood, and listened, and trembled with fear,/The song of the telegraph to hear."[33] The bodiless voice, resonating sonorously from the ocean depths, repeats its promise to promote international accord and eradicate warfare, since "With the olive-branch extended,/Swift I go to every shore;/Soon all nations shall be blended,/They shall learn of war no more." But this siren's promise of international amity darkens with the prospect that "Soon beneath the deep Atlantic,/Far beneath the swelling wave,/Will my still small voice be passing/To the land that owns the slave."[34] The poem interrogates triumphal assessments of telegraphic diplomacy more directly than would the 1858 poem from *Punch*, eventually asking whether "Now the world is growing better,/Now that Progress leads the van,/Is it not a strange injustice,/To enslave another man?" But at the same as it questions the sort of progress transatlantic telegraphy will represent, the poem hypothesizes that the globalized economy that transatlantic telegraphy would promote could well "annihilate" slavery rather than simply profiting from it. "Are ye not free traders,/Ye yourselves the brave, the free?" asks the telegraph, just before imploring these same "free traders" to "Rise—annihilate this horror,/This foul stain of slavery!"[35]

North Atlantic conversations about free trade would reconfigure U.S. relations with Britain during the later antebellum period, and through that reconfigured relationship, northern and southern partisans would rearrange their mutual antipathies as well. That trans- and cisatlantic rearrangement will be the subject of the next chapter. But apropos of the Atlantic telegraph, it is crucial to note that in the United States as well as England, popular optimism over transatlantic telegraphy was tinged with anxieties over the closer economic and ideological ties the technology would encourage between slave-holding southerners and freedom-loving northerners. In a January 15, 1857, speech in Worcester, Wendell Phillips depicted telegraphic technology as a conduit of southern influence upon northern legislative, economic, and religious institutions. "The New York pulpit," he argued, "is today one end of a magnetic telegraph, of which the New Orleans cotton market is the other. The New York stock market is one end of a magnetic telegraph, and the Charleston *Mercury* is the other."[36] Indeed, the telegraph struck Phillips not as the instrument for improved relations between North and South, but rather as further incitement for northern secession. A secession of the northern states, Phillips contended, would allow for continued commercial relations between northern manufacturers and southern plantations, but would nevertheless free abolitionist legislators such as William Seward and Henry Wilson from an untenable kinship with "the Slave Power" and hence from "considerations that take their rise in the cane-breaks and cotton-fields of fifteen States" (*WP* 18).

Phillips, of course, had argued for disunion along with William Lloyd Garrison since 1845, but in his 1856 remarks on telegraphy he made his pitch for secession using an analogy of transatlantic disconnection: "Break up this Union," he urged, "and the ideas of South Carolina will have no more influence on Seward than those of Palmerston. The wishes of New Orleans will have no more influence on Chief Justice Shaw than the wishes of London. The threats and party tactics of Brooks, Soule, Blair and Benton will have no more influence on the *Tribune* than the thunders of the London *Times* or the hopes of the Chartists" (*WP* 18). Continuing, Phillips imagined a disunited states maintaining a cordial separation akin to that dividing the United States from England:

> Bancroft will no longer write history with one eye fixed on Democratic success, nor Webster invent "the laws of God" to please Mr. Senator Douglas. We shall have as close connection, as much commerce; we shall still have a common language, a common faith and common race, the same common social life,—we shall intermarry just the same, we shall have steamers running just as often and just as rapidly as now;—but what cares Dr. Dewey, in New York, for the opinion of Liverpool? Nothing! What cares he for the opinion of Washington? Everything! [. . .] I mean to take Massachusetts, and leave her exactly as she is, commercially. She shall manufacture for the South just as Lancashire does. [. . .] What I would do with Massachusetts is this—I would make her, in relation to South Carolina, just what England is. I would to God that I could float her off, and anchor her in mid-ocean! (*WP* 18)

3. Rumor and Speculation

Anchoring Massachusetts in mid-ocean, bringing the Commonwealth that much closer to abolitionist England and that much further from slaveholding South Carolina, is for Phillips a trope representing the widening, apparently oceanic, gulf between the northern and southern sections. In this way Phillips's complaint about the telegraph recapitulates the description Thoreau included in *Walden* (1854) of a sectional divide so profound as to be unbridgeable even by telegraphy: "We are in great haste to construct a magnetic telegraph from Maine to Texas; but Maine and Texas, it may be, have nothing important to communicate."[37] As in Phillips's later statement, Thoreau's cranky assessment of telegraphy in 1854 imagines the technology highlighting sites of rupture and division between North and South; the silent telegraph stretching between Maine, a state that came into being with the Compromise of 1820, and Texas, whose admission to the Union in 1845 had in the eyes of many New Englanders upset the 1820 détente between North and South, only stresses the fact that the people populating these regions are, ideologically, no longer on speaking terms. But in relocating his sectional complaints upon the Atlantic—upon which he imagines Massachusetts steadily floating, as it were, eastward—Phillips repositions the damaged rapport between North and South as somehow triangulated with England. Such a triangulation would emerge appear more acrimoniously, moreover, in congressional deliberations over appropriations for the transatlantic telegraph.

These deliberations took place just as the Brooks/Sumner fracas cleared, in January of 1857 when William Seward introduced into the Senate Bill No. 493, which proposed matching British annual appropriations of $70,000 to the New York, Newfoundland, and London Telegraph Company in exchange for fifty years of shared use. Initially, many senators objected to the bill on the grounds that the proposed cable would extend between two terminuses within British territory; in the event of war between the two nations, these senators argued, the United States would certainly lose access to the telegraph, leaving Britain with the advantage of instantaneous communications between London military commanders and their field officers in Canada. Near the outset of the debate, Seward and other supporters of the bill rejoined such concerns by echoing popular assessments of international telegraphy as the harbinger of peace, destined to instill an era of diplomacy, a perspective many southern delegations frankly derided. But aside from the national security ramifications of enabling Britain telegraphic communication with a territory on the United States' northern border, many southern members of the Senate found other reasons to oppose the bill.

Senator John Burton Thompson of Kentucky, for instance, condemned it as a decadent expenditure at a time when Kentucky was receiving no federal funds to improve her own infrastructure (when Louisville and Charleston, for instance, lacked the benefit of direct telegraphic communication). After suggesting that the Senate instead appropriate revenues for domestic public works projects, Thompson insinuated that the transatlantic telegraph had become the pet of New England Anglophiles already engaged in unseemly confabulation with English cohorts. "There are [those] in Boston and New York," he derided, "un-Americanized as I regard them, who are in partnership with British subjects; and so far as enterprise and commerce are concerned, we can get everything we want to know that may come by this line cheaper than in any other way" (*CG* 34: 3: 419). Continuing, Thompson stated baldly, "I do not like the idea of this Government going into partnership in an enterprise like this, to lay down a submarine telegraphic line across the sea. If it is feasible, no doubt it will be done by individuals, and then let those who use it pay for it" (*CG* 34: 3: 419).

Thompson's objections to Seward's bill dismissed contemporaneous tropes of transatlantic telegraphic diplomacy as distractions from the sectional and moneyed interests behind Seward's proposal. Rather then trumpeting the peace-instilling propensities of international telegraphy, Thompson pointed out, simply, that the United States and Britain were "inclined to quarrel" while suggesting that partnerships like that proposed in Senate Bill 493 "will only be the occasion for another quarrel" (*CG* 34: 3: 419). While professing "great admiration for the progress of science and of art," Thompson characterized the opposition's glee over the wonders of telegraphy as "a cloak for appropriations of the public money" and "a scheme to get out of Uncle Sam so many dollars by tickling him and flattering him and talking to him about the progress of the age" (*CG* 34: 3: 419–20). Thompson's skepticism over the telegraph's potential to instill friendly relations between the United States and Britain struck to the core of contemporaneous discourses idealizing the technology as perhaps the most marvelous instance of "the progress of the age." More important, his objection to the appropriation of public dollars for what he considered a project benefiting "individuals" rather than the nation itself highlighted more deeply sectional divisions arising out of the Senate's consideration of Seward's bill. As an instrument of commerce, the transatlantic cable would certainly reconfigure the Anglo-American trade in, among other things, cotton. When Andrew Butler of South Carolina (he of the ineloquent "loose expectorations" and over whose diminished honor Brooks had caned Sumner only months before) seconded Thompson's speech, he voiced his intention to vote against the bill "on the surety that the sparse planters throughout the United States will never use this line. When used it will be by a combination of speculators and capitalists in Great Britain and in this country, with a common interest to make a sacrifice of the agricultural portion of the country" (*CG* 34: 3: 421).

Although in one respect, the transatlantic cable had the potential to disrupt rather than calm relations between the United States and Britain—two countries, as Thompson had insisted, "inclined to quarrel" and which would hence make of any complicated joint undertaking further occasion to antagonize one another—Butler and other southern senators saw further danger in the project's provision of an avenue though which northern speculators, acting as agents for English entrepreneurs, could more effectively swindle southern suppliers of cotton. Though senators Thomas Jefferson Rusk of Texas and Judah Philip Benjamin of Louisiana would assure their southern colleagues that the transatlantic telegraph would only benefit planters by enhancing the Euro-American marketplace ("The planters of the West and the South do not sell their products themselves on their own plantations," Benjamin would point out a month later [*CG* 34: 3: 870]), Thompson would join with Butler in condemning the project as, once again, the darling of "un-Americanized" northern speculators. The bill would eventually pass, but not before Thompson, voting against the measure with seventeen other senators (fifteen hailing from slave-holding states),[38] would denounce it as part of a northern economic strategy to disinherit southern planters. "The senator from Texas told us this line would be of great advantage to the cotton-planters," he opined. "I should like to know what the gentleman from Mississippi and the gentleman from Arkansas think about its advantage. What sort of advantage is it to be to the cotton-trade? Why, sir, everyone knows that a combination of New York merchants will control the line, and while the telegraph is as big a liar as Common Rumor, it will always lie to their side." For its potential to erode the interests of planters, Thompson declared, the measure "ought to be killed just as a Mississippi negro with a flail will kill a snake" (*CG* 34: 3: 754).

Thompson's metaphor, in which the agent of northern encroachment upon the southern economic system is executed through a quick stroke administered by a subject of that system, may have reminded some of the senators present of Brooks's assault on Sumner just months before. Thompson's reversal of popular discourses on international telegraphy, now presented as "as big a liar as Common Rumor," turned on the suspicions of many southern delegations that the primary effect of the transatlantic cable would be to transfer wealth produced on southern plantations to the ledgers of northern merchants who were themselves already partnered with British manufacturers. In the House of Representatives on February 5, 1857, William Smith of Virginia complained,

> I know it is alleged that this line will benefit the agricultural and planting and commercial interests of the country. In what manner? . . . How is commercial intelligence to be transmitted? By the Governments of England and the United States? No. Commercial intelligence is to be transmitted by those engaged in trade between the two countries. Suppose there is a fluctuation in the price of cotton in England: the English merchant, in connection with the trader of this country, will of course send the intelligence over this wire, and in this way it will become a question of competition between us just as at present. How, then, are we to be benefitted by this telegraph? Can it protect us against speculators? Certainly not. I maintain that, instead of being a corrective of speculation, it will be the ministering angel to it. (*CG* 34: 3: 587)

Rumor and speculation came to constitute a crucial semiotic relay in congressional discourse over appropriations for the transatlantic telegraph. While in some ways, the two words function as synonyms—each word describing, under one sort of usage, a propagation of what is either untrue or unconfirmed—the movement from rumor to speculation also describes a shift in emphasis whereby the slander or rumor to which the telegraph might serve as ministering angel comes to infiltrate global trade, the speculation it will certainly amplify. Questions over whether the telegraph would function as an effective conduit of factual information in this way became intertwined with questions over whether it would function as an effective conductor for economic reimbursement: whether, as a new conduit for the trade in cotton, it would serve to more effectively transfer wealth to producers of the crop, or rather divert that wealth to northern "speculators" into whose hands the telegraph will have fallen. This semiotic compression of rumor with speculation not only redescribed commodities trading itself as a form of lying. As the harbinger of a technologically enhanced traffic in fabrications and machinations conducted to the disadvantage of the South, the intercontinental telegraph posed for southern congressional delegations the threat of transatlantic alliance between the two Englands, old and New. The northern speculators Thompson denounced, after all, were already in his view "un-Americanized";

as in Wendell Phillips's happy vision for abolitionist Massachusetts, these northern speculators were already hearkening steadily across the Atlantic, drifting along the proposed route of gutta-percha cable toward economic alliance with England.

4. Legislative Bodies

Through its apparent disembodiment of communication, the telegraph reconfigured antebellum dichotomies of mind and body.[39] Telegraphy disarticulated eloquence—it brought into popular conception the removal of spoken language from the site of its enunciation, provoking considerations of vocal presence and absence visible in works such as Christopher Cranch's "An Evening with the Telegraph Wires" and Beecher's 1858 commentary in the *Independent*. In congressional discussions over the transatlantic cable project, southern resistance to appropriations rested most consistently upon assertions, such as Andrew Butler's, to the effect that the telegraph was "a gossip and a liar," a characterization also developed in an August 1, 1857, piece in the *Saturday Evening Post* maintaining that, in reporting "the state of markets, [the telegraph] serves private interests by transmitting messages . . . but it does imp's work likewise, when it becomes the courier of trifles, carries fibs and fabrications."[40] In the context of the Sumner affair, embodiment and its relation to eloquence—or for that matter, to fibs and fabrications—became crucial to Andrew Butler as he addressed the Senate in defense of Brooks's caning of Sumner. Butler's defense of Brooks, that is, not only repeated the charge that it was Sumner who had committed violence in his ungentlemanly and personal spoken attack upon Butler; further, he extended his denunciation of Sumner by describing the latter's speech on Kansas as itself a disembodied and transatlantic speech act. In this way, Butler's defense of Brooks intertwined Sumner's allegedly injurious words with the tropes of disembodiment and rumor in popular telegraphic discourse even as it intimated the prospects of transatlantic dispossession that would so rankle southern legislators in their consideration of Seward's transatlantic communications bill at the outset of the following session.

The relay for this connection was provided, at least in part, by the era's privileging of spoken over written eloquence, which Butler implicitly called upon in his assertion that Sumner had published his speech on Kansas prior to actually delivering it on the Senate floor. On June 12, Butler made the accusation in order to suggest that Sumner's Kansas speech did not qualify as protected discourse under congressional rules of conduct, and hence that Brooks's attack on Sumner did not violate the senator's freedom of speech. "It has been said," Butler scoffed, "that the liberty of speech has been violated." Continuing, Butler denounced Sumner for having abused the Senate's tradition of deliberative and embodied oratory:

Our ancestors were a people of hardy morality. Generally, when they spoke, they spoke directly from the heart. Such a thing as printing speeches beforehand, of having them printed without being uttered in the Senate, was unheard of in their day. They were men who stood on their legs, and spoke out. They had hearts and mouths. They did not resort to the appliances of paper and printing before they brought their speeches here. If the Senator from Massachusetts were present, and would answer me, I would put the question to him, "Was not that speech of yours printed and published before you spoke it in the Senate of the United States?" (*CGA* 34: 1: 630)

According to Butler, not only did Sumner publish the speech on Kansas before delivering it on the Senate floor; more damnably, he transmitted the speech to England. "Has it come to this," he asked, "that a Senator upon this floor can claim such an extensive privilege, under the law of Parliament, that he can send off, by the twenty thousand, speeches to England and to the four corners of the globe, where I am not known, and then claim protection upon the ground that he has a privilege that precludes him for being questioned elsewhere for words spoken in debate?" (*CGA* 34: 1: 630).

Butler's assertion that Sumner's speech was already in circulation in England at the time he delivered it in the Senate remains difficult to verify, though it capitalized upon Sumner's reputation as an Anglophile who was, in the words of the London *Examiner* after the assault, "hardly less well known in London than in his own town of Cambridge."[41] But in charging Sumner with the impropriety of printing the speech prior to its delivery, Butler did not merely accuse Sumner of libel in addition to slander. More to the point, Butler accused Sumner of violating a congressional priority given to voice over print, a priority authorizing the special protections accorded words spoken in Congress. These protections, as Butler pointed out, derive from the British parliamentary tradition according to which no member of either house could be questioned outside of Parliament for words spoken in debate.[42] In other words, Sumner's prepublication of his speech, according to Butler, had the effect of removing from the site of their enunciation words whose extraordinary right-of-way was contingent upon their congressional setting.[43] And in thus detaching his words from himself, in placing them in iterable form at a distance from the scene of their enunciation and indeed from his own body, Sumner transports those words beyond the Capitol to play international havoc with Butler's reputation. To quote Butler once again,

Will you tell me that a member rising here and handing a speech to a reporter, and telling him to print it, comes within the purview of the Constitution? Has he uttered words in debate? Will you tell me that a member who has made a speech of five sentences may append it to a newspaper like the Tribune, which has libeled me, and has the right to send through the post offices of this government, and have folded up by the persons employed [. . .]

at the public expense, into my daughter's parlor, that which would cost him his life if he told it to me? (*CGA* 34: 1: 630)

Sumner's published words would cost Sumner his life, in other words, were he to speak them directly to Butler, but only if spoken outside the Capitol, since Butler's intent is not to challenge the extraordinary protections placed upon words spoken by statesmen in the Plato's pharmacy of congressional debate.

The promise of these protections, indeed, were what the Massachusetts Legislature, communicating through a set of resolutions presented by representative Anson Burlingame on June 10, 1856, protested were violated in Brooks's attack on Sumner: because Brooks had indicated that he had carried out his attack on Sumner in retribution for the latter's speech before the Senate, the attack was not simply a criminal assault but more specifically a violation of the Senate chamber as a sanctum of free speech.[44] Once removed from that context, Sumner's words constitute a more ordinary form of language for which he would then be more personally liable. But for Butler, who again is dealing with Sumner's words in light of parliamentary precedent, the real threat of Sumner's disembodied, transported words concerns the damage they can inflict once transmitted across the Atlantic. "Perhaps not more than five hundred or a thousand people heard the Senator on the occasion when he assailed me," Butler supposed, "and I venture to say that, of the number who were present and who knew me, not one believed a word of what he said. It is a different thing when he has printed a package of twenty thousand of the documents, franked them, and sent them to England, where, I suppose, he will be highly praised" (*CGA* 34: 1: 630). To be sure, part of Butler's point is to charge Sumner with having violated the congressional code of ethics in abusing his franking privileges, and to exonerate Brooks by depicting Sumner's speech as having been delivered, in some sense, beyond the protected space of the Capitol. But in locating that unprotected discursive space between the United States and England—imagining its conduit across the Atlantic, paid for "at the public's expense"—Butler figures the speech on Kansas as a transatlantic speech act akin to the sort of rumor and speculation to which the transatlantic cable, according to many southern senators during the next session, would become ministering angel.

Certainly, however, telegraphy is not writing. Though both communication technologies obviate the corporeal presence of speakers—disembodying the word, as I have argued—to collapse either medium into the other risks effacing material distinctions between the printed grapheme and the modulated baud rates of Morse code. And yet such elisions were constantly under way in antebellum culture, as with Cranch's and Beecher's depiction of telegraphy as a flow of words beneath the soundless Atlantic depths. Edward Everett yoked the telegraphic to the discursive most dramatically at the April 22, 1857, inauguration of Washington University in St. Louis, as he brandished before his audience a segment of gutta-percha-wrapped copper wire. "I hold in my hand a portion of the identical electric cable," he mused, "which is now in the progress of manufacture, to connect America with Europe."[45] Continuing, Everett proclaimed, "this amazing apparatus is but another form of language; it transmits intelligence only as it transmits words. It is like speech, like the pen, like the press, another piece of machinery by which language is conveyed from place to place."[46] Raising his other hand, in which he now juxtaposed an edition of Homer, Everett drove home his point: that telegraphic cables merely transported across space what printed texts had for 3,000 years borne through both space and time. "Behold another phenomena," he stated, "an intellectual telegraph—if I may call it so—not less marvelous."[47]

In some ways Butler's anxieties over Sumner's abolitionist words, flowing unregulated across the Atlantic to wreak havoc on southern reputations in England, resonates with that circumstance most essential to transatlantic literary production and distribution virtually throughout the nineteenth century, the lack of an international copyright treaty between the United States and England until 1891.[48] It was the absence of such an agreement, of course, that allowed abolitionist novels like *Uncle Tom's Cabin* (and other "negro" "poetry" to which Butler had mockingly compared Sumner's discourse in 1852) to circulate much more widely in England than they otherwise might have. In like manner, Butler envisions Sumner's abolitionist words, themselves a form of poetry or creative literature much like *Uncle Tom's Cabin*, flowing unregulated, beyond the reach of U.S. libel laws, to shape public opinion in England. Answering Butler's accusation, Massachusetts senator Henry Wilson, speaking on the floor of the Senate on June 13, retorted, "The Senator [from South Carolina] says that twenty thousand copies have gone to England. Here, again, is his accustomed inaccuracy. If they have gone, it is without Mr. Sumner's agency. But the Senator foresees the truth. Sir, that speech will go to England; it will go to the continent of Europe; it has gone all over the country, and has been read by the American people as no speech ever delivered in this body was read before. That speech will go down to coming ages" (*CG* 34: 2: 1403).

No wonder, then, so many southerners viewed Brooks's gutta-percha cane as an instrument of literal rebuttal. At issue in Butler's protest over Sumner's disembodied words was the Socratic complaint according to which face-to-face communication (the "hardy morality" given voice by those prior legislators who, possessed of "hearts and mouths," "stood on their legs, and spoke out") provides for the deliberative discursive formations that check gossip, speculation, rumor, and lying. The tensions upon which Butler articulated his defense of Brooks thereby complicated parliamentary and congressional understandings of the role of the word in the constitution of national deliberative bodies, but these complications also reverberated more broadly through popular representations of the Sumner assault. In James Magee's lithograph of the caning, Sumner's raised pen in the upper right-hand corner of the illustration aligns with the printed speech on Kansas, visible beneath Sumner's felled body, in the lower right. Representing Sumner's oratory as a form of writerly disembodiment, these elements juxtapose with the left side of the lithograph, dominated by Brooks, the frantic assailant whose body is captured in the apogee of exertion. Sumner's body, by contrast, appears unusually relaxed, passive, composed, even as it falls under the onslaught of Brooks's gutta-percha cane. The illustration's emphasis upon Sumner's tranquil pose was repeated throughout journalistic accounts of the assault in the North, where Americans were constantly informed that during the attack Sumner was unable to defend himself, since he was confined in the narrow writing desk where he had been working as Brooks commenced his attack.

The *Washington Star* reported that "[Mr. Brooks] went up to Mr. S., who was at his desk writing, and said: 'I have read your speech carefully . . . and I feel myself under obligations to inflict on you a punishment for this libel and insult.' Mr. Sumner thereupon essayed to rise from his seat, as though to resist what Mr. Brooks had said, when he (Mr. Brooks) struck Mr. S. with rapid and repeated blows about the head with a gutta percha cane."[49] The *New York Evening Post* reported that at the instant of the attack, "Mr. Sumner was sitting in his place, writing very busily" and unable to extricate himself from his Senate chair and desk, the latter of which was screwed to the floor.[50] The *National Era* similarly explained that as Brooks approached Sumner, the latter "was so absorbed, that he saw nobody, was unconscious of the presence of anybody in the Chamber. He had drawn his armchair close up to his desk, and his legs were stretched out under it, in such a way that he was in a most defenseless position."[51] The picture emerging from such reports was consistent: a northern, abolitionist senator, trapped within the confines of his writing desk— absorbed in the process of composing the written speech he will then, according to Butler, transmit by the tens of thousands across the Atlantic—is felled under the blows of a gutta-percha cane wielded by a southern slaveholder, who utters the only audible words of the transaction. In their emphasis upon Sumner's trapped position, such reports of the assault provide more than an attempt to redeem Sumner's manhood, which was then under constant ridicule in the southern press.

In such depictions of Sumner confined within his writing desk, Brooks and Sumner enact a violent contest between the spoken and the written, as if in ferocious reinterpretation of Jacques Derrida's image of Plato and Socrates in *La Carte Postale* (where Socrates the speaker sits composing at the writing desk, his back to Plato, who is now stands over Socrates, directing him). Sumner's literal speech, muffled by a printed rendition purportedly already in passage to England (itself the inversion of Emerson's "Eloquence," which was first delivered as oratory in England in 1847 only to pass into print by way of return to America, via the conduit of the *Atlantic* in 1858), remains inaudible in these depictions; it is Brooks who speaks and then strikes Sumner before the latter can utter a word.

As with Christopher Cranch's transcendentalist narrator, who grasps the vibrating iron string of the telegraph and thus transforms himself to the medium of transatlantic communication and sentiment, Brooks's application of his own gutta-percha instrument transforms Sumner's body to a node for southern fury. Intensely embodied, vehemently cisatlantic, Brooks's attack retrieves congressional deliberation to the Capitol through the here and now of physical assault, a violent reassertion of Butler's congressional "ancestors" who had no use for "appliances of paper and printing." Butler's acclamation of free speech, of course, would efface certain historical details: that southern legislators maintained a gag rule on antislavery utterances in Congress from 1835 to 1843, for instance, or that several southern states instituted laws prohibiting the transportation of abolitionist printed materials into their borders throughout the same period. Completing its circuit to millions, as Richard Dana would say, Brooks's cane reasserted the ethos behind such restrictions. Indeed, it offered an alternate interpretation of the transatlantic cable itself, one irreducible to the peace-giving stream of diplomatic and disembodied voices so many commentators would imagine beneath the soundless Atlantic, ushering a new age of electrical eloquence and expanded human freedom.

Henry Timrod's Global Confederacy

1. From Empire to Globalization

The anxieties registered in congressional deliberations over telecommunication with Britain—especially southern members' worries over economic confabulation between English textile manufacturers and northeastern U.S. speculators—took shape alongside the alternative prophesy of a powerful economic relationship between those same English manufacturers and their southern suppliers. That anticipation engendered globalist notions of a new geopolitical reality built to engender such economic relationships, and that form of prophesy—along with the political and economic eventualities that thwarted its realization, and the literary formations both the prophesy and its failure provoked—are the subject of this closing chapter. U.S. sectional thinkers through three decades, I have tried to demonstrate, seized upon a series of renditions of historical England, a place of roundheads and cavaliers who were themselves the descendants of Normans and Saxons as well as the sires of Confederate slaveholders and Yankee abolitionists. Moreover, they reveled in a stylized idea of Anglo-American space, sparsely populated with ahistorical yeoman rustics and pregnant with grandeur, and these spaces configured sectional consciousness for North American thinkers in places like Massachusetts and Virginia. But with the advent of the transatlantic cable and the impending state of international proximity toward which its closures of space seemed to hearken, new prospects of cultural, social, and economic connectedness jerked U.S. sectional engagements with England into the present tense and into redefined transnational realities. Medievalist and pastoral renditions of Englishness, with which northerners and southerners imagined themselves more strikingly connected than their rivals, permitted many Americans to reformulate their own regional and political identities as partisans in the conflict over slavery even while situating the cisatlantic conflict within English histories, genomes, and landscapes. The very cisatlantic and sectional antipathies under negotiation in these histories, genomes, and landscapes also charged those questions, reopened by the transatlantic telegraph, concerning rumor and speculation, printing and writing, eloquence and violence.

And certainly the cable drew a newly realizable transatlantic economic space into the welter of sectional conflict. The North Atlantic economic horizon encircling much congressional rancor over the cable was also a forerunner of what is now often referred to as globalization: in the anxious predictions of the southern opposition to Seward's appropriations bill, international economic partners confabulating through instantaneous telecommunication networks and operating at levels beyond governmental supervision obviate national borders while shaping economic circumstances that may well redetermine both the government and the borders. Over the course of the war between the states, northerners and southerners perceived emergent economic potentials in their relations with England even as they were embroiled in a process of national atomization that indicated a transformation of their own geopolitical and economic frontiers. Indeed, by 1861, southern thinkers had come to conceive their own national model as if rooted not in a Jacksonian promise of geographical expansion, but rather in a scheme of globalized transnational economics.

This sort of claim about southern national prophesy may seem odd for at least two reasons. First, the history of sectional conflict in the United States is in obvious ways bound up with a classically imperial model of territorial expansion which contemporary theorists currently, if with varying degrees of polemic, tend to contrast with globalization. Certainly in a broad sense, the course of the antebellum period was punctuated by outbreaks of sectional antagonism provoked, very often, by the absorption of territory. For this reason, senator Salmon Chase of Ohio, speaking in opposition to senator Stephen Douglas's Kansas-Nebraska bill (which, once passed in 1854, permitted settlers in both territories to adopt pro-slavery constitutions), denounced the Slave Power for having gorged itself upon western lands. "It is Slavery that again wants more room," he declared. "It is Slavery with its insatiate demand for more slave territory and more slave States."[1] From the late 1840s through the '50s, in fact, territorial acquisition proved the continual flashpoint for sectional enmity. The Missouri Compromise of 1820 was fashioned in order to maintain a political stability between the sections as the nation expanded, but the dismantling of that détente over the decades to follow occurred along a curve plotted across moments of geographical acquisition: in 1845, as Texas was granted statehood; in 1847–48, as California and the Southwest were annexed; in 1850, as Texas's borders were settled and California was admitted as a free state; and most ferociously in 1854–58 as border ruffians and radical abolitionists waged de facto civil war over the future of slavery in Kansas. Douglas's Kansas-Nebraska bill, indeed, came to condense the entire antagonism between North and South as a struggle over territory in the decade after the dissipation of the Free-Soilers. All of which is to say that national territorial acquisition became the trajectory along which, as Frederick Douglass would say, "the more the question [of slavery] has been settled, the more it has needed settling."[2]

The larger history of continental conquest of which sectionalism is therefore a part concerns a second circumstance putting pressure on my claims about southern national prophesy near the end of the antebellum period, because that larger history has in many ways served as a fundamental object of study for nineteenth-century literary studies since the formation of the discipline, but in accentuated ways over the past three decades I must review now at some length. While the motif of westward expansion has oriented the field since Frederick Jackson Turner, anti-imperialist Americanist criticism came into ascendancy out of the recognition that, as Amy Kaplan put it in her introduction to *Cultures of United States Imperialism* (1993), "The study of American culture has traditionally been cut off from the study of foreign relations,"[3] a circumstance *Cultures* attempted to redress by taking "for its subject . . . the multiple histories of continental and overseas expansion, conquest, conflict, and resistance which have shaped the cultures of the United States and the cultures of those it has dominated within and beyond its geopolitical boundaries."[4]

Since the publication of Kaplan's and Pease's influential collection, a major strain of the New Americanist series that anthology inaugurated has enlisted the study of American literature and culture into a broader critique of western empire, repositioning both classic and underread works of American literature within the historical coordinates of national expansion: the Monroe Doctrine, manifest destiny, the Trail of Tears, the annexation of Texas, the conquest of the Philippines. Indeed, viewed through the anti-imperial lenses honed by the New Americanists, it has become apparent that the history of American Studies as an academic discipline has, throughout much of the twentieth century, enjoined an imperial metanarrative through its traditional emphasis upon the exceptionalism of the Puritan errand into the wilderness, the prepossession of the democratic project, or the call of North American, and especially western, landscapes. As Donald Pease put it in his own introduction to *Cultures*, this prior tradition of Americanist scholarship was formed "[i]n keeping with the myth-symbol school of interpretation," engaging "a protypical American self (*American Adam*) to liberate 'our' native land (*Virgin Land*) from 'foreign' encroachment (*The Power of Blackness*)."[5] Altering that course of triumphalist scholarship, anti-imperialist Americanists have reoriented the field in ways that lay bare, for instance, Richard Chase's view of the benign bent of American literary production: "The English novel, one might say, has been a kind of imperial enterprise. . . . By contrast . . . the American novel has usually seemed content to explore, rather than to appropriate and civilize, the remarkable and in some ways unexampled territories of life in the New World and to reflect its anomalies and dilemmas. It has not wanted to build an imperium but merely to discover a new place and a new state of mind."[6]

More recently, a rising interest in economic globalization as an emergent paradigm for transnational hegemony has caused some scholars to contest the key terms grounding anti-imperialist critique. The publication in 2000 of Michael Hardt and Antonio Negri's *Empire* brought out the terms of disagreement between globalization studies and anti-imperialism in its suggestion that "in contrast to imperialism," the globalizing project "establishes no territorial center of power and does not rely upon fixed boundaries or barriers. It is a decentered and deterritorializing apparatus of rule that progressively incorporates the entire global realm within its open, expanding frontiers."[7] While imperialism describes both the process and the culture of national absorption of allegedly virgin lands—in Said's explanation, "the practice, the theory and the attitudes of a dominating metropolitan center ruling a distant territory"[8]—the emblematic mechanism of globalization is not the military annexation but rather the economic and transnational conglomerate.

Hardt and Negri's suggestion that postcolonial definitions of empire no longer aptly conceptualize machineries of international coercion has been suggestive for a growing number of Americanist scholars. The editors of one recent collection of essays call for a reorientation around globalization, a move "to consider American cultural production not in terms of a singular narrative of the progressive expansion of U.S. territory, modes of production, or forms of government, but rather of multiple and often conflicting *geographies*," a maneuver that would seem to contest several points of anti-imperialist emphasis.[9] The resonance of the challenge posed in the advent of globalization studies is indicated in the insistence with which some anti-imperialist Americanists maintain, with John Carlos Rowe, that "little has changed since Horkheimer and Adorno argued in 1944 that 'even the aesthetic activities of political opposites are one in their enthusiastic obedience to the rhythm of the iron system'"—that, in other words, globalization is only the latest modality of imperial rule.[10] For Rowe, nothing in recent history suggests a departure from the fundamental narrative of U.S. territorial absorption, since "[i]n its inevitably globalized forms, the U.S. culture industry continues to produce the deep divisions between local resistance and subaltern imitation so characteristic of colonial conflicts from the age of traditional imperialism to the neo-imperialisms of our postindustrial era."[11] Hence Rowe cautions Americanists to avoid "alienat[ing] new global phenomena from their complex histories," a warning sounding much like an admonition of either Paul Jay, who confesses, "I think [Arjun] Appadurai is right that globalization cannot be reduced to Westernization or Americanization," or Giles Gunn, who observes that, in light of globalization studies "it has become widely recognized that the national paradigm as applied to literary history has been significantly weakened."[12]

One recalls John Dewey's statement in 1927, that "imperialism is a result, not a purpose and a plan." The most significant obstacle for any critique of empire, Dewey suggested, is "precisely the consciousness of the public that is innocent of imperialistic desires."[13] Because, as Dewey elaborated, "[t]he average citizen of the United States has little knowledge of the extent of American business and financial interests in" nations of lesser economic prowess, "[w]e are not aware of the change in conditions brought about by our development into a nation possessed of enormous capital seeking investment, a fact which make the countries to the south much more afraid of us than they are of Europe."[14] Imperialism is easiest, according to Dewey, when its missionaries remain unaware of the articulation of consumerism, free trade, and broadening spheres of capital with policies of diplomatic and military force. And so if the advent of globalization studies produces a sense of resistance amongst anti-imperialist Americanists like Rowe, perhaps part of the problem is produced by the implicit proposition that if the United States once operated along imperial vectors, very recent history has indicated a reorganization of U.S. hegemony in accordance with postimperial, because globalizing and hence deterritorializing, principles of rule.

As if in implicit assent to the notion that in globalization, something new in underway, akin to a break with older models of state hegemony, the emergent body of literary scholarship formed at the globalist turn has found the late nineteenth and early twentieth centuries the richest ground for its critical mode. Thus, as Brückner and Hsu acknowledge, "[t]he twentieth century has thus become a key period for studies of geographical phenomena such as globalization, deterritorialization, and the troubling articulation of national ideology and global capital that Neil Smith calls 'American Empire.'"[15] In such treatments, the dawn of globalization becomes the dusk of isolationism and national exceptionalism, leading Thomas Peyser, for instance, to characterize the turn of the twentieth century as that moment at which "it was no longer possible to define American civilization, or indeed nationality itself, without reference to the rest of the globe."[16] A tendency to treat the twentieth century as the era of globalized capital has the effect of foreclosing, or at least rendering marginal, exploration of globalizing impulses at work during the formative decades of U.S. nationhood, thus shoring up what Gretchen Murphy calls "the ideological framework of traditional isolation that has made this context [of American international relations during the early nineteenth century] invisible, or at least not worth talking about."[17]

What might it mean, rather than imagining a sudden outdating of the expansionist paradigm sometime in the late nineteenth or early twentieth century or—the alternative—describing the consumerist subject of information economy as only the newest subject of empire, to locate economic globalization and the subjectivity it instills within that very antebellum past New Americanists have taught us to regard, as Kaplan once recommended, through "the study of foreign relations"? Such a maneuver would not render economic globalization *simply* legible as another mode of imperial expansion, but would rather attempt to discern the history of globalized capital even at the points where it has never coincided with expansionist rhetoric or theory. Such an undertaking, moreover, would portend obvious stakes for the examination of America's transatlantic past. If, aside from the model of national absorption known as imperialism, globalization indicates other national models serving the interests of rule through multidirectional and transnational intercourse, not only in material but also in intellectual production, how might reckoning those alternative models renew inquiry into antebellum conceptions of national becoming, and especially the forms of nationalism that developed at the American peripheries of the North Atlantic rim?

2. The Snows of Southern Summers

Take the example of the Confederate poet Henry Timrod, the title of whose 1861 "Ethnogenesis" declares itself the generative act by means of which the southern people become a People, or by means of which the Confederacy suddenly coheres as if through divine gesture, or through the shudder and flush of shared blood. "Ethnogenesis" imagines its iambic pulse as the throbbing of the Confederacy's birth, a palpitation not only through which Timrod constitutes himself poet laureate of the South, but through which the southern nation emerges upon the globe instantly woven, like cotton fibers, into the material of global commerce and culture. In this capacity "Ethnogenesis" serves as a continuation and development of the globalist themes Timrod developed in his prior poem "The Cotton Boll" (1860), and so, taken together, both poems constitute Timrod's vision of the Confederacy as a nation coming into being (in one sense) out of the soil, and yet (in another) unbound to mere locality, situated through multiple geographies simultaneously.

"The Cotton Boll" takes form in extended meditation over a single boll of cotton, which Timrod's speaker considers in a state of Whitmanesque relaxation:

> While I recline
> At ease beneath
> This immemorial pine,
> Small sphere!
> (By dusky fingers brought this morning here
> And shown with boastful smiles),
> I turn thy cloven sheath,
> Through which the soft white fibres peer,
> That, with their gossamer bands,

Unite, like love, the sea-divided lands,
And slowly, thread by thread,
Draw forth the folded strands,
Than which the trembling line,
By whose frail help yon startled spider fled
Down the tall spear-grass from his swinging bed,
Is scarce more fine;
And as the tangled skein
Unravels in my hands
Betwixt me and the noonday light,
A veil seems lifted, and for miles and miles
The landscape broadens on my sight,
As, in the little boll, there lurked a spell
Like that which, in the ocean shell,
With mystic sound,
Breaks down the narrow walls that hem us round,
And turns some city lane
Into the restless main,
With all his capes and isles![18]

Planted and harvested by slaves, whose "dusky fingers brought this morning here" to show "with boastful smiles," the cotton boll condenses dimensions of national meaning for Timrod, for whom the "soft white fibres" and "gossamer bands," visible through the shell of the seed pod, are every bit as multirepresentational as the leaves of grass over which Whitman had leaned and loafed five years earlier (and in second edition, the year Timrod wrote the poem). For one thing, the cotton boll signifies a promise of geopolitical union, since its "gossamer bands/Unite, like love, the sea-divided lands." Not, then, union between North and South: Timrod is beyond hoping for reconciliation between the sections in 1860, though in an earlier life he had remained a Unionist during the South Carolina nullification crisis of 1828–33.[19] Rather, then, a transaction through "love" that can "unite" nations separated by oceans.

The first movement of "The Cotton Boll" develops this transoceanic theme, if only somewhat. As the speaker unravels the "tangled skein"—spinning it to fine yarn and thus submitting its material to the refining process for which cotton is transported to textile mills across the Atlantic—"A veil seems lifted," after which the speaker's vision opens to broader panoramas as if, he explains, "in the little boll, there lurked a spell/Like that which, in the ocean shell,/With mystic sound,/Breaks down the narrow walls that hem us round." Like the telegraph, the cotton boll partakes of some power to dissolve barriers akin to that of a sea shell whose sound, the speaker then explains, "turns some city lane/Into the restless main,/With all his capes and isles!" Timrod's first section of the poem thus ends by linking, through simile followed by synecdoche, the cotton boll to the Atlantic Ocean, another of the "barriers" whose breach both the cotton boll and the seashell to which Timrod likens it seem to betoken. How could one not find such elisions of hemispheric expanse worthy of epic treatment? The transmogrification of simple "lane[s]" to "main[s]," even "restless mains," is what the cotton boll portends in its own metamorphosis from skein to yarn—the uplifting of the South through its commerce in King Cotton, now leveraged on behalf of an impending secession that will obviate the need for parasitic northern speculators and transatlantic merchants. Hence does the speaker's consideration of the cotton he holds lead to the "broaden[ing]" of his vision; it is cotton that allows Timrod to look beyond the South itself, beyond the northern states, indeed beyond the impending cisatlantic crisis toward lands beyond the sea, and to this end Timrod puns on the word "main," nominally signifying the restless main street supplanting the "lane" it once was, but whose alternate signification Timrod licenses through his reference to the coastal geography of "capes and isles." A simple city lane, in other words, becomes part of a mainland through the same oceanic economies that generate financially bustling thoroughfares.

This transformation of the lane into a main involves, for Timrod, the adjoining of southern landscapes with lands "leagues beyond" under the aegis of cotton. In the second movement of the poem, Timrod imagines that "Yonder bird," peering upon the landscape out of which Timrod composes his poem,

> Sees not from his high place
> So vast a cirque of summer space
> As widens around me in one mighty field,
> Which, rimmed by seas and sands,
> Doth hail its earliest daylight in the beams
> Of gray Atlantic dawns. (*PHT* 7)

Timrod's speaker characterizes his circularly proscribed space—conceptualizable as such only from his landlocked terrestrial viewpoint—as if from that perspective "rimmed" by Atlantic barriers. Within the remoteness of that viewpoint, "earliest daylight" arrives in the form of "beams/Of gray Atlantic dawns." But again, the bird's-eye view Timrod imagines here attaches the southern mainland, formerly "hem[med]" in and thus geographically discrete, to "realms made up of many lands" (*PHT* 7). In this reoriented cartography, the Atlantic rim no longer describes the perimeter of the South, formerly "lost afar/Behind the crimson hills and purple lawns/Of sunset" (*PHT* 7). This is because the Atlantic dawn provides only the first of two illuminating terms in the poem, shedding its light westward by longitudinal degrees and in the process measuring an oceanic expanse only to be condensed in the bird's wider perspective, which is also the broader "vision" afforded by Timrod's consideration of the cotton boll.

The poem's second source of illumination emerges in its third movement, which describes now, in widening panorama, the illumination of distant lands in the glow of southern cotton:

> Although I gaze upon no waste of snow,
> The endless field is white; And the whole landscape glows,
> For many a shining league away,
> With such accumulated light
> As Polar lands would flash beneath a tropic day! (*PHT* 7–8)

The "flash[ing]" cotton blanketing the southern landscape now illuminates the perimeters of the Atlantic rim, its white luminescence "shining leagues away," beaming eastward to meet and mingle with the Atlantic dawn. Timrod's elision of longitudinal expanse also entails a change of latitudinal ecology, a global climate shift wherein the "accumulated light" of the cotton fields illumines "Polar lands" that now "flash beneath a tropic day!" Timrod's tropic of cotton, with its attendant visions of southern snows—these fields of cotton lighting the Atlantic, warming "Polar" regions and in the process conflating the tropical with the arctic—also appears in "Ethnogenesis," where Timrod once again imagines the cotton fields of the Confederacy as "THE SNOWS OF SOUTHERN SUMMERS!" "Let the earth/Rejoice!" Timrod there intones.

> Beneath these fleeces soft and warm
> Our happy land shall sleep
> In a repose as deep
> As if we lay intrenched behind
> Whole leagues of Russian ice and Arctic storm! (*PHT* 151)

Timrod's is a metaphor of latitudinal climate shift he may have encountered in Poe's *The Narrative of Arthur Gordon Pym of Nantucket*, the first few chapters of which Poe had serialized in the *Southern Literary Messenger* over the course of 1837, prior to the novel's publication in two volumes the next year. That is to say, Pym's journey down the Atlantic rim, after bringing him into near-fatal contact with the "treacherous" and "subtle" black natives of Tsalal, finally terminates in a region of similarly polar and yet tropical whiteness. "Many unusual phenomena now indicated that we were entering upon a region of novelty and wonder," Pym tells us in his entry for March 1, as he proceeds southward into Antarctic regions.[20] Among these phenomena are sudden bursts of luminescence upon the southern horizon, "flaring up in lofty streaks, now darting from east to west, now west to east . . . in short, having all the wild variations of the Aurora Borealis" (*CWP* 3: 184). Also, "[t]he temperature of the sea seemed to be increasing momentarily, and there was a very perceptible alteration in its colour" (*CWP* 3: 184). The sea, Pym means to say, is turning hot, and it is also turning white. In his entry for

March 3, Pym reports, "The heat of the water was now truly remarkable, and in color was undergoing a rapid change, being no longer transparent, but of a milky consistency and hue" (*CWP* 3: 185). At the novel's sudden conclusion Pym, having arrived at a cataract marking the location of the South Pole, finds himself hurtling toward a great "veil," a "white curtain" out of which emerges "a shrouded human figure, very far larger in its proportions than any dweller among men. And the hue of the skin of the figure was the perfect whiteness of the snow" (*CWP* 3: 188).

Like "The Cotton Boll," *Pym* bases its discovery of radiant polar and yet tropical whiteness in an Atlantic context of speculation and commerce, the valuable *biche de mer* Pym's fellow crew attempt to secure from the inhabitants of Tsalal hearkening forward to Timrod's cotton boll, recently picked "by dusky fingers." Pym's vision of all-encompassing whiteness terminates his narrative unexplainedly; but Timrod's vision of the snows of southern summers affords him perspective not only upon the bucolic southern landscape but also the avenues through which its bounty will be transmitted elsewhere. For one thing, Timrod now beholds the "unhewn forest . . . /In whose dark shadow a future navy sleeps," while at another moment, he insists that "No fairer land" than the South "hath fired a poet's lays" (*PHT* 8, 9). Adjoining the prospect of future military might to prospective literary accomplishment, Timrod imagines that each measure of national legitimacy will appear in some future as both the product of southern plenitude and the vehicle for its global transmission. This is because the southern poet instills "grace" into the landscape, since "His be the meed whose pencil's trace/Hath touched our very swamps with grace," but also because Timrod's southern poet becomes

> The source wherefrom doth spring
> That mighty commerce which, confined
> To the mean channels of no selfish mart,
> Goes out to every shore
> Of this broad earth, and throngs the sea with ships
> That bear no thunders; hushes hungry lips
> In alien lands;
> Joins with a delicate web remotest strands. (*PHT* 9, 9–10)

Like the cotton it celebrates, at once condensing the "strands" that make up the boll with the coastal "strands" skirting the Atlantic rim, southern poetry will in Timrod's prophesy become a global export, itself a "mighty commerce."[21]

Among other eventualities, such commerce will "feed the cottage-smoke of English homes," Timrod predicts. His reference to the picturesque English hovel marks another relocation of Timrod's transatlantic and prospective gaze, resulting in an extended simile through which Timrod compares his own labor as a poet to the toils of Cornish miners, tunneling from England's

westernmost peninsula to furrow under the Atlantic as if hearkening toward
Timrod's South:

> As men who labor in that mine
> Of Cornwall, hollowed out beneath the bed
> Of ocean, when a storm rolls overhead,
> Hear the dull booming of the world of brine
> Above them, and a mighty muffled roar
> Of winds and water, yet toil calmly on,
> And split the rock, and pile the massive ore,
> Or carve a niche, or shape the archèd roof;
> So I, as calmly, weave my woof
> Of song, chanting the days to come,
> Unsilenced, though the quiet summer air
> Stirs with the bruit of battles, and each dawn
> Wakes from its starry silence to the hum
> Of many gathering armies. (*PHT* 10–11)

Likening his situation as a contemplative poet who must persevere "Unsi-
lenced" through "days to come" (detached from though not oblivious "to the
hum/Of many gathering armies") to the plight of the Cornish miners whose
labor proceeds leagues beneath "the bed/Of ocean" from where the storm
above is audible only as "muffled roar," Timrod not only tinges "The Cotton-
Boll" with his anticipation of war between the states, nor merely adds to the
mix of things his tacit likening of poetic composition to the weaving of textiles
as he "weave[s his] woof."

He also figures his act of transatlantic and poetic commerce as a form of
subaqueous communication, partaking in the tropes of an eerie silence, a
"voice without sound" beneath the waves, that attended the deployments of
telegraphic cable linking England to France in 1850 and England to North
America in 1858. (In a way, Timrod's act of ventriloquism parallels Whitman's
in that year's edition of *Leaves of Grass*, the first containing the poem entitled
"A Word Out of the Sea.") Linking his own southern nationalist prophesy to
the heady futurism of that technology, Timrod ends his poem free of the anxieties voiced by many southern delegations in Congress who had predicted,
apropos of Seward's 1857 transatlantic telecommunications bill, that the transatlantic cable would only strengthen a coalition of New York merchants bent
upon the appropriation of southern cotton. More confident than they, Timrod
ends "The Cotton-Boll" imagining a bankrupt and abandoned New York,
"where some rotting ships and crumbling quays/Shall one day mark the Port
which ruled the Western seas" (*PHT* 11).

"Ethnogenesis," which Timrod wrote in the throws of inspiration following
the inauguration of the Southern Congress at Montgomery in February of 1861
("Hath not the morning dawned with added light?" Timrod asks, rhetorically,

in the poem's opening line [*PHT* 150]), develops further Timrod's globalist vision for the Confederacy. More so than "The Cotton-Boll," "Ethnogenesis" is a confused poem. Perhaps transported to giddy heights by the official birth of the Confederacy of which he now imagines himself laureate, Timrod at one point accuses northern abolitionists of having "warred with God" in making unholy "creeds" of "What Christ and Paul refrained to preach"—presumably, Timrod's way of pointing out that the Bible does not condemn slavery—before he then wanders, haplessly, into an allusion to Exodus:

> That we must pass a redder sea
> Than that which rang to Miriam's holy glee,
> Will surely raise at need
> A Moses with his rod! (*PHT* 151, 153)

As a reference to the archetypal liberation story of the Bible, this is surely an unfortunate move on Timrod's part. But "Ethnogenesis" also continues in the vein of "The Cotton-Boll" inasmuch as it delineates a prospective globalized commerce as the guarantee of a Confederate future. This global commerce is not only based in cotton, the snows of southern summers hailed in both poems, but in chattel slavery itself, what Timrod now imagines will become the South's most precious export. Elevating his perspective once again, now upon "Some mighty Alp" from which he can discern his nation's future as if from European heights, Timrod rejoices

> Not only for the glories which the years
> Shall bring us; not for lands from sea to sea,
> And wealth, and power; and peace, though these shall be;
> But for the distant peoples we shall bless,
> And the hushed murmurs of a world's distress:
> For, to give labor to the poor,
> The whole sad planet o'er,
> And save from want and crime the humblest door,
> Is one among the many ends for which
> God makes us great and rich!
> The hour perchance is not yet wholly ripe
> When all shall own it, but the type
> Whereby we shall be known in every land
> Is that vast gulf which lips our Southern strand,
> And through the cold, untempered ocean pours
> Its genial streams, that far off Arctic shores
> May sometimes catch upon the softened breeze
> Strange tropic warmth and hints of summer seas. (*PHT* 154)

In Timrod's rewritten manifest destiny for the Confederacy, the republic of slavery will not only stretch westward to the Pacific in fulfillment of its prior

Jacksonian mission, but also eastward, toward the "English homes" mentioned in "The Cotton-Boll" as the foreign beneficiaries of southern cotton and verse. "[T]o give labor to the poor,/The whole sad planet o'er," the Confederacy is now poised to reestablish the Atlantic slave trade, a prospect Timrod now symbolizes in the Gulf Stream as the conduit for the South's exportation of the slave system to distant lands. In its simultaneous occupation of multiple cartographies, "Ethnogenesis" disperses the geographically linear spread of democracy described by manifest destiny, the illumination of dark regions made iconic, for instance, in John Gast's 1872 painting *American Progress* (in which a personified Liberty marches westward, bringing Enlightenment and telegraphic cable as Native Americans flee before her glow) or for that matter Albert Bierstadt's 1864 *Valley of the Yosemite* or 1869 *Oregon Trail* (both of which similarly depict the West as a darkened region succumbing to the dawning light of progress). In Timrod's vision of national ascension, the progressive annexation of lands westward does not require euphemistic presentation—nor hardly any presentation at all—because such axes of Jacksonian conquest are incidental to the global vectors he rather imagines will chart his country's map of national becoming.

3. Charleston and Kennsington, India and Lancashire

The configuring effects of westward expansion upon nationalist and sectionalist discourses over the decades prior to the Civil War make it all the more striking that the formation of the Confederacy was attended with such redirection of national prophesy. And yet, the globalist themes Timrod sounded in "The Cotton Boll" and "Ethnogenesis" were an amplification of ideas that had penetrated southern nationalism for decades. This is to say that though the globalized southern nationalism of these poems reflected a swerve from prior alignments of southern sovereignty with annexed soil to be worked by slaves, the antifederal economic self-determinism informing Timrod had enjoyed a venerable history in the South by 1860.[22] South Carolinians in the Charlestonian circles that shaped Timrod, in fact, had linked separatism to free trade since 1828, when the so-called Tariff of Abominations, put in place by the Adams administration, imposed duties of up to 40 percent on imported manufactured goods. The 1828 tariffs bill favored northern manufacturers who had up until then competed only poorly with European imports, but the effects of the bill's protectionist measures were experienced very differently by South Carolinians, who were now compelled to pay higher prices for northern manufactures, but whose agricultural exports faced a hardened market among English textile producers whose own exports—lethargic since the elevated tariff reduced demand in North America—naturally reduced their own demand for raw materials such as southern cotton.

John C. Calhoun, who had become vice president under the Jackson administration, denounced the tariff in his anonymously authored *South Carolina Exposition and Protest* (1828), which described southerners as "the serfs of the system, out of whose labor is raised, not only the money paid into the Treasury, but the funds out of which are drawn the rich rewards of the manufacturer and his associates in interest."[23] Calhoun continued:

> The duty on imports which is mainly paid out of our labor, gives them the means of selling to us at a higher price; while we cannot, to compensate the loss, dispose of our products at the least advance. It is then, indeed, not a subject of wonder, when understood, that our section of the country, though helped by a kind Providence with a genial sun and prolific soil, from which spring the richest products, should languish in poverty and sink into decay, while the rest of the Union, though less fortunate in natural advantages, are flourishing in unexampled prosperity.[24]

In spite of Calhoun's opposition, President Jackson remained supportive of the tariff. In July 1831, Calhoun amplified his complaints in his published Fort Hill Address, in which he asserted the Constitutional right of South Carolina to nullify the tariffs within its borders; that same month, nullifiers in Charleston formed the States Rights and Free Trade Association, mobilizing their movement to radicalize the state legislature. The resulting ascendancy of the nullifiers to the legislature led to that body's vote, in November 1832, to abrogate the federal tariffs within the state.[25]

The crisis was eventually defused in early 1833 with a compromise tariff reducing duties on imports to an average of 20 percent, but not before Congress also passed Jackson's "Force Bill," which called for the relocation of duties collection in Beaufort and Georgetown to federal ships deployed into those harbors, and for closing the customhouse in Charleston in order to enforce tariffs at two federal forts also located off the coast. Moreover, the bill provided for the enforcement of these measures by federal troops.[26] While most nullifiers in Charleston, appeased by the reduction in tariff rates, claimed victory (and voted in Columbia in March to repeal the prior ordinance of nullification), others warned that the federal tariffs had never been the primary source of conflict. Speaking at the legislative convention that repealed the nullification ordinance of the prior year, state representative Robert Barnwell Rhett warned that the tariffs had represented the northern section's hostility to broader southern institutions. "Every stride of this Government, over your rights, brings it nearer and nearer to your peculiar policy," he insisted. According to Rhett, the federal government had not been motivated by mere pecuniary interests, but rather by its "despotic nature," in accommodation of which "there is no liberty—no security for the South."[27]

William Gilmore Simms, who was a lifelong friend of Timrod's, had similarly remained a Unionist throughout the nullification crisis (in fact, his unpopular stance may have cost him his newspaper, the *Charleston Daily Gazette*, which collapsed in 1832), but like virtually all prominent Charlestonians in the early 1830s, he remained vexed by the tariff itself.[28] Simm's dramatic poem *Atalantis*, published in 1832 and then in second edition in 1852, places South Carolina's turmoil over free trade in a phantasmagorical Prospero's isle in the mid-Atlantic. Atalantis, whom Simms identifies as "a princess of the Nereids," has been taken captive by Onesimarchus, "King of Sea-Demons" who has also snatched Atalantis's magic wand, depriving her of her powers. In an attempt to coerce his captive into marriage, Onesimarchus places Atalantis within an impenetrable "circle" ("Most fit for thee to flutter in,—not fly," he gloats), impervious to both military rescue and, he points out, commerce:

> ONESI. [. . .] All in vain
> Thy hope, whether within thyself it be,
> Or in the armies which thy brothers raise—
> Here, powerless in the conflict, useless all;—
> For, in the air, I've thrown a circling spell,
> Borrow'd from night and silence,—which, being gross,
> Far grosser than the elements which make
> Your finer tempers, ye may not withstand!
> [. . .] All around
> our island limit, where the ocean breaks,
> This element is scattered,—like a wall,
> Shutting out all invasion,—closing all,
> Within, from commerce with the realm without!
> Thus art thou girdled now.
> [. . .]—thou canst not break
> The narrow circle of thy prison bound,
> And taste the finer element, whose breath
> Might thee to thy power.[29]

Even as Atalantis denounces him for his arrogance and malice, Onesimarchus insists that his measures are necessary for the preservation of his rule. Responding, Atalantis accuses Onesimarchus of overstepping the "fair deserving" of "just tribute":

> ATAL. Thou cruel king!
> Hadst thou by other qualities of grace
> Master'd the heart that feels for thee but scorn,
> This merciless act of thine had set it free;
> Had robb'd it of persuasion of thy worth
> In every office; and, from virtuous meed,
> Had pluck'd all fair deserving, that else
> Been yielded by just tribute.

> ONESI. Thou wrong'st me;—
> And chid'st too harshly the o'ercoming sway,
> Which keeps dominion safe, and makes it strong. (*WS* 128)

Though Onesimarchus describes his imprisonment of Atalantis as a matter of prudent statesmanship—"keep[ing his] dominion safe, and mak[ing] it strong"—he also confirms her accusations in revealing his intent, a few lines later, to dominate Atalantis's every thought and "inclination," depriving her the last shreds of freedom:

> ONESI. 'Tis well! But thou shalt feel,—
> So shalt thou know better,—how great the power
> Thou mock'st at, in thy ignorance and pride!
> And though, unless by wanton will of thine,
> I may not gain possession of thy form,
> Yet shall I so constrain thee by my arts,
> So work upon thy weakness—so forbid
> All bent of inclination,—all desire,—
> Curtailing every thought that does not tend
> To the fierce satisfaction of my want,— (*WS* 128–29)

For all his references to the exigencies of rule—for instance, the many "tribute realms" he must monitor and regulate—Onesimarchus as it turns out is simply tyrannical. Atalantis remarks,

> Till now, my thought had been that, with thy power,
> There was a sense to give it dignity,
> And marshal thy gross attributes with state
> Into considerable order. But not now,—
> When I look on thee, so incapable,—
> [. . .] all my hate
> Subsides into a feeling less than scorn,
> Which cannot yet be pity. (*WS* 129)

Brushing off her contempt, Onesimarchus gloats over the impenetrability of the prison in which he has placed Atalantis, and so, dismissing "The aid thou look'st for from thy tribute realms," he exults that his magically erected "barriers shut out hope from thee" (*WS* 135). *Atalantis* thus allegorizes the Atlantic Ocean as a setting of political turmoil unleashed by a despotic ruler who, in an effort to enforce an unwanted union, isolates his captive from the oceanic aid and "commerce" through which she would otherwise secure power and independence. Atalantis herself spends much of her imprisonment envisioning a restored seascape "Unvex'd by contact with rebellious power,/Such as offends us here." If the despotism to which Onesimarchus subjects Atalantis bears some resemblance to what Charlestonians experienced as a striding federal despotism (in accommodation of which, as Rhett warned in his 1833 speech, "there is no liberty—no security for the South"), the poem also imagines an overcoming of that repression. As in "The Cotton Boll" and "Ethnogenesis," Simms's poem envisions liberation as the opening of oceanic barriers and the restoration of commerce, after which Atalantis returns to the bosom of the ocean, presumably to rule the archipelago beneath the Southern Cross described toward the end of the poem (WS 200).

It is crucial to understand that works such as *Atalantis* and "Ethnogenesis" were widely read and reviewed. The *New York Times* described Timrod's *Poems* (1860), published by Ticknor and Fields, as "very uncommon poems; full of delicacy without weakness, and power without coarseness" while praising the "picturesque clearness" of Timrod's "conception," comparing him to Tennyson, and "rejoic[ing] in the future before him."[30] "Ethnogenesis," moreover, was published in *Littell's Living Age*.[31] For that matter, and for decades after its initial appearance, *Atalantis* was discussed nationally as a literary masterpiece. According to a review in *De Bow's*, it was through the aesthetic accomplishments of *Atalantis* that Simms earned the respect of his New York circle of writers and editors;[32] the poem was frequently compared to Shakespeare and Milton in both northern and southern journals (the *Philadelphia Album and Ladies Literary Portfolio* gushed, "The plot is so wild and extravagant, but is agreeably so, and has that charm which belongs to the creations of SHAKSPEARE'S 'Tempest' and Milton's 'Comus,'" even as the *Southern Literary Messenger* reported, "A scholar of no mean attainments in literature, and of cultivated critical skill, pronounced the 'Atalantis' of Mr. Simms not unworthy of comparison, as a poem and a work of art, with the immortal 'Comus' of Milton").[33] Even the hostile reviewer of the Cincinnati *Weekly Herald and Philanthropist*, while characterizing Simms's *Areytos, or Songs of the South* (1846) as a form of "autorial diarrhea" bringing "discredit upon American Literature," conceded that "in his 'Atalantis,' a dramatic poem, we find wildness of fancy, true poetry, and much skill in the management of the machinery of the tale."[34] The concerns Timrod and Simms registered in their work were not limited to the margins of the publishing world, nor relegated to some regional marketplace, but on the contrary enjoyed recognition at the highest levels.

All of which is to suggest that the predominance of the critique of imperialism in antebellum Americanist literary studies over the past two decades has left this essential fact unexamined: not only that the Confederacy pronounced its emergent mythos in a globalist rather than imperial lexicon, but also that the secession provoked for both sides a reconsideration of the national project as now staked in the vicissitudes of a globalized economy. If westward expansion would obviously continue to represent, for Americans on both sides of the Mason-Dixon, an entire Jacksonian promise of continental dominion, that promise was also unrealizable through sheer imperial conquest, and this consideration prompted a resituating of the idea of the nation to now occupy manifold and worldwide spaces simultaneously. For that matter, though the acquisition of territory had remained a constant spur to the process through which the federal union destabilized through the 1840s and '50s, the emergence of a newly technologically and economically intraconnected Atlantic rim also bore witness to a shift in southern political rhetoric from an emphasis upon soil—whether "free" or "southern"—to a projection of dilating economic zones. Slightly more than a year after the Senate passed Seward's telecommunications bill, in the midst of deliberations over the Lecompton Constitution, South Carolina senator John Henry Hammond boasted, "If we never acquire another foot of territory for the South, look at her. Eight hundred and fifty thousand square miles; as large as Great Britain, France, Austria, Prussia, and Spain. Is not that territory enough to make an empire that shall rule the world?"[35] But the "empire" Hammond envisioned was not an empire of the west, the slaveholding imperium Free-Soilers of the late 1840s had feared in Texas, nor indeed what more recent Republicans had denounced in Kansas. Hammond's South was a transnational economic entity that accounted for more than two-thirds of American exports. "[T]he strength of a nation depends in a great measure upon its wealth, and the wealth of a nation," he said, "like that of a man, is to be estimated by its surplus production."[36]

If globalization amounts to a broad dispersal of the imagined frontier—or a fragmentation of that leading edge known as the frontier into multiple zones of economic encounter—the breadth of this dispersal as envisioned in the bellum South was predetermined by the template of the British Empire. In the case of the Confederacy, which from the first moments of secession formulated its strategy around Jefferson Davis's hopes for British recognition (which would hence break the federal blockade and introduce into the theater of conflict the potential for British interference), the strategy for gaining such recognition was built entirely upon the perception of England's need for southern cotton. The story of that strategy's failure provides, perhaps, an analog of Salman Rushdie's quip over England's ignorance of its own history being understandable: most of that history, after all, having occurred overseas. Apropos of the Confederacy, much of the history that came to displace the prospective one generated out of Timrod's cotton boll indeed occurred well overseas, far beyond the Atlantic rim Timrod had imagined as the promised sphere of influence for the Confederate States of America.

One such setting appears yet within that rim: the 1862 London International Exhibition on Industry and Art, which had been planned to eclipse prior World's Fairs in Paris as well as to mark the tenth anniversary of the first Great Exhibition in London during 1851 (the South Kensington event had been originally planned for 1861 before it was postponed). The 1862 exhibition in many ways achieved the regal scope it set forth for itself. The building housing the Grand Exhibition Hall was of an astounding magnitude. Indeed, the Exhibition

Picture Hall alone, attached to the building in continuation of a tradition set by
the French seven years earlier, was 350 meters long, as expansive as the grand
gallery at the Louvre. Two massive domes, measuring 49 meters in diameter
(larger than the domes of either St. Paul's or St. Peter's), capped the east and
west wings of the structure, whose front façade was 350 meters across. The
entire Exhibition Palace covered 16.1 acres. Over six million visitors entered the
Exhibition Palace between its opening on May 1 and its closure on November 1,
each paying admission fees between a shilling and a pound, depending on the
time of day they entered. Still, the profits generated by the exhibition were neg-
ligible (only £790 beyond the event's costs of £458,842), while the enormous
scale of the Grand Palace made it difficult for visitors to experience most of the
exhibits within a reasonable period. The building itself was criticized as un-
gainly, even ugly, by many of the attendees. In *Revue des Deux Mondes*, Alphonse Esquiros wrote, "The shape of the building received criticism from all
quarters: as indicated by the origin of the word itself, every monument should
be the expression of an idea, but that building in South Kensington could just
as easily be used for a railway station, a military barracks or a model prison."[37]
The widely beloved Prince Albert, who had been central in the planning of the
1851 exhibition and in whose honor the 1862 event had been conceived, died in
December of the prior year, casting a pall over the proceedings (and preventing
Queen Victoria, still in mourning, from attending). But most serious of all for
the exhibition's planners, the outbreak of hostilities between the formerly
United States meant not only that the American presence at the exhibition,
which had been considerable in 1851, would this time be greatly diminished.
Beyond that, by the exhibition's opening, halted cotton supplies from America
had resulted in a production crisis centered in the textile district of Lancashire,
where many English manufacturers were now forced to scale back their participation if not cancel their exhibits altogether.[38]

Alfred Lord Tennyson, England's poet laureate since Wordsworth's death
two years earlier, presented the choral ode at the public opening of the Exhibition Palace. It was an act that in itself transformed the tenor of the office of
poet laureate, as Wordsworth, laureate since 1843, had written no official
poetry during his tenure. Leaving behind that Wordsworthian reclusion, the
opening lines of Tennyson's poem sounded the great themes behind the exhibition itself, according to which international commerce and innovation laid
the conditions for a universal peace:

> Uplift a thousand voices full and sweet,
> In this wide hall with Earth's inventions stored,
> And praise th'invisible, universal Lord,
> Who lets once more in peace the nations meet
> Where Science, Art and Labour have outpour'd
> Their myriad horns of plenty at our feet.[39]

Closing his benediction, Tennyson amplified its depiction of global commerce as the symbol of man's progress from militarism:

> O ye, the wise who think, the wise who reign,
> From growing commerce loose her latest chain,
> And let the fair white-winged peacemaker fly
> To happy heavens under all the sky,
> And mix the seasons and the golden hours,
> Till each man finds his own in all men's good,
> And all men work in noble brotherhood,
> Breaking their mailed fleets and armed towers,
> And ruling by obeying Nature's powers,
> And gathering all the fruits of peace and crown'd with all her flowers.[40]

Commerce, in Tennyson's ode and in the coded universe of the exhibition itself, provides the mechanism for a burgeoning global, fraternal sympathy. At the 1847 annual soiree of the Manchester Athenæum, where Emerson had delivered the address that would form the closing chapter of *English Traits*, regaling the English as possessed of the "vigor" and "pulse" required to overcome that season of commercial crisis, other speakers had intoned themes in anticipation of Tennyson's. The keynote speaker on that occasion, the historian Sir Archibald Alison, proclaimed, "There was a natural connexion which had made itself manifest in every age, and had proclaimed itself in every period of history, between the powers of intellect and the energies of commerce, and many of the greatest efforts of the human mind and the greatest impulses to human improvement had arisen from that glorious alliance."[41] The economic reformer and free-trade advocate Richard Cobden, taking the podium after Alison, insisted that through global commerce North Atlantic nations

> were enlarging the circle of their sympathies, that the sphere in which political action was working was widening in their day; that instead of separate nations viewing each other with that narrow, jealous spirit which once was mistaken for the particular patriotism, they were willing to enter into more generous calculations of their own and their neighbors' interests; and the whole wide world was approaching the time when it would, as he hoped and believed, be discovered that the interests of all were identical.[42]

Recited against the backdrop of the manufacturing crisis provoked by the cessation of cotton shipments from the American South, as well as reports from America of virtually mind-expanding violence in April (24,000 Union and Confederate troops were killed that month at Shiloh alone), Tennyson's ode captured a similarly sanguine air permeating the exhibition's official confidence in commercial progress coupled with international harmony.

The exhibition's organizers acknowledged deepening anxieties over the supply of cotton in the *Handbook to the Industrial Department of the International*

Exhibition, published as a guide to the thirty-six industrial and agricultural classes comprising the exhibition, noting that "[t]he present state of the cotton trade, owing especially to the failure of the supply of this article from the Confederate States of America"—this reference to the Confederacy as a national entity, though here made by a Royal Commission, did not reflect the position of the Ministry of State—"renders these collections of great value. The Cotton Supply Association are clearly proving that we have but to encourage the growth of cotton in other countries to render ourselves free from those difficulties which arise from an exclusive dependence upon one."[43] In 1860, cotton exports from the American South had totaled 40 million bales, 85 percent of world production for international trade. But what the exhibition demonstrated, according to the *Handbook,* was that "our colonial possessions, and many foreign countries, are exhibiting remarkably fine specimens of cotton," thus indicating alternative prospects for the supply of the Lancashire mills.

Detailing the qualities and futures of cotton grown in Austria, Italy, Egypt, Syria, Trinidad, Jamaica, Bermuda, the Bahamas, India, Australia, and South Africa, among other regions, the *Handbook* and the exhibits it described attempted to calm fears over the possibility that the war in America might continue for years, and in many cases implied that—developed and "encouraged" properly—some such suppliers would provide an improved base of supply for the English textile industry. For instance, "The cotton plant is a perennial in the Bermudas," the *Handbook* explained, "enduring for a period of from twelve to twenty years, grows to a height of eight to ten feet, producing abundantly during the whole term of its existence, and bears two crops a year." Indeed, "if the plant was cultivated with the care that is bestowed upon it in the Southern States of America, abundant crops of the long stapled variety could be grown here, possessing all the silky fineness so desirable in the fibre" (*H* 384–85). In Australia, "the vastness of the Queensland cotton field show them there is a colony in Australia from whence a supply of this staple, equal to any demand, can be furnished, as soon as labor and capital are introduced into it for the purpose" (*H* 340). Turning to South Africa, the *Handbook* observed that "[t]he cotton-plant grows readily in Natal. . . . The main difficulty for the present in the way of success seems to be the readiness with which the white colonists find more productive applications of their energies, and the unwillingness with which the Kaffir enters upon any system of work that ties him to the performance of a certain task at a certain time." The usual workforce behind the suspended Confederate cotton industry might well have been able to provide perspective upon the "unwillingness" of "the Kaffir." Nevertheless, the *Handbook* promised, "[t]he colonial government is at the present time making an attempt to encourage the Kaffirs to grow cotton" (*H* 398). Most promising of all was the Indian exhibition of cotton, presenting 166 samples grown from American, Egyptian, Bourbon, and Pernambuco seed, and revealing "a country gifted by nature with every product which can minister to the uses of man, or his luxuries" (*H* 391).

In August, representatives of cotton-producing countries and colonies held a conference at the Horticultural Society in South Kensington to plan for the global dispersal of the world cotton supply formerly centered in the American South. Acting as chair of the meeting, John Cheatham, who was president of the Cotton Supply Association of Manchester, expressed the association's anxiety over the pressures placed upon English textile manufacturers by the southern secession. As reported in the *Times*, Cheatham confessed, "At the moment when the representatives of industry, capital, and enterprise from every part of the world were gathered together here, this country, as regarded its leading manufacture—one upon the prosperity of which to a large extent depended the greatness of England—was in a position unexampled in its history, one to which he looked forward during the next few months with feelings almost of despair."[44] Still, the cotton exhibits at the exhibition provided prospects in the absence of southern cotton. Dr. Forbes Watson, who had organized the Indian portion of the exhibition, pointed out, "In India there was abundant labour, and the power of producing cotton more cheaply than in any country on the face of the earth." Continuing, Watson offered guarded optimism in observing that "India had at short notice doubled the usual quantity sent to this country, but this year the supply would be no more than last year, for they must not be expected to get more from a country which had not yet been tapped. As to the quality, abundant proof had been afforded that they could supply cotton of the exact kind required at Manchester."[45]

Such British pluck and soldiering through were not at all what commentators in the Confederacy had been banking upon. In his address to the Southern Planter's Convention a month prior to the opening of the London Exhibition, the convention president, Thomas J. Hudson, had lauded the gathered planters for having provided the economic basis for the secession. "In your cotton alone you have a monopoly of one of the world's greatest wants," he declared. "With this you give labor, cheap clothing and sustenance to millions in the old and new world. With this you maintain the commercial activity and control, to a great extent, the financial policy of the civilized world."[46] Writing for *De Bow's Review* in January 1861, W. H. Chase had advocated secession as the South's route to "entire freedom of trade with the whole world," predicting that an independent South would permit "a radical change in the political and commercial relations of the seceding States with the commercial world at home and abroad; by which a free market would be opened to general commerce." So vital would southern free trade prove to other markets, Chase argued, that "the men of the West and the East will pause in their threatened hostility to the revolution; *while England and France would send powerful fleets to insure its peaceful maintenance.*"[47]

The *Charleston Mercury* regularly promoted the view that a cessation of southern cotton would prove too much for European powers, especially Britain, which would quickly intercede in order to restore supplies. On January 25, 1861, the *Mercury* advised,

> Let the patriots and planters of the South keep back their cotton. In March Europe will need supplies. If our ports are blockaded, Europe will find a way to open them. . . . With all the Cotton States united, we can bind the world to pledges of recognition, and even alliance. We can declare our ports free to the trade of all the world, New England excepted; discriminate between Southern and Northern bottoms; issue letters of marque and reprisal, and play such a game with our blockading gentry as will cure them very soon of their warlike passions.[48]

Centering its predictions in Lancashire, the *Mercury* stated in its October 3 editorial:

> Manchester is the cog wheel, the stoppage of which, brings to a stand still, the 80 per cent. and odd of the total home industry of Great Britain. The trade and industry of Birmingham, Leeds, Huddersfield, Sheffield, Staffordshire, Bristol, Glasgow, Dublin, Belfast, Liverpool, London, and other towns and districts, would be utterly prostrated by the absence of the usual supply of Southern Cotton. The rail roads and mining property would feel the shock. The shipping interest of Liverpool, and the banking interest of London would fall into confusion, panic and ruin.[49]

Frederick Law Olmsted, in his 1861 *The Cotton Kingdom: A Traveller's Observations on Cotton and Slavery in the American Slave States*, quoted from a similarly confident source insisting that "[t]he civilized world is dependent upon the Slave States of America for a supply of cotton. . . . Such a monopoly under such circumstances must constitute those who possess it the richest and most powerful people on the earth. The world must have cotton, and the world depends upon them for it. Whatever they demand, that must be conceded them; whatever they want, they have but to stretch forth their hands and take it."[50] In February 1862, an anonymous "Confederate reporter" of the *Southern Literary Messenger* predicted that "[w]hen the blockade is raised by European nations, which may even be before this meets the public eye, there is last year's cotton crop to meet the demands of the manufacturers; and if it should so happen that we have more of 'the staff of life' than we shall need for home consumption, that also will find a ready market in thickly populated France and England."[51]

Southerners had expressed such truculent confidence in the supreme power of the cotton supply for years. In his speech of March 4, 1858, Senator Hammond had asked, rhetorically, "[W]ould any sane nation make war on cotton? Without firing a gun, without drawing a sword, should they make war on us we could bring the whole world to our feet."[52] For their part, commentators in the North expressed deep anxiety that Britain, driven by its need for cotton, would recognize the Confederacy. An editorial appearing in the October 3, 1861, issue of the *Independent* opined,

> There is still in England a class representing the old slaveholding interest in the West Indies; there is yet a larger class whose moneyed interests in the cotton manufactures are allied with slavery; and there is a class whose intense aristocracy of feeling leads them to look with allowance upon slavery as an institution of caste;—and these parties may do more to control the public sentiment of England, through the press and through Parliament, than either her evangelical Christians or her rude liberty-loving commonality. Hence it cannot be assumed of England as a power that she is as antislavery today as in the days of Clarkson and Wilberforce.[53]

The editors of the *Atlantic Monthly* were more sanguine, running a piece in the April 1861 issue imagining that transatlantic trade, far from favoring the South, would force it to reform or dissolve.

> The laws of trade must be the great teacher; and here, as elsewhere, England, the noble nation of shopkeepers, must be the agent for the fulfillment of those laws. It is safe to-day to say, that, through the agency of England, and, in accordance with those laws, under a continuance of the present profit on that staple, the dynasty of King Cotton is doomed,—the monopoly which is now the basis of his power will be a monopoly no more. If saved at all from the blight of this monopoly, the South will be saved, not in New York or Boston, but in Liverpool,—not by the thinkers of America, but by the merchants of England.[54]

Imagining that "the real danger of the Cotton dynasty lies not in the hostility of the North, but in the exigencies of the market abroad," the writer for the *Atlantic* insisted that Confederates "struggle not against the varying fortunes of political warfare, but against the irreversible decrees of Fate."[55]

Northerners had reasons for such varying expressions of anxiety and optimism concerning Britain's probable stance toward the Confederacy. It was true enough that the abolition of first the slave trade and then slavery itself within the empire had provided northern abolitionists with salient narratives and symbols through which to conceptualize their own efforts.[56] Further, abolitionists touring England during the 1850s had found sympathetic audiences among the population now most affected by the northern blockade of southern cotton, the workers of textile mills both in Lancashire and further north.[57] When Frederick Douglass spoke to an audience of abolitionist operatives at Newcastle upon Tyne in February of 1860, attendees adopted the following resolution:

> That this meeting being fully convinced that what is morally wrong cannot be commercially right, and being equally sensible of the importance to the people of this mighty empire, of obtaining an abundant supply of cotton,

rejoices in, and cordially sympathises with, the efforts made in Lancashire and elsewhere to procure this material from sources which are unpolluted with the foul taint of slavery, and would respectfully call the attention of the Chamber of Commerce at Manchester to the necessity which exists of putting an end, at once and forever, to the importation of slave-grown cotton.[58]

And yet, prominent voices in England also voiced skepticism about the northern cause. *Punch* ran a poem in its November 2, 1861, issue (reprinted in *Littell's Living Age* of December 14) entitled "King Cotton Bound; or, the New Prometheus," which argued that the northern blockade had eliminated the very export that had provided the United States its primary global economic footing. (The poem was accompanied by a lurid illustration depicting the bound king being disemboweled by a federal eagle.)[59] Especially critical was the *Times*, which came to be regarded in the northern United States virtually as the Confederacy's London ministry of information. On May 26, 1861, the *Times* insisted, "Honourable and true-hearted men will never consent to maintain the Union by shedding the blood of Southern people and the Southern States; therefore such men can never support the Administration of Lincoln."[60]

Jefferson Davis addressed the same issue in his April 29 speech to the provisional Confederate Congress, professing, "[W]e seek no conquest, no aggrandizement, no concession of any kind from the States with which we were lately confederated; all we ask is to be left alone; that those who never held power over us should not now attempt our subjugation by arms."[61] Even by January 19, 1863, more than two weeks after the enactment of Lincoln's executive order for general emancipation, the *Times* ran the following:

No one in England thinks that the citizens of the Atlantic cities, who are warring in order to recover the profits of slave labour, are honestly desirous to extinguish slavery. No one in England imagines that the President, who has over and over again declared that his object is to restore the Union, with slavery if he can, without slavery if he must, desires emancipation for itself. No one in England is dupe enough to credit that Mr. Seward, who has told his friends that if it would help to restore the Union he would force Massachusetts to become a slave State, has any horror of slavery.

In the same editorial the *Times* confessed, "[W]e look upon the American contest as a purely political quarrel, and tacitly hold out opinion that, as the cause of Italy against Austria is the cause of freedom, so also the cause of the South gallantly defending itself against the cruel and desolating invasion of the North is the cause of freedom."[62]

In September 1861 the U.S. consul in Manchester, Henry Lord, wrote to Seward that popular sentiment was "almost unanimously adverse" to the Union.[63] In July 1862, the *American Theological Review* published what was up until that point one of the most angry assessments of England's perceived commercialist stance, supposing that

> if the South succeeded, it would have free trade with England, and free trade is a very great blessing—for England, which has so many manufactured goods to sell in the dearest markets, and raw goods to buy in the cheapest. And would it not after all be better to have the new slave republic succeed . . . than to have the Great Republic subdue it; for in the latter case, the power of republicanism would be proved to be mightier than that of any other form of government; whereas, if the South established its independence, it would certainly need a stronger government than before, possibly an aristocracy in form as well as in fact—and this would go to show that aristocracy is conducive to the well-being of states.[64]

In the event of a Confederate victory, "Southern cotton could be directly exchanged for English manufactures," and "the Monroe Doctrine would become a dead letter" (497). "In all this, we say," proclaimed the anonymous author, "England has let slip a great opportunity of showing itself faithful to its loudly proclaimed principles. It has been tried and found wanting" (504). Finally, the author asks, "And is this the voice of Old England, whom we venerated, as we venerated no other people, and from whose loins it was our boast that we sprung?" (514). The *Continental Monthly* was similarly excoriating:

> England, the greatest of actual nations, had a part to act in our war, and that part a noble one. Not the part of physical intervention for the benefit of Lancashire and of a confederacy founded on slavery, which both Earl Russel and Lord Palmerston inform the world will not take place "at present." Not the part of hypercriticism and misconstruction of Northern "Orders," and affectionate blindness to Southern atrocities. But such a part as was worthy of the nation, one of whose greatest glories is that it gave birth to a Clarkson, a Sharpe, a Wilberforce.[65]

4. Benign Markets

Reading such commentaries, one would almost suppose that Britain *had* conferred the recognition Jefferson Davis sought. That Prime Minister Palmerston would not extend recognition (even if merely, in the phrase that become the byword of the British policy, "not at present") was loudly declaimed in the southern press as the war entered its second year. But in the North, even Emerson joined in directing some of the harshest criticism of his career at what he now perceived as the insufficiently decisive British policy. In his first delivery of the lecture "The Fortune of the Republic" at Tremont Temple in December 1863, he proclaimed, "To say the truth, England is never out of mind. Nobody says it, but all think it and feel it." Delivering the lecture two decades after his

1844 speech on emancipation in the West Indies (an event Emerson had attributed as much to the "[t]he genius of the Saxon race, friendly to liberty" as to the commercial disadvantages of slavery—"Unhappily, too, for the planter," he mused, "[t]he moral sense is always supported by the permanent interest of the parties"[66]), Emerson now decided that the English "are insular, and narrow. They have no higher worship than Fate. Excellent sailors, farmers, ironsmiths, weavers, and potters, they retain their Scandinavian strength and skill; but their morals do not reach beyond their frontier. The old passion for plunder: England watches like her old war-wolf for plunder."[67] "Never a lofty sentiment," Emerson continued, "never a duty to civilization, never a generosity, a moral self-restraint is suffered to stand in the way of a commercial advantage. In sight of a commodity, her religion, her morals are forgotten" (*LL* 2: 323). Declaring his country's moral supremacy over England, he continued:

> We are coming,—thanks to the war,—to a nationality. Put down your foot, and say to England, we know your merits. In past time, we have paid them the homage of ignoring your faults. We see them still. But it is time that you should hear the truth,—that you have failed in one of the great hours that put nations to the test. When the occasion of magnanimity arrived, you had none: you forgot your loud professions, you rubbed your hands with indecent joy, and saw only in our extreme danger the chance of humbling a rival and getting away his commerce. When it comes to dividing an estate, the politest men will sometimes quarrel. Justice is above your aim. Stand aside. We have seen through you. Henceforth, you have lost the benefit of the old veneration which shut our eyes to the altered facts. We shall not again give you any advantage of honor. We shall be compelled to look at the stern facts. And, we cannot count you great. Your inches are conspicuous, and we cannot count your inches against our miles, and leagues, and parallels of latitude. We are forced to analyse your greatness. We who saw you in a halo of honor which our affection made, now we must measure your means; your true dimensions; your populations; we must compare the future of this country with that in a time when every prosperity of ours knocks away the stones from your foundation. (*LL* 2: 327)

Emerson's rebuff of the English in 1863 was an echo of other anti-English sentiments to which many northern journalists were at that moment giving vent; and as with those other expressions of disaffection, what should be striking here is the fact that the Lancashire operatives, their local leaders, and their representatives in Parliament had by this point revealed themselves strongly supportive of the Union cause, and under trying circumstances. Take for instance Timrod's mention of "the cottage-smoke of English homes" that would, he promised, be nourished by the productive forces of his globalized Confederacy. Timrod's alignment of southern cotton production with the lifeblood of the English home and hearth was an attempt to represent with pastoral flourish the economic interdependence of the two Atlantic regions, the intense localism of the picturesque cottage now rendered global because warmed, Timrod might say, by strange warmth from tropic seas.

But of course such assertions of shared economic interest elided much when configured through domestic or familial imagery. Since the beginning of the industrialization of textile production in England, and even after the formal prohibition of factory workers under six years old in 1833, many of the Lancashire operatives were in fact child laborers between six and eighteen years old. While most of these workers were paid little more than their subsistence, still others were literally slaves—even if the word was not applied to them (that is, in either England or the northeastern United States; though in the South, of course, critiques of "wage slavery" thrived as a counterabolition-ist discourse), child workers at the Quarry Bank Mill at Styal, for instance, signed or otherwise marked legal documents consenting to become the property of the mill owner. At Quarry Bank, child workers were not paid nor permitted to leave unless found to be unfit, and in that case, sent back to the urban workhouses from which they came (a more dire fate, most of these workers would consider, than the fifteen-hour workdays, and hours of additional chores, making up their lives at the textile mills and attached "apprentice" houses). And like other slaves, child workers across northern England were subject to systems of enforcement including solitary isolation, extended work hours, and corporal punishment.

Even as child labor declined in England, the importance of the female workforce increased, causing Evangelical factory reformers to opine the breakup of the family unit. In other words, Timrod's linkage between southern cotton production and a pastoral English existence hearkened both prophetically and anachronistically; and moreover, the actual operatives whose nonexistent cottages were to be warmed by a flow of southern cotton subsisted in a relationship with American slaves that was rife with potentials for sympathetic identification. And in terms of what Emerson and other northeastern commentators failed to recognize in their own chagrin with Britain's official disinclination to denounce the Confederacy prior to 1863, it bears noting that both Lancashire textile workers and their political representatives agreed to endure work stoppages in order to lend support to American slaves. This is a remarkable thing when we consider that when the adult operatives of English textile mills were told by U.S. abolitionists during the 1840s and '50s that in America, men could be kept as property, many could have responded that they themselves were treated as little more than human chattel.[68] Similar discourses, indeed, had informed the Chartist movement during the prior decade. When Timrod imagined in "Ethnogenesis" an exportation of the slave system to England, the child operatives at hundreds of mills across Lancashire and the northern counties could well have responded that the American South mightn't bother.

That the Lancashire operatives, instead of being unimpressed by the reports of slavery in America, endured shortages and stoppages in order to support what they saw as a war to extinguish the oppression of slaves separated from them by oceanic, national, and biological divides might have stirred the same northern Anglophilia as had energized prior identifications with Saxon England.[69] In an address to President Lincoln adopted at Free Trade Hall on December 31, 1862, citizens of Manchester had praised the president and Congress for the abolition of slavery in Washington and, preemptively, for the "complete uprooting of slavery" in the United States.[70] Imploring the president "not to faint in [his] providential mission," the Manchester operatives closed their address declaring, "We are truly one people, though locally separate. And if you have any ill-wishers here, be assured they are chiefly those who oppose liberty at home, and that they will be powerless to stir up quarrels between us from the very day in which your country becomes, undeniably and without exception, the home of the free."[71]

Here indeed was the liberty-loving Saxon of whom Emerson, Douglass, Child, and so many others had written. But Emerson's statements in 1863, his repudiation of English "moral self-restraint" (formed, he wrote, in accommodation of "commercial advantage"), acknowledged none of this, and instead redoubled on his earlier projections for a morally guided globalized economy, published under the title "Wealth" in his 1860 volume *The Conduct of Life* but also delivered frequently through the 1850s, during the period when southern statesmen were formulating their own "Cotton Is King" vision of a transatlantic southern nationalism through public lectures, published articles, and Congressional speeches. In the 1860 rendition of that essay, and echoing the most deferential passages of *English Traits*, Emerson had expressly lauded the English for an ancient mercantilist spirit built upon the same "iron law which Nature thunders in these northern climates," a principle of self-sufficiency predominant in New England and according to which "each man should feed himself." Elaborating his theme, Emerson turns to the illustration provided, he says, by English individualism and prosperity:

> The strong race is strong on these terms. The Saxons are the merchants of the world; now, for a thousand years, the leading race, and by nothing more than their quality of personal independence. No reliance for bread and games on the government, no clanship, no patriarchal style of living by the revenues of the chief, no marrying-on,—no system of clientship suits them: but every man must pay his scot. The English are prosperous and peaceable, with their habit of considering that every man must take care of himself, and has himself to thank, if he do not maintain and improve his position in society. (*LL* 2: 48)

In imagining the "iron law" of New England independence as the same principle guiding English prosperity "for a thousand years," Emerson once again (and for the last time) triangulates the cisatlantic sectional conflict against his own construction of Englishness, re-codifying the struggle between the states by removing its terms to the Eastern periphery of the Atlantic rim. In linking the English, with their eschewal of "reliance" and their "pecuniary independence" to "prosperous and peaceful" habits that are themselves the hallmark of a skill for imaginative identification with others ("their habit of considering that every man must take care of themselves"), Emerson thus enshrines the pecuniary history he valorizes in the English as also providing the moral standing of his own "northern climates." Obviously, by 1863 Emerson had reconsidered the characterization. But the theory of a civilizing global commerce Emerson would articulate in "Wealth" in many ways reflects the ethos that had driven England's free trade policies since the repeal of the Corn Laws in 1846, when Parliament voted to reduce tariffs on imported grains (it should be said, to the immediate detriment of domestic producers).

One of the speakers who had preceded Emerson in his 1847 address at the Manchester Athenæum was Richard Cobden, who had been instrumental in the repeal, and whose advocacy of free trade was based in his belief that unfettered commerce between nations would in turn promote a more pacifistic set of foreign relations carried out among free traders who were possessed of common economic (and eventually, humane) interests. Cobden's remarks on the night of the Manchester Athenæum event, to the effect that the English were increasingly "willing to enter into more generous calculations of their own and their neighbors' interests; and the whole wide world was approaching the time when it would . . . be discovered that the interests of all were identical," expressed this keystone conviction of his career: that through free trade, private and commercial actors would build their own networks of international rapport that would come to displace the territorial diplomacies carried out by national governments.[72] Driven by their desire for uninterrupted commercial relations between suppliers and manufacturers, producers and consumers, free traders would exhibit greater capacities for imaginative sympathy with their international partners, acting upon economic motives that would prove conducive to placid relations.

Cobden's views were inherently cosmopolitan and internationalist, since the free traders he envisioned were not so bound by identifications formed in the kith and kin of merely local allegiances as they were impelled to apprehend and obligate themselves to the priorities of their transnational commercial partners. But there was nothing in Cobden's cosmopolitanism to guarantee the virtues he predicted, those "generous calculations" that would in his view lead to the discovery that "the interests of all were identical." Cobden had founded his free trader's ethos on the promise of a new internationalist subjectivity, detached from the ties that hinder nationally constrained lives, imagining instead a view from above that obviated national allegiances and jealousies. What he never fully confronted was the extent to which the globalized economies he regarded as the machinery of such cosmopolitanism, with their underlying focus upon peculiar forms of "interests," would remain available to agents of coercive transnational experiences. For this reason, his view on the American crisis formed apart from his personal repugnance for slavery. At the outbreak of the war, for example, Cobden exercised the kind of unofficial diplomacy he advocated in sending his friend Charles Sumner a barrage of letters urging the senator to convince the Lincoln administration to turn over two Confederate diplomats a U.S. naval frigate had removed from the HMS *Trent* in November 1861, a seizure that had outraged the British public and that nearly resulted in war. Even as he outlined the British position to Sumner, Cobden revealed that his own antipathy toward the northern cause was founded mainly in his distaste for economic strictures. "There are two subjects on which we are unanimous and fanatical—*personal freedom and Free Trade*," he explained. "These convictions are the result of fifty years of agitation and discussion. In your case we observe a mighty quarrel: on one side protectionists, on the other side slave-owners. The protectionists say they do not seek to put down slavery. The slave-owners say they want Free Trade. Need you wonder at the confusion in John Bull's poor head? He gives it up! Leaves it to the government."[73] Earlier in the month, he wrote to Sumner, testily, "I hope the result of this war will lead to the abolition of blockades."[74]

5. The Wealth of Nations

In some ways, Emerson's "Wealth" indicates a view of global economy much in concert with Cobden's highest ideals, surmising a steadily expanding globalism as the engine of increasing levels of freedom. The poem heading the essay as published in *The Conduct of Life* peers backward to a primordial earth preparing itself for the productive engagements of human industry. Surmising that, over the course of "dizzy æons," "the creeping centuries drew/The matted thicket low and wide . . . The granite slab to clothe and hide,/Ere wheat can wave its golden pride," Emerson composes a teleology of natural processes ranging from the microscopic ("what wind the lichen bore,/Wafting the puny seed of power) to the tectonic (the "ferns and palms" eventually "pressed/Under the tumbling mountain's breast" to form "the safe herbal of coal"), all choreographed as it were to provide a base of production for human trade.[75] Eons after the extinction of "races" whose eradication has served to "pave/The planet with a floor of lime," arrives what Emerson calls "the wise selecting will," a human agency that "Draws," from the "slime and chaos," "threads" (*CW* 7: 45). Much like Timrod's cotton boll, whose similarly unraveling threads embroider panoramic visions of globalized economy, the wise selecting will of "Wealth" draws its threads from Nature in order to establish "temples . . . and towns, and marts,/The shop of Toil, the hall of Arts;/Then flew the sail across the seas/To fed the North from tropic trees" (*CW* 7: 45). Plotting the course of commerce latitudinally, as in both Timrod's "The Cotton Boll" and "Ethnogenesis," Emerson similarly imagines a Nature harnessed by what he calls "the poet's dream"; and yet in Emerson's account, the burgeoning civilization of commerce relies for its "fulfill[ment]" upon "New slaves": "Galvanic wires, strong-shouldered Steam" (*CW* 7: 45). As technologies of transoceanic communication and transportation, galvanic wires and steam engines apparently displace prior "slaves" who pass unnamed in both the poem and the essay; and so, the poem ends in homage to the principle of "conscience" instilled in the shift from human to technological slavery:

> But, though light-headed man forget,
> Remembering Matter pays her debt:
> Still, through her motes and masses, draw
> Electric thrills and ties of Law,
> Which binds the strengths of nature wild
> To the conscience of a child. (*CW* 7: 45)

The electricity thrilling through galvanic wires, this new slave that, in its service of global commerce, effectively outdates—and hence, one would suppose, liberates—other slaves, also recalls "wild" "nature" to its moral principle. Defining that electric thrill is the aim of "Wealth." From its first passages, the essay reads as if in repudiation of the moral economies articulated by Emerson's friend Thoreau. Though Emerson intones a kind of Thoreauvian lesson as he insists, "He is no whole man until he knows how to earn a blameless livelihood," he just as quickly rebuffs one of the key motifs of *Walden* and "Resistance to Civil Government" as he states, flatly, "Every man is a customer, and ought to be a consumer. He fails to make his place good in the world, unless he not only pays his debt, but also adds something to the common wealth" (*CW* 7: 45). In asserting that every man ought to be a consumer, Emerson is not speaking metaphorically. We are not on earth, he explains, to live by "bare subsistence"—for instance, off in a hut on Walden Pond—since we are "by constitution expensive, and [need] to be rich" (*CW* 7: 45). Whereas Thoreau's ethics of economy urges conscientious individuals to withdraw their consent from coercive structures by withholding their economic participation, Emerson's insistence that "[e]very man is a consumer, and ought to be a producer" builds toward his notion that wealth orders Nature around principles of self-sufficiency. Wealth, he explains, "is in applications of mind to Nature," as when "[t]he steam puffs and expands" to bring sustenance to "hungry New York and hungry England" (*CW* 7: 46). Through such transactions, as for Timrod, both national borders and latitudinal parallels dissolve: the shipment of coal "carries the heat of the tropics to Labrador and the Polar circle . . . to make Canada as warm as Calcutta" (*CW* 7: 46). And paradoxically, the advent of wider circles of commerce are the expression, not the nullification, of self-assertion and individual will. This is because, Emerson says, while "[w]ealth begins in a tight roof that keeps the rain and the wind out," it eventuates "in a boat to cross the sea, in books to read; and so, in giving, on all sides, by tools and auxiliaries, the greatest possible extension to our powers, as it added feet, and hands, and eyes, and blood, length to the day, and knowledge, and goodwill" (*CW* 7: 46–47). Wealth, it seems, supplements the corporeal reach of individuals through its supply of additional bodies: feet, hands, eyes, and blood. No wonder Emerson thought of steam and electricity as "new slaves," since in his view they served as more efficient prostheses than the literal bodies serving the purpose on southern plantations.

With such considerations Cobden might well concur, citing the tendency of commercial relations to transform imaginative identification between commercial agents into "prosperous and peaceful" relations. But Emerson's investment of global commerce with a power to enlarge freedom parts way with Cobden at this very point, because unlike Cobden, Emerson fully recognizes the "tyrannical" principles at work in such globalizing transactions of power. Untrusting of Cobden's speculator-cum-diplomat, Emerson confronts the probability that, exercised without check, the will that produces all wealth "would bring us to barricades, burned towns, and tomahawks, presently" (*CW* 49). "Power is what they want," Emerson admits, and the power that progenitors of wealth seek is not on its own a socially cohesive or culturally productive force. The "men of the mine, telegraph, mill, map, and survey," Emerson explains, are "monomaniacs," inherently dangerous, but their monomania is checked by the "prudent men" with whom they transact their designs, those who "keep down" an otherwise "tyrannical" ambition. "How did North America get netted with iron rails, except by the importunity of these orators, who dragged all of the prudent men in?" Emerson asks. "Is party the madness of many for the gain of a few?" On the contrary, Emerson imagines that

> [t]his *speculative* genius is the madness of few for the gain of the world. The projectors are sacrificed, but the public is the gainer. Each of these idealists, working after his thought, would make it tyrannical, if he could. He is met and antagonized by other speculators, as hot as he. The equilibrium is preserved by these counteractions, as one tree keeps down another in the forest, that it may not absorb all the sap in the ground. (*CW* 50; emphasis original)

So through such a system of action and counteraction, the projectors of wealth are "sacrificed, but the public is the gainer," much as with the "races" of the opening poem whose extinction provides the loam and lime of the earth. In 1860, Emerson imagined that global commerce provided the congress for such a leveling of "tyranny" while still opening channels for tyranny's most productive energies. As with the industrial technologies of the poem, those "new slaves" coming to displace others, Emerson's system of globalized wealth seems structurally inimical to the economics of slavery itself. "If you take out of State-Street the ten honestest merchants," Emerson supposes, "and put in ten roguish persons, controlling the same amount of capital,—the rates of insurance will indicate it, the soundness of the banks will show it: the highways will be less secure: the schools will feel it: the children will bring home their little dose of poison." Corruption is the enemy of wealth in this scheme, since it endangers the stability upon which wealth depends. Returning to the arboreal metaphor according to which global commerce "keeps down" monomania in the manner of "one tree [that] keeps down another in the forest," Emerson continues:

> An apple-tree, if you take out every day for a number of days, a load of loam, and put in a load of sand about its roots,—will find out. An apple tree is a stupid kind of creature, but if this treatment be pursued for a short time, I think it would begin to mistrust something. And if you should take out of the powerful class engaged in trade a hundred good men, and put in a hundred bad, or what is just the same thing, introduce a demoralizing institution, would not the dollar, which is not much stupider than an apple-tree, presently find out? (*CW* 55–56)

Emerson's reference to the "demoralizing institution" whose effects register even in the "stupid" dollar taps wider convictions amongst free trade advocates who believed that unfettered international commerce would in the end expel slavery. In one such expression, an 1862 review of Olmsted's *Journeys and Explorations in the Cotton Kingdom* supposed that with "the markets of England and France supplied with bales that have not come down the Mississippi" now instead furnished with cotton from India and Egypt, "it will be found that negro slavery is unremunerative and—indefensible."[76] But Emerson also establishes a moral register that, he concluded by 1863, England had failed to meet. The verdict was shared by many other northern statesmen who, especially in the aftermath of the *Trent* debacle, regarded England's stance throughout the war as unhelpful, either practically uncommitted to the goal of emancipation or actually hostile to republicanism.

Touring the United States in 1864, in the hopes of repairing damaged relations between northern U.S. society and England, Oxford professor of history Goldwin Smith repeatedly urged northerners to recall their ancient connections to England, even going so far as to suggest the two geopolitical entities had always remained, in effect, one country. Goldwin capped his tour with a piece in the *Atlantic Monthly* in which he recognized the desire of all "[n]ewcomers among the nations" to "have a history." But, he explained, "you have a real and glorious history, if you will not reject it,—monuments genuine and majestic, if you will acknowledge them as your own. Yours," he wrote, "are the palaces of the Plantagenets." In view of this shared transnational past, Smith explained, "It would as ill become you to cultivate narrow national prejudices at present. You have come out, as from other relics of barbarism which still oppress Europe, so from the barbarism of jealous nationality."[77] Indeed, in promoting his view of an Anglo-American history that obviated national barriers, Smith alluded to the Confederate and northeastern racial theories that had codified the cisatlantic dispute in terms of an epic Norman and Saxon struggle, suggesting that "[t]he real origin of your nation is the key to the present relations between you and England. This is the old battle waged again on a new field." Updating and transforming that discourse, Smith wrote, "We will not talk too much of Puritans and Cavaliers. The soldiers of the Union are not Puritans, neither are the planters Cavaliers. But the present civil war is a vast episode in the same irrepressible conflict between Aristocracy and Democracy; and the heirs of the Cavalier in England sympathize with your enemies, the heirs of the Puritan with you" (*GS* 751).

Smith's transnational appeal converts the ethnic antagonisms of the past, or rather, reconstitutes the political and economic struggles of the present, as an "irrepressible conflict between Aristocracy and Democracy" with which both the United States and Britain were still beset in 1864. If England itself was torn by the same divisions of interest afflicting the United States, how could Americans expect England to speak with one voice on the contest to end slavery? The divisions between the United States and England, arising out of miscommunications and misrepresentations flowing across the North Atlantic over the prior three years, would be patched up as had other divisions of the past, he explained: through free trade. Even after the American Revolution, Smith insisted, England's loss of its former colonies "emancipated commerce and gave free course to those reciprocal streams of wealth which a restrictive policy had forbidden to flow" (*GS* 750). And "[t]he inauguration of free trade was in fact the renunciation of the only solid object for which our ancestors clung to an invidious and perilous supremacy, and exposed the heart of England by scattering her fleet and armies over the globe" (*GS* 740). But at the same time, U.S. inhabitants of this great Anglophone civilization must evolve beyond a vulgar class resentment: "It would be most unworthy . . . to preach vulgar hatred of an historic aristocracy," Smith explained, since "we have friends of the better cause among our English capitalists as well as among our English peers." Upon such members of the better class Smith built his hopes for restored transatlantic "community," since "[t]he course taken by such men at this crisis is an earnest of the essential unity of interest which underlies all class-divisions,—which, in onward progress toward the attainment of a real community, will survive all class-distinctions, and terminate the conflict between capital and labor, not by making the laborer the slave of the capitalist, nor the capitalist the slave of the

laborer, but by establishing between them mutual good-will, founded on intelligence and justice" (*GS* 755).

Perhaps sensing that his argument left much of the animosity unhealed,
Smith pointed out that northern Unionists had often failed to codify the conflict in morally clear terms. "In justice to my country," he argued, "let me
remind you that you did not—perhaps you could not—set the issue between
Freedom and Slavery plainly before us at the outset; you did not—perhaps
you could not—set it plainly before yourselves." Thus, he continued, "You
cannot be surprised, if our people took your rulers at their word" in defining
the purpose of the war in Unionist rather than abolitionist terms (*GS* 763–64).
Nevertheless, with the war now apparently drawing to its close, Smith urged
his northern audience to imagine with him a great Anglo-American, North
Atlantic Commonwealth whose prosperity would heal the wounds of 1861–
64."Other thoughts crowd upon my mind," he wrote, closing the *Atlantic*
piece,

> thoughts of what the two nations have been to each other in the past,
> thoughts of what they may yet be to each other in the future. . . . A century
> hence, the passions which caused the quarrel will be dead, the black record
> of the quarrel will survive and be detested. Do what we will now, we shall
> not cancel the tie of blood, nor prevent it from hereafter asserting its under-
> lying power. The English men of this day will not prevent those who come
> after them from being proud of England's grandest achievement, the sum of
> all her noblest victories,—the foundations of this great Commonwealth of
> the New World. (*GS* 768–69)

Attempting to contextualize England's stance toward the American crisis,
and tacitly referring to the American Republic as a part of a North American "Commonwealth," Smith wrote for a northern U.S. readership that was
smarting in 1864 over a perceived English partiality toward the Confederacy. For their part, southerners saw no evidence of such bias. After Lincoln
made emancipation the official policy of the government, Parliament voted
to confirm Palmerston's ongoing position of neutrality "at present," and
indeed, Lancashire's representatives in the House of Commons remained
in the preceding debate solidly supportive of Palmerston's policy, in apparent reality check for the southern cotton strategy. (Indeed, in a January 19,
1863, letter to the textile workers of Manchester, Lincoln thanked the operatives for their staunch support of the Union throughout their long
season of economic hardship. "I cannot but regard your decisive utterances
upon the question [of slavery] as an instance of sublime Christian heroism
which has not been surpassed in any age or in any country," he wrote.)[78] At
a loss, writers in southern journals and newspapers denounced England, as
in the North, for hypocrisy and treachery. There was, first, a period of disbelief: after the Confederate capitulation at Vicksburg, for instance, in

a dirge over the destruction of an estimated 300,000 bales of cotton in western Tennessee and northern Mississippi (burned in anticipation of Federal invasion), the *Memphis Appeal* addressed itself to a bystanding world through a chorus including the exclamation "Nations! . . . 'Tis for liberty we fight!" before then narrowing the appeal to an "England" who might yet intercede:

> England! see our sacrifice—
> See the Cotton blaze!
> God of nations! now to Thee,
> Southrons bend th' imploring knee;
> 'Tis our country's hour of need—
> Hear the mothers intercede—
> Hear the little children plead![79]

Upon full realization that there would be no British interference with the federal blockade, disbelief turned to outrage. In a poem entitled "England's Neutrality," published first in the *Southern Illustrated News* and then in *Punch* before reappearing in both the *Wilmington Journal* and the *Southern Literary Messenger*, John R. Thompson opined the "dream that England soon will drop her long miscalled Neutrality,/And give us, with hearty shake, the hand of nationality."[80] The poem distributes invective liberally among Palmerston's cabinet and England's leading advocates of free trade. To John Bright, who had been Richard Cobden's partner in the repeal of the Corn Laws but who now believed that the flow of cotton would be restored only through a Union victory, the poem attributes a blank hostility toward the South and a hope for its annihilation: "Why, let 'em fight," he exclaims, "these Southerners, I hate 'em,/And hope the black Republicans will soon exterminate 'em."[81]

Palmerston, speaking with "pitiless severity," appears aloof in the face of northern atrocities: "Let arts decay, let millions fall, for aye let Freedom perish,/With all that in the Western World men fain would love and cherish,/Let Universal Ruin there become a sad Reality:/We cannot swerve, we must preserve our rigorous Neutrality." But the poem reserves its most scathing satire for Lord Russell, the architect of Palmerston's policy who had, during the month of the *Trent* fiasco, intimated the opening of a second front with the North by more than tripling British forces near Maine's border with Canada.[82] No longer particularly favoring either side, Russell intones, "Yes, let 'em fight, till both are brought to hopeless desolation,/Till wolves troop round the cottage door, in one and t'other nation,/Till, worn and broken down, the South shall prove no more refractory,/And rust eats up the silent looms of every Yankee factory—."[83] In its attribution to Russell of a feckless ambivalence, not only for the travails of the South but also for the decaying textile mills of the North, the poem strangely enough redirects hostility from the North—now imagined as a fellow victim of English apathy—and toward England itself, which surveys from a patrician distance American landscapes of desolation:

> "Til bursts no more the cotton boll o'er fields of Carolina,
> And fills with snowy flosses the dusky hands of Dinah;
> Till war has dealt its final blow, and Mr. Seward's knavery
> Has put an end in all the land to Freedom and to Slavery" [. . .]
> "So shall our 'merry England' thrive on trans-Atlantic troubles,
> While India on her distant plains her crop of cotton doubles;
> And as long as North or South shall show the least vitality,
> We cannot swerve, we must preserve our rigorous neutrality."

Russell's speech, the poem surmises, "might well become a Saxon legislator," voicing a viewpoint as barbaric as if from "Vikings" who "quaffed from human skulls their fiery draughts of honey mead."

Flinging the Normanist discourse of southern nationalism at the English themselves was, of course, the contumely of a truly lost cause. The snows of southern summers, evaporating from the plantations of the South, are now transferred to the plains of India, harvestable by other dusky fingers, spirited away through the very commercial mechanisms Timrod had imagined would deliver independence to the Confederacy. Its envoys no longer granted audience in Russell's Ministry of State, both its promises and its threats no longer considered by the operatives of the Lancashire mills, the Confederacy, we might say, learned the hard way the vicissitudes of globalized economies. As Hardt and Negri explain in their analysis of contemporary global transnationalism, "With the decline of national boundaries, the world market is liberated from the kind of binary divisions that nation-states had imposed, and in the new space a myriad of differences appears. These differences of course do not play freely across a smooth global space, but rather are regimented in global networks of power consisting of highly differentiated and mobile structures."[84] Like contemporary geopolitical players staking similar hopes in today's transnational world economy, in 1863 the Confederacy found what such myriads of "differentiated and mobile structures" portend for those regions that are—as, we might say, the Confederacy from 1861 to 1863—subject to that most euphemistic of all geopolitical designations: that of the developing nation.

Coda

Here is a lithograph published in August 1858 by Baker and Godwin Printers of Manhattan, commemorating the successful transmissions made that month over the newly deployed transatlantic telegraphic cable connecting Britain with the United States (figure C.1). Yankee Jonathan and John Bull clasp hands across the Atlantic as the U.S.S. *Niagara* and H.M.S. *Agamemnon* unspool over three thousand miles of cable joining two continents. In many ways the image is conventional, presenting the cable as the instrument of diplomacy and peace—themes propounded in the inaugural transmissions of Queen Victoria and President Buchanan as well as thousands of printed commentaries in both the United States and Britain. "Glad to grasp your hand, uncle John!" exclaims Jonathan from the shore of North America. "I almost feel like calling you father, and will if you improve upon acquaintance! May the feeling of Friendship which comes from my heart, and tingles to the very ends of my fingers, be like the electric current which now unites our lands, and links our destiny with yours!" For his part, Uncle John cannot but reciprocate Jonathan's declarations of biological and electrical kinship: "Happy to see you and greet you, Jonathan! You feel like 'bone of my bone and flesh of my flesh!'" Promising, for his part, not to "think of quarreling any more," John Bull prophesies a transatlantic rapport between equals, but also expresses his esteem in terms of Union: "How good and pleasant a thing it is," he remarks, quoting from Psalms, "for brethren to dwell together in unity."

Here, a far less conventional representation of the cable, published by another New York lithographer the following month, in honor of the New York celebrations on September 1 (figure C.2). Again, the *Niagara* and *Agamemnon* pay out leagues of the cable that now frames the image. But in its first departure from the nomenclature established through other representations of international telegraphy, Adam Weingärtner's *Torchlight Procession Around the World* makes clear that the wiring of the North Atlantic is only the

THE LAYING OF THE CABLE---JOHN AND JONATHAN JOINING HANDS.

FIGURE C.1 *The Laying of the Cable—John and Jonathan Joining Hands, 1858.* Woodcut with letterpress, 42.5 × 56.5 cm. Library of Congress, Prints & Photographs Division, LC-DIG-pga-00117.

beginning, that the geopolitical ramifications of this accomplishment ripple well beyond the telegraphic plateau now joining the United States and Britain. Hence, the project of networking the planet in high-speed communication technology is here undertaken not by the familial Jonathan and Uncle John, but by a multinational procession composed of Chinese, Middle Easterners, Native Americans, Africans—heathens of the world, now enjoined in technological revolution as they hoist telegraphic cable around the earth. If even in this eccentric way, the image reiterates common associations established throughout the 1850s between international telegraphy and a dilating prospect for global liberty, its expansion of the telegraph's scope diminishes whatever propinquity may exist between John and Jonathan, deliberately misplacing a more conventional emphasis upon the importance of that relationship in the welter of a more global movement toward liberation.

Strangely, perhaps—to twenty-first-century eyes—the dreamlike, eponymous procession works under the direction of a fire brigade whose helmets are emblazoned with the initials of the United States—as if to imply that this mob of racial and national others heeds American instruction as it both binds the world in networked communication technology and extinguishes some conflagration—the cable now resembling by association with the fire brigade

FIGURE C.2 *Torchlight Procession Around the World, 1858. Lithograph, 18 × 14 in.; 45.72 × 35.56 cm. Division of Home and Community Life, National Museum of American History, Smithsonian Institution, Harry T. Peters lithography collection.*

some enormous water hose, the heavenly mists enshrouding the process now looking like smoke. That cable also joins portraits of Franklin, the revolutionary father famously associated with the electricity powering the telegraph; Samuel Morse, the inventor of telegraphy itself; the international entrepreneur Cyrus W. Field, the father of the transatlantic cable project who was feted through New York on the September 1 celebrations; and William Levereth Hudson, captain of the *Niagara* (whose ship, five years prior to its more historic transaction with the *Agamemnon*, had ferried Nathaniel Hawthorne to his consulship in Liverpool). Whereas other images published in honor of the opening of the cable touted the international partnership symbolized in this pinnacle of Anglo-American cooperation, Weingärtner's includes no British figures in its honor roll. Instead, the Atlantic cable is an American achievement, a victory for republicanism and Yankee ingenuity.

Many contemporary Britons might find that omission typical, recalling more recent American claims to have prosecuted the Second World War all but unilaterally or invented the automobile. But Weingärtner is not simply inaugurating that form of U.S. amnesia through which Britain appears as the ineffectual cousin of the United States, a stultified genteel forever behind the curve of things; both his omissions and his imagery are guided by much more confrontational impulses. After adorning those portraits of Franklin, Morse, Field, and Hudson, the cable follows the arch formed at the meeting of the two hands of Liberty and Britannia, or perhaps Columbia and Victoria, where a most prominent member of the fire brigade straddles an eagle, directing his attention toward the *Agamemnon* and the Union Jack, showering both with arrow-tipped electrical current emanating from his fingertips. The cloud from which he and the eagle emerge—perhaps from which his electricity has arced—is itself emblazoned with electric bulbs spelling the word "LIBERTY." The firefighter riding the eagle is electrocuting Britain, shocking it with currents of liberty.

So it's not simply that the telegraph will promote international understanding and hence quell conflict, and it's not simply that it will do so on a wider scale than other treatments such as Baker and Godwin's imagine; this new conduit of manifest destinarian energy will defibrillate the world, spreading liberty through a process galvanizing to that multiethnic, multinational procession but traumatic to Uncle John. If the Atlantic really was, as Emerson had indicated in *English Traits*, like a galvanic battery through which England charged the United States with the former's most liberal energies, here the current of that arc is reversed. The relays of this switch have much to do with the firefighters who populate Weingärtner's image, figures who manifest an even more complicated iconography, the barest metonym of which emblazons the unfurling scroll beneath Franklin's portrait, which reads, "What th' B'hoys intended by the Atlantic Cable."

As historians such as Sean Wilentz and Edward Widmer have shown, popular associations circulated in 1850s New York between fire brigades and so-called Bowery boys, the "b'hoys" mentioned here (and indeed, Weingärtner's studio address, published at the bottom of the page as 87 Fulton Street, places him just south of the Bowery district where the so-called b'hoys held sway). Themselves often members of volunteer fire brigades, Bowery b'hoys were associated with the red shirts and massive boots of fire companies, which many donned as a sort of gang uniform. Between the 1840s and '50s the b'hoys incarnated a certain Whitmanesque swagger, positioned somewhere between artisans and laborers, but were also figures of thuggish confrontation and urban violence.[1] These traits were bound to an ever-evolving political ideology whose details shifted in relation to sectionally polarizing questions such as popular sovereignty or the rights of fugitive slaves, for example, but which more constantly (if abstractly) opposed aristocracy and privilege—the Bowery b'hoys, to put it another way, were more consistently politicized by the evils of wage slavery than of chattel slavery. But if Weingärtner's text and imagery links the b'hoys to the Atlantic cable and hence reduplicates those associations between telegraphic eloquence and physical violence that were rehearsed in the Sumner assault and its rhetorical aftermath, the b'hoys are also here yoked to the movement named in the image's dedication. Connecting his image "to

Young America," Weingärtner now ties the rowdy b'hoys to public figures such as John O'Sullivan, Franklin Pierce, or Stephen Douglas, advocates of westward expansion who, like the Bowery b'hoys, declared indifference to the slavery question but commitment to Union.

The upshot of this melding of Young America with the figure of the b'hoy is to conflate an expansionist triumphalism, resonant with broad swaths of the American public, with a form of urban localism not only averse to privilege, not only full of masculine contempt for anything hinting of aristocracy, but also—and because of these qualities—inherently hostile toward British structures of power and dispensation. No longer an occasion to celebrate a set of Anglo-American connections magnified in a networked North Atlantic expanse, the telegraph now announces the end of a geopolitical order controlled in London. This is not to claim a much greater degree of clarity for the intended resonance of the torchlight procession. Do these racially and geographically distant peoples await their own democracy delivered through the aegis of Young America and manifest destiny, conducted at the fingertips of the b'hoys (as if in fulfillment of the prophesy voiced by David Dudley Field, brother to Cyrus Field, who predicted the telegraphy would become "the world's girdle" through which the United States would achieve dominion from the equator to the poles)?[2] Or are they instead subjects of the British Empire, current or former victims of an imperium guided not by the promise of liberty but by sheer monarchical power? If popular representations of the cable often provide fodder for an historiography of misunderstanding (for instance, in the widespread sense that what the Atlantic cable transmitted was not Morse code but rather actual voices, intoning sonorously along an otherworldly ocean floor), Weingärtner's vision of telegraphic progress entails its own blind spots (the Native American figures in the torchlight procession, for instance, presumably cannot regard Queen Victoria or Britannia as their primary antagonist). But those ambiguities notwithstanding, what is crucial here is that the disenthrallment to which Weingärtner gives vent involves the displacement of one semantics of liberty—associated with abolitionist politics, and through those fixated upon the meaning of Anglo-American rapport—favoring instead a syntax associated with Young America, expansion, and Union.

It is a common thing, at penultimate moments like this, to pan outward, to elaborate wide-ranging implications, even if it feels more to the point to historicize than to extrapolate. And so in that spirit, I'll end saying two things about the sentiment toward England Weingärtner's lithograph articulates—a view of England that runs counter to so much affinity this book has documented but that surveys the space toward which that cultural history of affiliation seems to have led, a place from where Emerson, in "The Fortune of the Republic," would urge Americans to count as very little England's inches against America's miles, and leagues, of accomplishment in the name of liberal progress.

Though it was published about five years prior to that statement of Emerson's, Weingärtner's lithograph speaks to the reversals toward which Atlantic sectionalism finally tended. One might say that over the course of the antebellum period, Americans could not but refer the crisis over slavery to England. Since the Revolution, Americans have often voiced a moral superiority with regard to the English, a nation of landed gentry and inherited titles, grounding their stance in the more enlightened ethos of republicanism. And yet, it was a British court that abolished slavery throughout the United Kingdom in 1772; it was the British Parliament that abolished the Atlantic slave trade in 1807 and the British navy that enforced the act; and it was the British Parliament that ended slavery peacefully, throughout the empire, in 1833 as the United States entered decades of life-threatening convulsions over its inability to resolve the same issue.

The point is not simply that many U.S. abolitionists throughout the first half of the century leveraged the theme of British moral supremacy with regard to slavery in order to effect reform in the United States, and nor is it that many of these same figures, and many others both within their approximate sectional and ideological camp *and* on the opposite side of the Mason-Dixon, generated increasingly detailed accounts of England and the English that seem to have served even more intricate demands. The larger point is that sectionalism and slavery are not domestic issues that prevent us from reading the early nineteenth century in its international mode. Sectionalism and slavery absolutely formed the ways in which Americans understood themselves as inheritors of a set of English legacies and as agents within a great North Atlantic civilization, because slavery and the sectionalism it produced marked the limits of U.S. claims to democratic virtue vis à vis England. Pitting one against the other—the "domestic" crisis of the Union or "international" cultural relations with Britain—runs counter to the aesthetic, political, historiographical, and economic lived experience of the period. Weingärtner's lithograph of the Atlantic cable attempts to reassign the sources of a globally civilizing energy; it evacuates significance from the Anglo-American relation to the extent that it sidesteps the sectional issues that have energized that significance. In its strained attempt to present the cable not only as a U.S. accomplishment but as part of a U.S. antidote to empire, the image registers the depth and resonance of the very patterns of association it seeks to neutralize.

That is one point I would underline here, the point to do with literary, cultural, and intellectual history. The second, more extrapolating point would be that the recoiling from England of which Weingärtner's is one expression is also a part of a perennial U.S. psychology. I am reminded in this sense of an insight Stanley Cavell once made of Emerson's self-reliant citizen who incessantly turns from his culture—one can incessantly, or repeatedly, turn *from* only if one is just as repeatedly turning *toward*, Cavell reminds us.[3] And there is a sense in which the England from which Emerson and others turned more decisively near the end of the Civil War was in the first place an American phantasm, as if former Anglophiles in the North and the South were now holding England accountable for not living up to qualities and virtues that in any case were not of England's own formulation. The terms of this American recall of affection are indeed incessant. The idea of an English-speaking geopolitical order, descended from Norman royalty, Saxon freedom fighters, or some conflation of the two—perhaps the ultimate conflation is simply the Magna Carta itself—arrests the American imagination when it is not shrinking from Britishness (as in recent U.S. deliberations over the efficacy of a single-payer health-care system) investing Americans in the fantasy of shared descent (as in the continued currency, on my own shores of the pond, of the phrase "special relationship").

One thinks of the Atlantic Charter, formulated by Franklin Delano Roosevelt and Winston Churchill on August 14, 1941, aboard U.S. and British warships anchored in Placentia Bay, Newfoundland, perhaps seventy miles from the 1858 Atlantic telegraph's western terminus. The charter was not a signed strategic alliance—it did not secure direct American involvement in the European war, as Churchill had hoped—but was rather a statement of "common principles" inherent "in the national policies" of the United States and Britain, a signal of North Atlantic allegiance grounded in political and philosophical differentiation from the Axis powers. The problem today for citizens of the former geopolitical entity, if it exists, is that the document reads as a repudiation of fascism *and* empire *and* globalized capital. The difference between members of Anglophone civilization and the Axis is that the former "seek no aggrandizement, territorial or other"; they "respect the right of all peoples to choose the form of government under which they will live; and they wish to see the sovereign rights and self-government restored to those who have been forcibly deprived of them"; "they desire to bring about the fullest collaboration between all nations in the economic field with the object of securing, for all, improved labour standards, economic advancement and social security"; and lastly, "they believe that all of the nations of the world, for realistic as well as spiritual reasons must come to the abandonment of the use of force," and will "aid and encourage all other practicable measures which will lighten for peace-loving peoples the crushing burden of armaments."[4]

The idea of a shared set of Anglo-American principles binding the republic to the realm at the deepest levels appears elsewhere in the history of the twentieth century, and indeed beyond: as Laura Doyle points out, George W. Bush made the idea thematic in a number of speeches he gave in the wake of 9/11 and later, in justification for war in Iraq.[5] As with those rhetorics of transatlantic kinship, in the Atlantic Charter the triumph of Anglo-American principles purport to expand the sphere of self-determination, bringing the planet closer to a state of global liberty. Even if Churchill would resist Roosevelt's repeated call for Indian self-determination as falling under the principles of the Charter; even if both leaders would choose not to press upon Soviet policy in the Baltics so long as fighting with Germany continued; even if the document's references to the need for widespread "abandonment of force" and "the crushing burden of armaments" ring hollow from the vantage of the post-Cold War, and post-9/11, world, the ideas of affiliation invoked in the Atlantic Charter speak to the fantasies of kindred ties Hawthorne imagined as roots, tendrils running beneath the Atlantic.

In this book I have tried to capture the cultural antecedents of this discourse of kinship as they emerged in the antebellum period, when the prospect of a dissolved republic freighted U.S. contests over Englishness in distinctive ways. It is, I would say, a price of U.S. investment in a larger North Atlantic cultural and geopolitical entity not only to promote visions of England that are essentially self-referential but occasionally to act on those visions with far-reaching consequences. So possibly the question left open concerns the potential for more reflective modes of emulation between the United States and England. We might concede that the idea of a special relationship is inevitable given the nations' significant overlapping of origins, political structures, and cultural production, but we can also render thematic those points that promote more complex accounts of transatlantic attachment and withdrawal. And so maybe the repetitive dilation and contraction of U.S. identification with England should no longer constitute the focus of transatlantic studies at all. Maybe—and perhaps this is the one valid lesson Weingärtner's lithograph can offer us—our critical and teaching practices ought better to focus upon what that incessant fantasy of kinship has covered over. By this I do not mean simply the violence for which Britain and America have been historically responsible, because that is a task for historians and in any case it is a task that has been readily and ably enjoined. That reality is, moreover, a level of the repressed contained in Weingärtner's illustration, which includes at its very center, much more lightly etched than the rest of the print, a veritable map of the triangular trade route, figuring it as something like the navel of this dream, the traumatic object around which this fantasy turns in its embroidered rendition of a Young America that is in actuality about to explode over the ramifications of that map.

As I say, I am not talking about dispelling ideology through historical illumination. I am thinking, rather, about assessing those terms for a more useable past that have been generated within the very transatlantic constellation of Anglo-American kinship. Most fundamentally, Weingärtner envisions a global, multinational, multiethnic movement harnessing the revolutionary potentials of high-speed information technology, redrawing a map still plotted along the coordinates of that old Atlantic transaction: Europe, Africa, the United States. Here in the young twenty-first century, how can such a vision of liberal progress, however wrong it may be, not also strike us for how much it may be getting right? In another transatlantic prophesy of liberty, Alan Moore's graphic novel *V for Vendetta*, an oppressed British citizenry can achieve freedom only through the destruction of Westminster, and the puppet Parliament within, in a final immolation of North Atlantic power (the United States having already succumbed to its most self-destructive tendencies, a smoldering waste across the water). V's Guy Fawkes mask has been more recently appropriated by Occupy protestors from Zuccotti Park to St. Paul's who are themselves children of the Arab Spring, the revolution whose executors, well beyond the peripheries of the telegraphic plateau, taught the 99 percent how to overturn a regime using iPhones, Twitter, Facebook.

Meanwhile, the new century's first Anglo-American adventure undertaken in the name of Anglo-American liberty has resulted in not one of the functional Middle Eastern democracies President Bush and Prime Minister Blair fervently, insistently, prophesied. Whether the achievements of the Arab Spring will endure and expand remains to be seen, just as it is now unclear whither will advance the Occupy movement. But one must take pause at the instruments of both, and in this sense, that ghostly procession of Weingärtner's, girdling their globe in telegraphic cable, offers some contemporary resonance of which we need not be dismissive. The problem and the opportunity is that master narratives of transatlantic kinship too often read univocally when in fact they are always contested from within, something Frederick Douglass, Lydia Maria Child, Henry Timrod, and Ralph Waldo Emerson understood as they turned the thematics of English racial origins toward their own contemporaneous and climactic ends. Accounting for the power of such maneuvers as these—grasping the implications of those contestations, both for the societies and the people who would otherwise inhabit those narratives—makes worthy work for Atlantic readers and citizens today.

{ NOTES }

Prelims

1. See Meredith McGill, *American Literature and the Culture of Reprinting, 1834–1853* (Philadelphia: University of Pennsylvania Press, 2003). Two recent review essays offer varying perspectives on the development of transatlantic literary studies over the past two decades: Amanda Claybaugh's "New Fields, Conventional Habits, and the Legacy of *Atlantic Double-Cross*," *American Literary History* 20: 3 (Fall 2008): 439–448, argues that Robert Weisbuch's tome by that name is both incredibly influential and almost universally ignored. Though citations of Weisbuch multiply by the year—such that the book has become by Claybaugh's estimation "one of the most often-cited works in trans-Atlantic studies" (441)—almost none of these later studies accept the book's model of literary rivalry. "In this way," Claybaugh points out, "*Atlantic Double-Cross* has presided over the development of a field that has moved away from many of Weisbuch's own presumptions" (442). In her "Transatlanticism Now," *American Literary History* 16: 1 (Spring 2001), Laura M. Stevens argues that transatlantic scholarship has developed in tandem with broader interests in the histories of colonization and slavery, but also that in its current form has opposed itself not as much to national as to exceptional models of literary production (94).

2. See Amanda Claybaugh, *The Novel of Purpose: Literature and Social Reform in the Anglo-American World* (Ithaca, NY: Cornell University Press, 2007). Claybaugh's scope extends well beyond the Civil War, encompassing the transatlantic copyright debates to which I allude above.

3. See Sam W. Haynes, *Unfinished Revolution: The Early American Republic in a British World* (Charlottesville and London: University of Virginia Press, 2010), and Leonard Tennenhouse, *The Importance of Feeling English: American Literature and the British Diaspora, 1750–1850* (Princeton, NJ, and Oxford: Princeton University Press, 2007). It bears pointing out that of these two recent texts, Haynes's remains most wed to the exceptionalist model I associate with Robert Weisbuch's *Atlantic Double-Cross* and which I see for the most part being undermined by current transatlantic scholarship. For Haynes, an early American appetite and fascination for all things British effectively rendered the antebellum U.S. "a cultural and economic satellite of the British Empire" (10), and though popular dispositions toward Britain were in constant flux during the period, Haynes depicts an antebellum culture of Anglophilia that subsisted in complex dialectic with the impulse to forge a national culture apart from that defined by British standards of taste. While Tennenhouse takes up the similar purpose of "exploring how the American tradition defined itself in an ongoing and yet changing relation to the British," suggesting that throughout the period "most writers and readers in America considered themselves to be members of the generic English culture that we generally mean by 'British culture,' and they thought of their literature as products of such a culture" (1), he also argues that the drive for cultural autonomy may not have been in place during the first half of the nineteenth century. Rather than being subject

to a British cultural hegemon, antebellum American readers and writers in Tennenhouse's estimation constituted a "British diaspora." In fact, Tennenhouse regards American literary history as distinctive for its "insistence on reproducing those aspects of Englishness that do not require one to be in England, so much as among English people" (9). Probably the most fulfilling book-length study of American deference to Britain, in this respect, is Elisa Tamarkin's *Anglophilia: Deference, Devotion, and Antebellum America* (Chicago and London: University of Chicago Press, 2008), which documents the patterns of endearment through which antebellum Americans affiliated with English abolition, education, and aristocracy.

4. See Robert Weisbuch, *Atlantic Double-Cross: American Literature and British Influence in the Age of Emerson* (Chicago: University of Chicago Press, 1986): "We will need many more books after this one to get to a satisfying assurance of major understanding. . . . Nevertheless, I will boast that this study represents something new. It means to inaugurate a field, or subfield, of literary study. The conventional habits by which departments of English and comparative literature organize themselves have made for a vacancy where a rigorous study of Anglo-American literary relations should have been occurring" (xx).

5. As Claybaugh explains, nineteenth-century literary historians tended to group literary texts from both nations within a category Claybaugh calls "literature in English" (12). Though the field of Anglo-American literary exchange in the nineteenth century was surely "overlaid with national prejudice and national self-assertion" (12), she points out, the literatures of that Anglophone world "have never been entirely distinct" (12), such that a general presumption of similitude undergirded most literary reviews and polemics. Similarly, Claybaugh reminds us that many of the twentieth-century pillars of Americanist literary scholarship, as late as Leavis and Matthiessen, read "across national borders as a matter of course" (13) long before transatlanticists such as Weisbuch urged late twentieth-century scholars to begin doing so. See Claybaugh, *Novel of Purpose*, 12–15. I also think here of Paul Giles's placement of Franklin's *Autobiography* within an Atlantic "ideology of exchange" in *Transatlantic Insurrections: British Culture and the Formation of American Literature, 1730–1860* (Philadelphia: University of Pennsylvania Press, 2001): "Just as commodities change places in the marketplaces of Philadelphia and London, so hypothesis and induction, print culture and oral tradition, Britain and America all change places within the circumference of the North Atlantic Enlightenment. These commercial circuits of exchange can thus be seen to work in parallel with a comparative idiom, since both depend for their efficient operation upon an intersection between two opposing forces, a process of mutual reciprocity where one side of the equation only makes sense in terms of the other" (86).

6. Giles, *Transatlantic Insurrections*, 189.

7. See Giles, *Atlantic Republic: The American Tradition in English Literature* (Oxford and New York: Oxford University Press, 2009), and *Virtual Americas: Transnational Fictions and the Transatlantic Imaginary* (Durham, NC: Duke University Press, 2002); Paul Gilroy, *The Black Atlantic: Modernity and Double Consciousness* (Cambridge, MA: Harvard University Press, 1993).

8. Ralph Waldo Emerson, "The Fortune of the Republic," *The Later Lectures of Ralph Waldo Emerson*, 2 vols., eds. Ronald A. Bosco and Joel Myerson (Athens and London: University of Georgia Press, 2001), 2: 323.

9. The record of southern conservative criticism of Emerson has been documented by Matthew Guinn, who convincingly depicts a review history beginning with the American Scholar Address and running through the war as a broad attempt "to justify and defend [the

slave-holding interest's] own precarious ideology from the outside threat that Emerson represented" (175). See Matthew Guinn, "Emerson's Southern Critics, 1838–1862," *Resources for American Literary Study* 25: 2 (1999): 175.

Introduction

1. Nathaniel Hawthorne, *The Centenary Edition of the Works of Nathaniel Hawthorne*, eds. William Charvat, Roy Harvey Pearce, Claude M. Simpson, et al., 23 vols. (Columbus: Ohio State University Press, 1962–95), 5: 38. Further references to this edition are cited parenthetically in the text and include volume and page numbers.

2. Hawthorne tried repeatedly to resolve his sense of transatlantic dislocation through the implement of romance, but without success. In *The Ancestral Footstep*, which he had begun and then abandoned in Italy, he wrote eighty-eight pages of a disillusioned American politician who discovers himself to be the rightful heir of an English estate abandoned by his family generations earlier. Having returned to Concord in 1861, he began two longer drafts around the same theme: in the first, the politician becomes a younger man; in the second (which Julian Hawthorne would edit and publish in 1882 as *Dr. Grimshawe's Secret*), the claimant's delusions stem from his childhood manipulation by the eponymous Grimshawe. And in *Septimius Felton*, which Hawthorne began and put aside during the same period, he reorients his story within the historical setting of the American Revolution. Here, the eponymous protagonist inherits the English estate of his long-lost brother, whom he has unknowingly killed not far from the battlefield at Concord—the Revolution thus becoming a rendition of fratricidal war or familial secession. Endlessly returning to the same ground, continual in his determination to build, perhaps, his final novel around this core notion of a displaced ancient line and its return to English soil, Hawthorne was nevertheless unable to bring any of his Anglo-American romances to completion. In a rut, he gave over his attentions to the American crisis, took a trip to Washington with his friend and publisher William Davis Ticknor, met Lincoln, and quickly wrote the sardonic "Chiefly About War Matters," which he published in the *Atlantic Monthly* in July 1862. Now back in stride, he abandoned the prior romances about England and began his memoir, revising the notebooks he had kept during his consular years first into a series of contributions for the *Atlantic* and then into a book, *Our Old Home*, which he published through Ticknor and Fields the following year. For useful overviews of Hawthorne's difficulties as he composed the American Claimant manuscripts, see Edward H. Davidson's and Claude M. Simpson's historical commentary included in volume 12 of the *Centenary Edition* (491–521), as well as Nina Baym, *The Shape of Hawthorne's Career* (Ithaca, NY, and London: Cornell University Press, 1976), 253–69; Brenda Wineapple, *Hawthorne: A Life* (New York: Alfred A. Knopf, 2003), 339–42; Edwin Haviland Miller, *Salem Is My Dwelling-Place: A Life of Nathaniel Hawthorne* (Iowa City: University of Iowa Press, 1991), 483–98; and Elisa Tamarkin, *Anglophilia: Deference, Devotion, and Antebellum America* (Chicago: University of Chicago Press, 2008), 76–86.

3. Hawthorne, *The English Notebooks by Nathaniel Hawthorne*, ed. Randall Stewart (New York and London: Pierpont Morgan Library, 1941), 92.

4. See Wineapple, *Hawthorne*, 342, 341.

5. See Tamarkin, *Anglophilia*, 83, who reads *Our Old Home*, along with the drafts comprising the American Claimant manuscripts, as Hawthorne's attempt to exercise "an affective loyalty" that has "been deplorably disused" (80).

198

6. See Wineapple, *Hawthorne*, 357–58.

7. My reading of *Our Old Home* alongside Hester's nativizing striking of roots parallels Doyle, who does not treat *Our Old Home* but who points out that this passage from *The Scarlet Letter* "echoes" Hawthorne's autobiographical passages from "The Custom-House." See Laura Doyle, *Freedom's Empire: Race and the Rise of the Novel in Atlantic Modernity* (Durham, NC: Duke University Press, 2008), 302. See also Sacvan Bercovitch, *The Rites of Assent: Transformations in the Social Construction of America* (New York and London: Routledge, 1994), 194–95, who remarks upon Hester Prynne's return to New England as the precondition of her charge as an "agent of socialization"—and who thus similarly binds Hester to processes of nativization.

8. Henry James, *Hawthorne* (1879; repr., Ithaca, NY: Cornell University Press, 1956), 121, 136.

9. Ibid., 121, 134.

10. Frederick Newberry, *Hawthorne's Divided Loyalties: England and America in His Works* (Cranbury, NJ, London, and Mississauga, Ontario: Associated University Presses, 1987), 17. I focus on Newberry here because his is still the defining book-length treatment of Hawthorne's transatlanticism, and because it is a masterful study to which I owe much. But in addition to the other studies I cite in this introduction, other landmark treatments of Hawthorne are relevant as well to the critical history I call into question here. See, for instance, Michael Colacurcio, *Doctrine and Difference: Essays in the Literature of New England* (New York and London: Routledge, 1997), 205–27, who demonstrates how far Hawthorne's entanglements of sexuality and authority commit him to a probing reading of Puritan jurisprudence. Edwin Haviland Miller, for his part, describes Hawthorne's attitude toward the Civil War in terms of withdrawal, attributing Septimius Felton's withdrawal from the battlefield as also an apt description of Hawthorne's disconnection from events as the war unfolded: "'I am dissevered; from 'the human race,' [Septimius] declares. 'It is my doom to be only a spectator of life, to look on as one apart from it. . . . How cold am I now, while this whirlpool of public feeling is eddying around me.'" See *Salem Is My Dwelling Place: A Life of Nathaniel Hawthorne* (Iowa City: University of Iowa Press, 1991), 492.

11. Laura Doyle, *Freedom's Empire: Race and the Rise of the Novel in Atlantic Modernity, 1640–1940* (Durham, NC: Duke University Press, 2008), 310–29.

12. See ibid., 310; Larry J. Reynolds, "*The Scarlet Letter* and Revolutions Abroad," *American Literature* 57: 1 (March 1985): 44–67. As Reynolds points out, "When Hester Prynne is led from the prison by the beadle who cries, 'Make way, make way, in the King's name,' less than a month had passed since Charles's Puritan Parliament had sent him what amounted to a declaration of war" (53). Moreover, "By the final scenes of the novel, when Arthur is deciding to die as a martyr, Charles I had just been beheaded (on January 30, 1649)" (53).

13. Newberry, *Hawthorne's Divided Loyalties*, 19.

14. Ibid., 197.

15. Washington Irving, *The Sketch Book of Geoffrey Crayon, Gentleman* (1820; repr., Paris: L. Baudry, 1825), 102, 103, 106.

16. See Paul Gilroy, *The Black Atlantic: Modernity and Double Consciousness* (Cambridge, MA: Harvard University Press, 1993), 25.

17. Amanda Claybaugh, *The Novel of Purpose: Literature and Social Reform in the Anglo-American World* (Ithaca, NY: Cornell University Press, 2007). At one point Claybaugh acknowledges the "imagined Britain of the cavaliers," a mythos that prevailed in the south

as "the counterpart and rival to the transatlantic ties that connected antislavery campaigners in both nations" (180), but this is simply to invoke the same southern cavalier mythology that has been the subject of critique since Twain.

18. Paul Giles, *Atlantic Republic: The American Tradition in English Literature* (Oxford: Oxford University Press, 2007), 72.

19. Giles, *Virtual Americas: Transnational Fictions and the Transatlantic Imaginary* (Durham, NC, and London: Duke University Press, 2002), 1–2.

20. In some ways, the discourses over Englishness I examine here served to depoliticize the sectionalism of the antebellum era in a manner similar to that isolated by Slavoj Žižek in his critique of western assessments of political strife in the former Yugoslavia—whose turmoil during the 1990s, one recalls, was often treated summarily as the outgrowth of "age-old" ethnic antagonisms rather than as a struggle over discrete and contemporaneous political objectives. As Žižek explains, "The fantasy which organized the perception of ex-Yugoslavia is that of 'Balkan' as the Other of the West: the place of savage ethnic conflicts long since overcome by civilized Europe; a place where nothing is forgotten and nothing is learned, where old traumas are replayed again and again" (212). See Slavoj Žižek, *The Metastases of Enjoyment: Six Essays on Woman and Causality* (New York and London: Verso, 1994), 210–13; also Christopher Hanlon and Slavoj Žižek, "Psychoanalysis and the Post-Political: An Interview with Slavoj Žižek," *New Literary History* 23: 1 (Winter 2001): 18–19.

21. See "Speech of Wendell Phillips," *Liberator*, March 29, 1850, 51.

22. In her work on nineteenth-century American Anglophilia, Tamarkin uses that word to describe a capitulation to English ways marking antebellum American society, especially among northern abolitionists. Anglophilia describes among other things a mythical Englishness—*Englishy* English, as Tamarkin calls it—an Englishness marking the moral rectitude not only of English racial and political attitudes but also (often, apparently, more pressingly) English habits, peccadilloes, mannerisms, accents, rituals, and values. This submission to Englishness, the great stock many antebellum Americans placed in the importance of being English, saturated American abolitionist circles to such an extent that not only nominal Anglo-Saxons such as Emerson, Charles Sumner, Margaret Fuller, or Wendell Phillips expressed enthrallment with English society and culture, but such that African-Americans as well found ways to "opt" for English lineage through ameliorative racial logic or through paying homage to English society, history, and royalty. Such habits of thought, as Tamarkin demonstrates, certainly comprise an important strain in antebellum-era American thought, a pattern of endearment through which American thinkers enshrined the English and situated themselves in relation to that enshrinement. I would suggest, however, that in the context of the sectional crisis, Anglophilia became a more fraught matter than even the conscious and unconscious gyrations undertaken by Anglophiles such as Frederick Douglass, Henry Brown, Samuel Ward, or Sumner would suggest. Indeed, it is precisely because England loomed so large in their imagination that antebellum Americans entered into contention amongst themselves concerning what "English" was, what it meant for an American to affiliate with a mother country whose defining traits seemed alternately to excoriate and apologize for slavery, and to what extent English example bore upon the sectional mind.

23. Quotes from a letter to William D. Ticknor, October 26, 1855, in *Letters of Hawthorne to William D. Ticknor, 1851–1864*, 2 vols. (1910; rpt., Washington, DC: NCR/Microcard Editions, 1972), 1: 111.

24. Quoted in Wineapple, *Hawthorne*, 275.

25. Ralph Waldo Emerson, in *The Collected Works of Ralph Waldo Emerson*, 10 vols., eds. Joseph Slater, Douglas Emory Wilson, et al. (Cambridge, MA, and London: Harvard University Press, 1971–2013), 5: 174.

26. Emerson, "The Fortune of the Republic," in *The Late Lectures of Ralph Waldo Emerson, 1843–1871*, eds. Ronald A. Bosco and Joel Myerson (Athens and London: University of Georgia Press, 2001), 327.

27. Ibid.

28. "The Once United States of America," *New Monthly Magazine*, September 1861, 3.

29. "The Old Dominion," *New Monthly Magazine*, August 1861, 388.

Chapter 1

1. Bernard Burke, *Vicissitudes of Families* (London: Longman, Green, Longman and Roberts, 1863), 288.

2. Ibid., 288–89.

3. "New England Historical and Genealogical Register," *North American Review*, April 8, 1856, 469.

4. Ibid., 469.

5. Ibid., 470.

6. Ibid., 472–73.

7. Elisa Tamarkin, *Anglophilia: Deference, Devotion, and Antebellum America* (Chicago: University of Chicago Press, 2007), 179; emphasis original.

8. Quoted in Tamarkin, *Anglophilia*, 192.

9. Ibid.

10. Ralph Waldo Emerson, *Journals of Ralph Waldo Emerson*, ed. Edward Emerson, 10 vols. (Boston: Houghton Mifflin, 1909–14), 8: 136. Parenthetical citations of Emerson's *Journal* are hereafter cited as *J* and include volume and page number.

11. See Paul Giles, "Transnationalism and Classic American Literature," *PMLA* 118: 1 (Spring 2003): 62–77, upon which I rely here. For an overview of the extent to which the Oregon issue galvanized American voters during the election of 1844, see Edwin A. Miles's "Fifty-Four Forty or Fight—An American Political Legend," *Mississippi Valley Historical Review* 44: 2 (September 1957): 291–309. For a useful analysis of the tensions between the United States and Britain from 1840 until the Civil War, see George L. Bernstein, "Special Relationship and Appeasement: Liberal Policy Toward America in the Age of Palmerston," *Historical Journal* 4: 3 (1998): 725–750.

12. Quoted in Giles, "Transnationalism," 67. See also John L. O'Sullivan, "The Great Nation of Futurity," *United States Democratic Review*, November 1839, 426–30; and O'Sullivan, "Annexation," *United States Democratic Review*, July–August 1845, 5–10; as well as David M. Pletcher, *The Diplomacy of Annexation: Texas, Oregon, and the Mexican War* (Columbia: University of Missouri Press, 1973), 320. As Giles and Pletcher note, O'Sullivan used the phrase "manifest destiny" in a prior commentary piece he published in the July–August issue of the *Democratic Review*, but he had also included this statement in the 1839 piece: "In its magnificent domain of space and time, the nation of many nations is destined to manifest to mankind the excellence of divine principles: to establish on earth the noblest temple ever dedicated to the worship of the Most High—the Sacred and the True" (427).

13. Richard Bridgman, "From Greenough to 'Nowhere': Emerson's *English Traits*," *New England Quarterly* 59: 4 (March–December 1986): 484; emphasis original. See also Julie Ellison, "The Edge of Urbanity: Emerson's *English Traits*," *ESQ* 32 (1986): 96–109; and Carle Hovde, "English and American Traits," in *Emerson and His Legacy*, eds. Stephen Donadio and Stephen Railton (Carbondale: Southern Illinois University Press, 1986): 66–83.

14. Hovde, "English and American Traits," 66.

15. Robert Weisbuch, *Atlantic Double-Cross: American Literature and British Influence in the Age of Emerson* (Chicago and London: University of Chicago, 1986), xii.

16. Emerson, *The Complete Works of Ralph Waldo Emerson*, ed. Edward Emerson, 12 vols. (Boston: Houghton Mifflin, 1903–1904), 5: 308; 1: 91. Further parenthetical citations to this edition are abbreviated as *W* and include volume and page number.

17. Philip Nicoloff, *Emerson on Race and History* (New York: Columbia University Press, 1961), 11–12. For a more recent rendition of this way of reading of *English Traits*, see Marek Paryż, "Beyond the Traveler's Testimony: Emerson's *English Traits* and the Construction of Postcolonial Counter-Discourse,"*ATQ* 20: 3 (September 2006): 565–90. Paryż reads *English Traits* within the context of postcolonial travel narrative, arguing that Emerson seeks "to work out [a] way of talking about England, the former colonizer, in order to construct a discourse about America" (566).

18. See Brenda Wineapple, *Hawthorne: A Life* (New York: Random House, 2004), 341–42.

19. Dana Phillips, "Nineteenth-Century Racial Thought and Whitman's 'Democratic Ethnology of the Future," *Nineteenth-Century Literature* 49: 3 (December 1994): 298.

20. As Anita Patterson points out, pamphleteers such as Allan Ramsey, writing in 1771, had praised Anglo-Saxon institutions as the pillars of an ideal community, supposing that "if ever God Almighty did concern himself about forming a government for mankind to live happily under, it was that which was established in England by our Saxon forefathers" (quoted in Patterson, *From Emerson to King*, 133). Indeed, in 1776, Thomas Jefferson described the impending revolution itself as an abolition of "feudal law" and a restitution of "the antient Saxon law [. . .] that happy system of our ancestors, the wisest and most perfect ever yet devised by the wit of man, as it stood before the 8th century." Quoted in Anita Haya Patterson, *From Emerson to King: Democracy, Race, and the Politics of Protest* (New York and Oxford: Oxford University Press, 1997), 134. For a more detailed discussion of Saxon ancient constitutionalism during the revolutionary period, see Reginald Horsman, *Race and Manifest Destiny* (Cambridge, MA: Harvard University Press, 1981).

21. H. D. Kitchell, "The Anglo-Saxon Element in English and American Society," *Wellman's Literary Miscellany*, February 1, 1850, 108.

22. George Bancroft, *History of the United States*, 10 vols. (Boston: Little, Brown & Co., 1834–74), 1: 366, 367.

23. Ralph Waldo Emerson, *The Later Lectures of Ralph Waldo Emerson, 1843–1871*, eds. Ronald A. Boscoe and Joel Myerson, 2 vols. (Athens and London: University of Georgia, 2001), 1: 11. Subsequent parenthetical references to this edition are cited as *LL*.

24. After the Civil War, Emerson rephrased his statement, omitting the sectionalist tenor: "I hope America will come to have its pride in being a nation of servants, and not of the served." Cf. Emerson's 1863 "The Fortune of the Republic," *W* 3: 541–42.

25. See George P. Marsh, *The Goths in New-England: A Discourse at the Anniversary of the Philomathesian Society of Middlebury College* (Middlebury, VT: J. Cobb., Jr., 1843), 14.

26. Marsh 13.

27. Lawrence Buell, *Emerson* (Cambridge, MA, and London: Harvard University Press, 2003), 264.

28. Emerson, *The Letters of Ralph Waldo Emerson*, ed. Ralph L. Rusk, 6 vols. (New York: Columbia University Press, 1939), 4: 332.

29. Thomas Babington Macaulay, *The History of England, From the Accession of James II* (Philadelphia: Porter and Coates, 1849), 1: 10. For an intriguing analysis of Macaulay's Whig bias in the *History* as a project in "reformist conservatism"—an argument with, I think, implications for his Saxonist bent in the first volume—see Bill Schwartz, "Philosophies of the Conservative Nation: Burke, Macaulay, Disraeli," *Journal of Historical Sociology* 12: 3 (September 1999): 183–217.

30. H. E. Garland, "England and the Slave Trade," *Western Journal and Civilian*, September 1854, 416.

31. John Mitchell Kemble, *The Saxons in England: A History of the English Commonwealth till the Period of the Norman Conquest* (London: Longman, Brown, Green, and Longmans, 1849), v.

32. George L. Craik and Charles MacFarlane, *The Pictorial History of England: Being a History of the People, as Well as a History of the Kingdom*, 4 vols. (London: Charles Knight & Co, 1841–44), 644. Charles Knight recorded in his autobiography that "Sir Henry Ellis, my old and valued friend, lent some aid [in *The Pictorial History*] to the literature of the Saxon period." See Charles Knight, *Passages from the Life of Charles Knight* (New York: G. P. Putnam & Sons, 1874), 379.

33. Robert Knox, *The Races of Men: A Philosophical Enquiry into the Influence of Race over the Destinies of Nations* (London: Henry Renshaw, 1850), v.

34. John Robertson, "Introductory Address, on Opening the Richmond Athenæum," *Southern Literary Messenger*, April 1852, 221.

35. William Archer Cocke, "The Puritan and the Cavalier," *De Bow's Review*, September 1861, 211.

36. "The Conflict of Northern and Southern Races," *De Bow's Review*, October–November 1861, 391.

37. William Falconer, "The Differences of Race Between the Northern and Southern People," *Southern Literary Messenger*, June 1860, 401–409.

38. George Fitzhugh, "Superiority of Southern Races—Review of Count De Gobineau's Work," *De Bow's Review*, October–November 1861, 375.

39. See "The Philosophy of Secession," *Southern Literary Messenger*, October 1862, 558.

40. See Richard Bonner, "Roundheaded Cavaliers? The Context and Limits of a Confederate Racial Project," *Civil War History* 48: 1 (2002): 34–59; and Ritchie Watson, "'The Difference of Race': Antebellum Race Mythology and the Development of Southern Nationalism," *Southern Literary Journal* 35: 1 (Fall 2002), 1–13. Indeed, Philip Guedalla briefly notes the emergence of Confederate nationalist racial theory in his 1936 volume: "Pursuing their researches, Southern genealogists detected a monopoly of Norman blood among themselves; and where Norman blood was present, it was pardonable to expect a Norman Conquest which might take the form either of a 'vast, opulent, happy and glorious slaveholding Republic throughout tropical America'" (86–87). Guedella's commentary seems to have escaped the notice of Bonner and Watson, whose investigations are in any case far more thoroughgoing. See Philip Guedalla, *The Hundred Years* (New York: Literary Guild, 1936). Lastly, William Taylor's classic intellectual history of the South prior to the Civil War, *Cavalier and Yankee*, acknowledges that sectional division prior to 1860 was often

considered "to be at least partly a matter of blood," though in Taylor's account, the most salient divisions marked differences of custom and culture. See William Taylor, *Cavalier and Yankee: The Old South and American National Character* (New York and Oxford: Oxford University Press, 1961), 15.

41. See "The Origin, and Political Life of the English Race," *Christian Review*, January 1850, 38.

42. Like other writers of the period, including Emerson, the author places the Normans as a race of "oppressors" while praising the Saxons for their democratic tendencies and supposing that these characteristics remain basically unchanged, since "The life of races outlives centuries of revolution, of progress and change" (37). Having relocated itself across the British Empire, "Not the wildest dreams of the poet could have anticipated the extend to which [the Saxon race] is now spread. . . . London is the financial centre of the civilized world, and if in the revolutions of time it shall cease to be so, where can this centre pass but to our own shores? Have all these endowments from the hand of God been given without an ulterior design? Surely he does nothing in vain. These capacities and endowments, of whatever kind, are held in trust for the world. One mission at least of this mighty race, is to be the teacher of all mankind in that political liberty whose enjoyment is restrained and protected by law" (52).

43. "The 'South-Side View of Slavery.'" *New Englander*, February 1855, 68; emphasis original.

44. "The New England Character," *Southern Literary Messenger*, July 1837, 413.

45. Reprinted as "The Puritan and the Cavalier," *Southern Cultivator*, March–April 1862, 53.

46. Ibid.

47. "Spence's American Union," *Blackwoods Edinburgh Magazine*, April 1862, 515–16.

48. Patterson, *From Emerson to King*, 126–27.

49. Gregg Crane, *Race, Citizenship, and Law in American Literature* (Cambridge: Cambridge University Press, 2002), 98.

50. Ian Finseth, "Evolution, Cosmopolitanism, and Emerson's Antislavery Politics," *American Literature* 77: 4 (December 2005): 730.

51. Though Robert Richardson characterizes Emerson's response to Chambers as mildly disdainful (Richardson deals with Chambers in one sentence: "Emerson read Chambers' *Vestiges of Creation* and disliked its theology" [395]), Nicoloff describes Emerson's "rather casual acceptance of virtually all the speculations which this 'scandal-rousing' book contained" (107). Similarly, Patterson describes Emerson as "deeply affected" by Chambers, "a work that set forth the general principle of ameliorative evolution" (144). See Robert Richardson, *Emerson: The Mind on Fire* (Berkeley: University of California, 1995).

52. Emerson, *W* 1: 40.

53. Cornel West, *The American Evasion of Philosophy: A Genealogy of American Pragmatism* (Madison: University of Wisconsin, 1989), 34. See also Peter Field, *Ralph Waldo Emerson: The Making of a Democratic Intellectual* (Lanham, MD: Rowan & Littlefield, 2002), 173–75; and Patterson, *From Emerson to King*, 141–47.

Chapter 2

1. Frederick Douglass, *The Frederick Douglass Papers, Series One: Speeches Debates, Interviews*, 5 vols., eds. John W. Blassingame and John R. McKivigan (New Haven, CT, and London: Yale University Press, 1979–92), 2: 70. Further references to this edition are cited parenthetically as *FD* and include volume and page numbers.

2. Francis Hargrave, *An Argument in the Case of James Sommersett, A Negro, Lately Determined by the King's Bench: Wherein it is attempted to demonstrate the present unlawfulness of domestic slavery in England* (London: W. Otridge, 1772), 26–27; emphasis original.

3. See Hargrave, *Argument*, 50: "The first case on the subject, is one mentioned in Mr. Rushworth's Historical Collections; and it is there said, that in the eleventh of Elizabeth, one Cartwright brought a slave from Russia, and would scourge him; for which he was questioned; and it was resolved, that England was too pure an air for a slave to breathe in."

4. Printed in "Massachusetts Legislature," *Liberator*, May 1, 1840, 1.

5. Synopses of this address were also published in "Meeting in Faneuil Hall—Tuesday Evening, May 30," *Liberator*, June 9, 1848, 91; and "New-England Anti-Slavery Convention," *North Star*, June 16, 1848, 2.

6. "Expatriation," *North Star*, December 22, 1848, 2; emphasis original.

7. Allen's address was published in *Frederick Douglass' Paper* (October 22, 1852), 1; emphasis original; as well as the *Liberator* (October 29, 1852), 176. For more on Allen's profile at New York Central College and subsequent emigration to England, see Benjamin Quarles, *Black Abolitionists* (Cambridge, MA: Da Capo Press, 1991), 138–39; and Philip Sheldon-Foner and Robert J. Branham, eds., *Lift Every Voice: African American Oratory, 1787–1900* (Tuscaloosa: University of Alabama Press, 1997), 229–30.

8. Harriet Beecher Stowe, "Chapter XIX: Topsy," *National Era*, November 6, 1851, 177.

9. Reprinted as "Southern Cavaliers vs Northern Puritans," *Douglass' Monthly*, July 1862, 680.

10. William Wells Brown, *The Black Man: His Antecedents, His Genius, and His Achievements* (New York: Thomas Hamilton, 1863), 34.

11. Lydia Maria Child, "The Black Saxons," *Liberty Bell*, January 1, 1841, 19–20. Further references are cited parenthetically in the text.

12. In her groundbreaking *Southscapes*, Thadious M. Davis examines a series of southern locales, including swamps, as spaces of "liminality and flux" that serve "an alternate way of enunciating and translating a productive space of alterity, otherness, and difference." See *Southscapes: Geographies of Race, Region, Literature* (Chapel Hill: University of North Carolina, 2011), 4.

13. Child, "Our Anglo-Saxon Ancestry," *Philanthropist*, December 8, 1841, 2.

14. See Sharon Turner, *The History of England During the Middle Ages* (London: Longman, Brown, Green, and Longmans, 1853), 124–25; Thomas Babington Macaulay, *The History of England from the Accession of James II* (Philadelphia: Porter & Coates, 1849), 1: 10–11.

15. Macaulay, *History of England*, 17.

16. Ibid., 10.

17. See Henry William Herbert, David Wright Judd, and Thomas Picton, *Life and Writings of Frank Forrester (Henry William Herbert)* (New York: Orange Judd Company, 1882), 51.

18. After the fifth episode of *The Saxon Serf*, published in the December 29 issue, the *Era* suddenly ceased serialization, apparently because Herbert had failed to supply a next installment of the developing manuscript. (The lapse resulted in a dispute between Herbert and the *Era*, much of which Bailey published.) Somehow or other the problem was worked through; with its October 12, 1854, issue, the *Era* began reserializing the novel under the title *Sherwood Forest*, starting again with a slightly revised first chapter, but this time reaching

completion of the novel with the April 12, 1855, issue. See "Mr. Herbert and His Story," *National Era*, May 4, 1854, 70; "To Our Readers," *National Era*, August 31, 1854, 138.

19. "New Books," *Albion*, December 15, 1855, 597.

20. "Literary Notices," *Godey's Lady's Book and Magazine*, January 1856, 86; "New Books," *Plough, the Loom, and the Anvil*, January 1856, 444.

21. "New Publications," *Evangelist*, November 1, 1855, 176; *Peterson's Magazine*, January 1856, 96.

22. "A Synopsis," *National Era*, January 4, 1855, 2.

23. Henry William Herbert, *Wager of Battle: A Tale of Saxon Slavery in Sherwood Forest* (New York: Mason Brothers, 1855), vi. Further references to this edition are cited parenthetically in the text.

24. For more on the *National Era*'s profile as an abolitionist publication in the 1850s, see Barbara Hochman, "*Uncle Tom's Cabin* in the *National Era*," *Book History* 7 (2004): 143–69.

25. I quote from Reginald Horsman, *Race and Manifest Destiny* (Cambridge, MA: Harvard University Press, 1981), 17, which includes a detailed discussion of American praise for Saxon ancient constitutionalism during the revolutionary period. For more on revolutionary-era interest in Saxon liberty, see Anita Patterson, *From Emerson to King: Democracy, Race, and the Politics of Protest* (Oxford: Oxford University Press, 1997), 133–34.

26. See Horsman, *Race and Manifest Destiny*, 9.

27. "The First of August," *Liberator*, August 6, 1841, 127.

28. "Speech of Wendell Phillips," *Liberator*, March 29, 1850, 51; emphasis original.

29. Theodore Parker, *Discourses of Slavery: The Collected Works of Theodore Parker*, 14 vols., ed. Frances Power Cobb (Whitefish, MT: Kessinger, 2004), 5: 62.

30. Much of Parker's account of Saxon liberties under the Norman regime resonates with a later account published in *Russell's* in 1859: "It had early been established, in favor of commerce, that if a villein escaped into a borough town, and remained a whole year, he was to be free, and the same privilege was allowed to a residence, for that length of time, upon any of the king's demesnes." See "Slavery in England," *Russell's Magazine*, April 1859, 25.

31. Parker, *Discourses of Slavery*, 5: 70. The passage was also extracted for the April 21, 1848 issue of the *North Star*. See "Selections from Parker's Letter on Slavery: Effects of Slavery on Law and Politics," *North Star*, April 21, 1848, 1.

32. For more on the subject of codification, see Charles M. Cook, *The American Codification Movement: A Study of Antebellum Legal Reform* (Westport, CT: Greenwood Press, 1981).

33. See John J. Crittenden and Chapman Coleman, *The Life of John J. Crittenden, with Selections from His Correspondence and Speeches*, 2 vols. (Philadelphia: J. B. Lippincott, 1873), 1: 377. Further references to this edition are cited parenthetically in the text.

34. Peleg Sprague, *Speeches and Addresses* (Boston: Phillips, Sampson and Company, 1858), 469.

35. Reprinted as "Refuge of Oppression" in *Liberator*, June 20, 1851, 1.

36. Reprinted in "Personal Liberty," *Liberator*, April 9, 1852, 58.

37. "No. 16—An Act Relating to the Writ of Habeas Corpus to Persons Claimed as Fugitive Slaves, and the Right of Trial by Jury," in *The Acts and Resolves Passed by the Legislature of the State of Vermont at the October Session, 1850* (Montpelier, VT: E. P. Walton and Sons, 1850), 9–10. The bill was also widely published in the popular press. See, for instance,

"Law for Slaves," *National Era*, December 19, 1850, 203; *Boston Evening Transcript*, December 19, 1850; *Richmond Whig*, December 27, 1850; *Richmond Enquirer*, April 1, 1851.

38. Writing in defense of the bill in the January 23, 1851, issue of the *National Era*, an anonymous Vermonter pointed out that "[i]f the Fugitive law suspends or nullifies the *habeas corpus*, it is itself a nullity, as conflicting with the Constitution. If, as is claimed by Mr. Attorney General Crittenden and other advocates of the fugitive law, the *habeas corpus* is not thereby suspended, then the Vermont act violates herein neither law nor Constitution." See "The Habeas Corpus in Vermont," *National Era*, January 23, 1851, 16. Moreover, a number of other state judiciaries offered decisions against the Fugitive Slave Law throughout the early 1850s. In Ohio, a state judge issued a writ of habeas corpus in order to release a suspected fugitive slave who had been arrested under the law, while the Wisconsin Supreme Court declared the fugitive slave law unconstitutional in an 1854 decision freeing Sherman M. Booth, a white abolitionist who had been imprisoned for assisting in the rescue of an accused fugitive slave. For useful overviews of the Vermont Personal Liberty Bill of 1850 as well as other state-passed remedies for the fugitive slave law, see Norman L. Rosenberg, "Personal Liberty Laws and Sectional Crisis: 1850–1861" in *Abolitionism and American Law*, ed. John R. McKivigan (New York and London: Garland, 1999), 321–40; and Horace K. Houston, Jr., "Another Nullification Crisis: Vermont's 1850 Habeas Corpus Law," *New England Quarterly* 77: 2 (June 2004), 252–77.

39. For more on Higginson's role—in coordination with Parker and other members of the Boston Vigilance Committee—in fomenting the riot, see Harold Schwartz, "Fugitive Days in Boston, *New England Quarterly* 27: 2 (June 1954), 204.

40. See "Appendix M: Speech of Theodore Parker at the Faneuil Hall Meeting," in Charles Emery Stevens, *Anthony Burns: A History* (Boston: John P. Jewett and Company, 1856), 291–92.

41. Eden B. Foster, *The Rights of the Pulpit, and Perils of Freedom. Two Discourses Preached in Lowell, Sunday, June 2nd, 1854* (Lowell, MA: J. J. Judkins, 1854), 9–10. For an extended treatment of Foster's sermon, see Albert von Frank, *The Trials of Anthony Burns: Freedom and Slavery in Emerson's Boston* (Cambridge, MA: Harvard University Press, 1998), 249–52.

42. *Congressional Globe*, 33rd Congress, 1st Session, 1515.

43. Ibid., 1517.

44. On *North Carolina v. Mann*, see Helen Tunnicliff Catterall, *Judicial Cases Concerning American Slavery and the Negro*, 5 vols. (New York: Octagon, 1968), 2: 2.

45. *Congressional Globe*, Appendix, 33rd Congress, 1st Session, 1015; emphasis original. Sumner's speech was also published in the *National Era* under the title "Fugitive Slave Bill" (July 6, 1854, 106).

46. See *Congressional Globe*, Appendix, 33rd Congress, 2nd Session, 211.

47. See "The Intentions of the Free States," *National Era*, March 15, 1855, 41, 41.

48. *Congressional Globe*, Appendix, 33rd Congress, 2nd Session, 246.

49. Also see "Sherwood Forest," *National Era*, March 8, 1855, 37. Subsequent references to *Wager of Battle* are cited as *Wager* and include parallel passages in the *National Era*, cited as *NE*.

50. Sumner, "The Demands of Freedom," *National Era*, March 8, 1855, 40; also *Congressional Globe*, Appendix, 33rd Congress, 2nd Session, 246.

51. Sumner, "The Demands of Freedom," *National Era*, March 8, 1855, 40; also *Congressional Globe*, Appendix, 33rd Congress, 2nd Session, 245. Sumner's delivery of the speech in

Congress during the evening of February 23 is also described in Charles Sumner, *Recent Speeches and Addresses* (Boston: Ticknor and Fields, 1856), 450.

Chapter 3

1. *War Poetry of the South*, ed. William Gilmore Simms (New York: Richardson and Company, 1867), v, 21–22.

2. Henry Herbert, *Wager of Battle: A Tale of Saxon Slavery in Sherwood Forest* (New York: Mason Brothers, 1855), 161.

3. Ralph Waldo Emerson, *The Collected Works of Ralph Waldo Emerson*, 10 vols., eds. Joseph Slater, Douglas Emery Wilson, et al. (Cambridge, MA, and London: Harvard University Press, 1971–2013), 5: 18. Further references to this edition are cited parenthetically as *CW* and include volume and page number.

4. John Locke, *Two Treatises of Government*, 5th ed. (London: A. Bettesworth, J. Pemberton, and E. Symon, 1728): 170–71, 167; emphasis original.

5. Brown's composed vistas swept aside the neoclassical garden styles of the early eighteenth century in favor of an "improved" nature of rolling panoramas, curvaceous bodies of waters formed by invisible dams, strategically cleared dales, and meadows. Describing his "grammatical" conception of landscape to Hannah More in 1782, Brown had once gestured toward a view from Hampton Court to explain, "Now there . . . I make a comma, and there . . . where a more decided turn is proper, I make a colon; at another part, where an interruption is desirable to break the view, a parenthesis; now a full stop, and then I begin another subject." See Peter Willis, "Capability Brown in Northumberland," *Garden History* 9: 2 (Autumn 1981): 158. As John Dixon Hunt explains, Brown's success was to efface the evidence of his manipulation of landscape, remaking nature through "judicious manipulation of its components, adding a tree here or a concealed head of water there. His art attended to the formal potential of ground, water, trees and so gave to English landscape its ideal forms, *la belle nature anglaise*. The difficulty was that less capable imitators and less sophisticated spectators did not see nature perfected . . .; they saw simply what they took to be nature." See John Dixon Hunt, *Gardens and the Picturesque: Studies in the History of Landscape Architecture* (Cambridge, MA: Massachusetts Institute of Technology, 1992), 42–44.

6. William Gilpin, *Three Essays on Picturesque Beauty* (London: R. Blamire, 1792), 8; emphasis original.

7. Ibid., 28; emphasis original.

8. Ibid., 8; emphasis original.

9. Ibid., 57.

10. Uvedale Price, *Essays on the Picturesque*, 3 vols. (1794; London: J. Mawman, 1810), 1: 10.

11. Price, *An Essay on the Picturesque: A New Edition*, 2 vols. (London: J. Robson, 1796), 1: 53.

12. Price, *Essays on the Picturesque*, 1150–51.

13. Indeed, one risk in speaking of "the picturesque school" is that of installing a more doctrinaire state of agreement among picturesque thinkers than the record will quite bear out. In her otherwise penetrating *Passions for Nature: Nineteenth-Century America's Aesthetics of Alienation* (Athens: University of Georgia Press, 2009), Rochelle Johnson sometimes errs in this direction—for instance, when she speaks of "practitioners of the

picturesque in Europe" for whom "ancient ruins were reassuring in that they signaled the immense strides of civilization" (72). In fact, ruins signaled a range of ideas for English picturesque thinkers and artists. Gilpin, for example, tended to speak of ruins as visual phenomena that helped impart roughness to a panorama, not only through their broken appearance but by virtue of being artificial objects in the midst of nature. See Gilpin, *Three Essays*, 28. For his part, Price considered ruins chiefly as a nexus of civilization and the natural world. See Price, *Essays*, 1: 18, 51–52, 199. For that matter, picturesque theorists were not equally strident in their condemnation of prior modes. Humphry Repton, for instance, while responsible for the widespread execution of Gilpinesque principles, was also an ardent defender of Capability Brown and the formal lawn. In the first pages of his 1795 *Sketches and Hints on Landscape Gardening*, Repton praised Brown for having "acquired, by degrees, the faculty of producing *effects*; partly from repeated trials, and partly from the experience of those to whose conversation and intimacy his genius has introduced him." See Humphry Repton, *The Landscape Gardening and Landscape Architecture of the Late Humphrey Repton, Esq.*, ed. J. C. Loudon (London: Longman, 1840), 30.

14. Emerson, *The Journals of Ralph Waldo Emerson*, 10 vols., ed. Edward Waldo Emerson (Boston and New York: Houghton Mifflin, 1909–14), 3: 5–6. Further references to Emerson's journals are cited parenthetically as *J* and include volume and page number.

15. Robert Weisbuch, "Post-Colonial Emerson and the Erasure of Europe," *The Cambridge Companion to Ralph Waldo Emerson*, eds. Joel Porte and Saundra Morris (Cambridge: Cambridge University Press, 1999), 193. For that matter, Weisbuch goes on to say that "Emerson could praise and particularize Europe only when he took his eye from the central and tyrannical notion of the idea of Europe in relation to an imitative America that, despite some bluster, agreed to its indebtedness by its inferiority." Emerson's aims while in Europe, Weisbuch claims, were oriented around "the crucial necessity to dignify the New World" (194).

16. Alfred von Frank, *An Emerson Chronology* (New York: G. K. Hall, 1994), 64.

17. *An Address Delivered on the Dedication of the Cemetery at Mount Auburn, September 24, 1831* (Boston: Joseph T. & Edwin Buckingham, 1831), 28.

18. Ibid., 17. For more on Mount Auburn Cemetery as a picturesque space, see Blanche M. G. Linden, *Silent City on a Hill: Picturesque Landscapes of Memory and Boston's Mount Auburn Cemetery* (Amherst: University of Massachusetts Press, 2007) and, especially, on Joseph Story's vision of the cemetery as a space of mourning, pp. 149–53.

19. See John Conron, *American Picturesque* (University Park: Pennsylvania State University Press, 2000), 14.

20. William Combe, *The Tour of Doctor Syntax in Search of the Picturesque* (London: Ackermann and Co., 1838), 6–7; emphasis original.

21. See Thomas Jefferson, *The Works of Thomas Jefferson*, 12 vols., ed. Paul Leicester Ford (New York and London: Knickerbocker Press, 1904), 3: 453.

22. Washington Irving, *History, Tales, and Sketches* (New York: Library of America, 1983), 797.

23. James Fenimore Cooper, *Gleanings in Europe: England* (Albany: State University Press of New York, 1982), 167.

24. "The Hudson River School," Hugill points out, "reflected the English love of gothic romantic landscapes" even at a time when English painters such as John Constable and William Turner "were moving rapidly toward the impressionistic style that later characterized

French landscape painting." See Peter J. Hugill, "English Landscape Tastes in the United States," *Geographical Review* 76: 4 (Oct 1986): 416, 413–14. Thomas Cole himself was born in Lancashire, and other prominent painters of the era, like Benjamin West and Samuel Morse, honed their technique in England. As John Conron has demonstrated, the spirit of eclecticism that pervaded American incorporation of English landscape aesthetics resulted in a broad embrace of the terms developed by theorists such as Gilpin, Price, and Repton, even to the extent that the terms over which they conducted decades of debate—the beautiful, the sublime, the picturesque—became blurred under the single term "picturesque," which itself expanded to a vanishing point. "During the 1830s" in America, he explains, "'beauty' comes to mean 'picturesque beauty' and 'sublimity,' 'picturesque sublimity'" (xvii). For more on the history of what Conron calls this "semiotic" blurring of categories, see Conron, *American Picturesque*, chapter 2.

25. A. J. Downing, *The Architecture of Country Houses; Including Cottages, Farm-Houses, and Villas* (1850; New York: D. Appleton, 1859), 268–69. For more on Downing's impact upon antebellum tastes, see Angela L. Miller, Janet C. Berlo, Bryan J. Wolf, and Jennifer L. Roberts, *American Encounters: Art, History, and Cultural Identity* (Upper Saddle River, NJ: Prentice Hall, 2008), 248–49. For more on Downing's associations between cottage architecture and republican morality, see Sarah Burns, *Pastoral Inventions: Rural Life in Nineteenth-Century American Art and Culture* (Philadelphia: Temple University Press, 1989), 80.

26. *Brook Farm: The Amusing and Memorable of American Country Life* (London: Wertheim, Macintosh, and Hunt, 1859).

27. Robert Conron's adept approach to the picturesqueness of *Walden* argues that Thoreau's presentation of nature, as well as his sense of rapt rejuvenation within it, extended from his study of Gilpin, who "presides over the conversion of Thoreau's journals from commonplace books to verbal sourcebooks" (*American Picturesque*, 291). In his own assessment of Thoreau's relationship with the picturesque, Lawrence Buell provides a rich sense of Thoreau's attraction to an aesthetic with which he was nevertheless impelled to tamper. "Thoreau," he well puts it, "manipulated picturesque cliché with gusto even as he put it under pressure" (410). Pointing out "the frequency with which the later Journal records aesthetic pleasure at points when the day or landscape seemed to organize itself as a composition: sunsets, distant views, vegetational patterns, and so on," Buell finds the trace of such composition, also, in Thoreau's "dual strategy of discovering wildness near home and stylizing the mundane, like the Irish ice harvesters." But at the same time, Thoreau's habit of transcending place would strike Robert Lowell (as someone who "liked and even wrote in this genre") as a "violation of an obvious decorum." See Lawrence Buell, *The Environmental Imagination: Thoreau, Nature Writing, and the Formation of American Culture* (Cambridge: Harvard University Press, 1995), 410, 412. Lastly, H. Daniel Peck argues that Thoreau's synergetic arrangements of the natural world place him in epistemological agreement with Gilpin and Ruskin. See "The Crosscurrents of *Walden*'s Pastoral," *New Essays on "Walden,"* ed. Robert F. Sayre (New York: Cambridge University Press, 1992), 73–94.

28. Henry W. Cleveland, William Backus, and Samuel D. Backus, *Villages and Farm Cottages: The Requirements of American Village Homes Considered and Suggested; With Designs for Such Houses of Moderate Cost* (New York: D. Appleton and Co., 1856), 38.

29. Gilpin, *Three Essays*, 44. Much of the desired effect in picturesque apprehension, of course, consisted in finding the right point of view. This is to say that English picturesque

theory was not only a complex apparatus for the practice of landscape architecture, but also a set of prescriptions on finding the best vantage from which to behold nature. Perhaps the best symbol for this criterion of the picturesque school was known as the Claude glass, a device manufactured to allow picturesque tourists to frame the natural vistas they encountered in their most pleasing—because picturesque—aspect. The handheld glass was a slightly concave, tinted mirror held so as to reflect the scene under consideration: that is, with the viewer facing *away* from the scene, peering instead into the somewhat distorted reflection in the mirror. Bending the scene along its elliptical contour, exaggerating distances and dulling contrasts, the Claude glass recomposed natural scenery for stationary viewing—framing the world, as it were, as if rendered in a painting—making nature suddenly and literally picturesque. By muting natural colors and contrasts otherwise more obviously discernable, the glass heightened the effects Gilpin and other picturesque theorists valued in the picturesque prospect: the projection of dramatic distance, the effacement of natural detail in favor of a unified whole. For more on the Claude glass, see Hunt, *Gardens and the Picturesque*, 174–79. As Hunt explains, the mirror "was the privileged metaphor of artistic representation, authorizing—according to one's emphasis—either accuracy of vision or the capture of the *belle nature*. To the picturesque tourist and amateur artist, it reflected the real world, yet also collected carefully chosen images within the oval or rectangular frame and colored them with its one, coordinating tint. It was both an objective, cognitive activity and a private, creative one, as the mirror's user turned his back upon the scene and withdrew into his own reflections" (178). It bears mentioning that Gilpin found the glass merely "novel" in his *Observations on Several Parts of Great Britain* (London, 1789), where he wrote, "The only picturesque glasses are those, which the artists call Claude Loraine glasses. They [. . .] give the objects of nature a soft, mellow tinge, like the colouring of that master. [. . .] In general, I am apt to believe, that the merit of this kind of modified vision consists chiefly in it's novelty; and that nature has given us a better apparatus, for viewing objects in a picturesque light, than any, the optician can furnish" (124–25).

30. Gilpin, *Observations* 47.

31. In her keen study *West of Emerson: The Design of Manifest Destiny* (Berkeley, Los Angeles, and London: University of California Press, 2003), Kris Fresonke argues that the attraction of the picturesque for antebellum Americans was in its apparent ideological friendliness to westward expansion. In the American reception of the picturesque travel narrative, Fresonke explains, "Lands imagined to be virgin . . . were simply waiting their picturesque destiny. It is otherwise difficult to account, in nineteenth-century exploration narratives, for the fashionableness of the picturesque—a literary mode that aims not high, but middle—unless we grasp how it flattered American destiny. . . . How else to narrate a landscape that welcomed its absorption into an empire than to describe in picturesque aesthetics its immemorial longing to do so? Such designs are sham judgments on the far West, and contain all the wonder and calamity of Jacksonian propaganda" (10). Thus the picturesque, Fresonke argues, was "an ideal tool for ordering discovery in America" (52).

32. Warren Burton, *The Scenery-Shower, with Word-Paintings of the Beautiful, the Picturesque, and the Grand in Nature* (Boston: Thurston, Tory, & Emerson, 1844), 10–13.

33. See Kenneth John Myers, "On the Cultural Construction of Landscape Experience: Contact to 1830" in *American Iconology: New Approaches to Nineteenth-Century Art and Literature*, ed. David C. Miller (New Haven, CT, and London: Yale University Press, 1993), 58–79.

34. Henry David Thoreau, *The Writings of Henry David Thoreau*, 20 vols. (Boston and New York: Houghton Mifflin and Company, 1906), 9: 370. For a more extensive treatments of Thoreau's engagement with Gilpin and the picturesque, see William D. Templeman, "Thoreau, Moralist of the Picturesque," *PMLA* 47: 3 (September 1932): 864–89; and Gordon V. Boudreau, "H. D. Thoreau, William Gilpin, and the Metaphysical Ground of the Picturesque," *American Literature* 45: 3 (November 1973): 357–69.

35. Thoreau, *Walden*, ed. Edward Hoagland (New York: Library of America, 1991). 231.

36. Thoreau, *Writings of Thoreau*, 6: 103.

37. In a most penetrating analysis, Maurice Lee demonstrates that Thoreau's ecological writings comprise a "statistical aesthetic" through which Thoreau surveys the natural world in a most literal sense, inferring and approximating that world on the basis of aggregate data. See chapter 5 of Maurice S. Lee, *Uncertain Chances: Science, Skepticism, and Belief in Nineteenth-Century American Literature* (Oxford: Oxford University Press, 2012). For Lee's sense of Thoreau's complicated reception of Gilpin, see 132.

38. Gilpin, *Observations on the Western Part of England, Relative Chiefly to Picturesque Beauty, To Which Are Added, A Few Remarks on the Picturesque Beauties of the Isle of Wight* (1798; London: T. Caldwell and W. Davies, 1808), 246.

39. Gilpin, *Three Essays*, 49.

40. Price, *An Essay* (1796), 1: 156.

41. Ibid., 1: 159.

42. Ibid.

43. Ibid., 286.

44. Repton, *Landscape Gardening*, 184.

45. All landscape architecture, Repton explained in *Observations on the Theory and Practice of Landscape Gardening* (published posthumously from various manuscripts in 1803) must accommodate the fact that the human eye apprehends more breadth than height in a single glance (since, as Repton illustrated through precise diagrams, the brow obstructs upward peripheral vision). From this circumstance Repton induces that the line of sight along which objects are beheld (that is, the axis of vision) must form the base of a right triangle whose adjacent axes (running from the foot to the summit of the beheld object, and—the triangle's hypotenuse—from that point to the spectator's eye) form an angle of approximately 30 degrees. See *Observations on the Theory and Practice of Landscape Gardening* in Repton, *Landscape Gardening*.

46. See Gilpin, *Three Essays*, 7: "A piece of Palladian architecture may be elegant in the last degree. The proportion of it's [sic] parts—the proportion of it's ornaments—and the symmetry of the whole, may be highly pleasing. But if we introduce it in a picture, it immediately becomes a formal object, and ceases to please. Should we wish to give it picturesque beauty, we must use the mallet, instead of the chissel: we must beat down one half of it, deface the other, and throw the mutilated members around in heaps."

47. After visiting the Ornithological Chambers on July 13, Emerson filled pages in his journal, now declaring, "I wished I had come only there. . . . The limits of the possible are enlarged, and the real is stranger than the imaginary" (*J* 3: 161–62). Continuing, Emerson records, "I saw black swans and white peacocks; the ibis; the sacred and the rosy; the flamingo, with a neck like a snake; the toucan rightly called *rhinoceros;* and a vulture whom to meet in the wilderness would make your flesh quiver, as like an executioner he looked." In still other rooms, Emerson notes, "I saw amber containing perfect mosquitoes, grand

blocks of quartz, native gold in all its forms of crystallization,—threads, plates, crystals, dust; and silver, black as from fire. Ah! Said I, this is philanthropy, wisdom, taste,—to form a cabinet of natural history" (*J* 3: 162–63). The variety of natural forms contained in the Jardin provoked Emerson to expound upon the "occult relation" connecting all objects and that *Nature* would render thematic. "Here we are impressed with the inexhaustible riches of nature," he wrote. "The universe is a more amazing puzzle than ever, as you glance along this bewildering series of animated forms,—the hazy butterflies, the carved shells, the birds, beasts, fishes, insects, snakes, and the upheaving principle of life everywhere incipient, in the very rock aping organized forms. Not a form so grotesque, so savage, nor so beautiful but is an expression of some property inherent in man the observer,—an occult relation between the very scorpions and man. I feel the centipede in me,—cayman, carp, eagle, and fox. I am moved by strange sympathies; I say continually, 'I will be a naturalist'" (*J* 3: 163).

48. In his masterly treatment of Emerson's visit to the Jardin, Lee Rust Brown argues that Emerson found there a model of classificatory unity answering his own needs as a composer of texts. The Jardin presented not simply nature—that "Not Me" Emerson makes the apparent subject of his first major essay—but also a mode of presentation and understanding as homologous with the organization of an Emerson essay as it also conveyed through cabinets and plant beds, nominal separations and groupings that may indicate (for some visitors to the museum of natural history) something of the quasi-divine. As Brown points out, taxonomy was akin to typology, for both Louis Agassiz and for Emerson, who felt himself "moved by strange sympathies" in the various chains of plant and animal being. In other words, the classificatory systems guiding Emerson in the Jardin and that Agassiz helped to develop were not experienced by either man as contingent or arbitrary human devices, even though Emerson for his part was completely capable of noting the extent to which divisions between races (and so, one would suppose, species as well) were always "drawn" imperfectly by investigators who were unable to "settle the true bounds" (*CW* 5: 24)—rather, they are incipient in the very forms of the natural world, suggested in the system of repetition and variation that is nature. See Lee Rust Brown, *The Emerson Museum: Practical Romanticism and the Pursuit of the Whole* (Cambridge, MA, and London: Harvard University Press, 1997), 58–59, 61–62. In some ways Brown is anticipated by Elizabeth A. Dant, who takes up Emerson's visit to the Jardin (which she describes, even two decades ago, as having "achieved the mythic inevitability of Newton and the apple") in order to examine "the assumptions underlying the construction of these ingenious scientific models," assumptions also "governing the enclosed world of Emerson's essays." See Elizabeth A. Dant, "Composing the World: Emerson and the Cabinet of Natural History," *Nineteenth-Century Literature* 44: 1 (June 1989): 18, 19. For a still prior treatment of Emerson's visit to the Jardin, and an early suggestion that his "experience at the Paris Museum is the clearest example" of "the contribution of pure science to the pattern of [Emerson's] development," and an instance that "culminat[ed] one phase of his thinking and initiat[ed] another," see David Robinson's "Emerson's Natural Theology and the Paris Naturalists: Toward a Theory of Animated Nature," *Journal of the History of Ideas* 41: 1 (January-March 1980): 69–88.

Like Brown, Laura Dassow Walls sees Emerson's visit to the Jardin as crucial for having presented him raw evidence of a massive, indeed all-encompassing, connectedness. The museum's importance was not to have "present[ed] him with the *idea* of nature's creative order, for that had long been familiar to him; rather, the Muséum gave him the *reality* of that idea, the complete chain, offering in material form the keystone that locked the arch of reasoning into place." See Laura Dassow Walls, *Emerson's Life in Science: The Culture of Truth* (Ithaca, NY and London: Cornell University Press), 13, 86. As Emerson's journal entry makes clear, the display of natural cabinets drove home an emphasis on taxonomy through resemblance between specimens. Robert Richardson makes the point in his own way as he explains, "Not only were the specimens in the exhibits linked to each other, they were also linked to him" (98), especially inasmuch as "[t]he central point, the pivot of Emerson's understanding of nature, is his conception of the all-encompassing relationship that exists at all times between the mind—understood as a more or less constant, classifying power—and the infinite variety of external nature." See Robert D. Richardson, Jr., "Emerson and Nature," *The Cambridge Companion to Ralph Waldo Emerson*, eds. Joel Porte and Saundra Morris (Cambridge: Cambridge University Press, 1999), 98, 102.

Recent work on Emerson's experience in the Jardin des Plants by readers such as Walls and Brown represents a departure from a venerable strain in Emerson scholarship that treats Emerson as a Manichean who was nevertheless driven to prove that the world exists. For this earlier era of Emerson scholarship, *Nature*'s chapter on "Idealism" defined the preeminent challenges of the essay, and anecdotes illustrating Emerson's habit of quipping whether the world was real rose to the status of definitive moments. So, Joel Porte would maintain that "Emerson was driven to accept the Ideal theory because he found sense experience distasteful, but not at all because he really believed that the world was an illusion." Rather, "[c]onvinced by temperament and training that the mind and the body, the spirit and nature, were not only separate but unequal, that the would was higher, finer, truer, than matter, he needed a theory, other than Christianity, that would bestow intellectual dignity upon these sentiments." Joel Porte, *Emerson and Thoreau: Transcendentalists in Conflict* (Middletown, CT: Wesleyan University Press, 1966), 53. For that matter, the earlier focus upon Emerson's equivocations between phenomena and noumena formed the prelude to Stanley Cavell's (spellbinding) work on Emerson, which after all treats Emerson as first of all wrestling with the challenge of philosophical skepticism, making him more properly the contemporary of Wittgenstein or Nietzsche than Agassiz or Audubon. The more recent focus upon Emerson's engagement with biological science, in other words, constitutes a large-scale reorientation of the field.

A similar shift against this idealist Emerson wrestling with skepticism is found in the reoriented current in Emersonian scholarship dealing with vision and optics. The postwar generation of Emerson scholars treated Emersonian optics as if linked to what Sherman Paul called Emerson's primary concern with "the relation of spirit and matter," or "the relation of man to the universe," the "need to see the universe as friendly, beneficent, lawful, and related," a set of problems Paul finds resolved in Emerson's definition of "the problem of insight in terms of the alignment of the axis of vision with the axis of things." See Sherman Paul, *Emerson's Angle of Vision* (Cambridge, MA: Harvard University Press, 1952): 1, 2, 71. F. O. Matthiessen's own focus upon Emerson's "almost exclusive absorption with seeing," and Emerson's various optative moods, for that matter, pitched *American Renaissance*'s casting of Emerson as if driven by a desire to "dispel the fogs of the romantic cultivation of the ego." See F. O. Matthiessen, *American Renaissance: Art and Expression in the Age of Emerson and Melville* (London and New York: Oxford University Press, 1941), 9. In *Emerson and the Orphic Poet in America* (Berkeley: University of California, 1978), R. A. Yoder speaks of *Nature* as a grafting of "the energy of vision onto a stable framework" (99). In *Spires of*

Form: A Study of Emerson's Aesthetic Theory (New York: Russell & Russell, 1965), Vivian Hopkins underwrote the "philosophical belief in the correspondence existing between man and external nature" with Emerson's detection of "a natural connection between light and the structure of the eye" (163). But more recently, optics has become for Emersonian scholars the touchstone of Emerson's engagement with the world rather than evidence of his need to bring the world into correspondence with abstractions. Christopher Windolph's *Emerson's Nonlinear Nature* (Columbia: University of Missouri Press, 2007) argues that the "transparency" of Emerson's transparent eyeball obtains only at moments of active or shifting focus—that what *Nature* presents, in other words, is a rendition of reason centered on the *process* of reasoning rather than the results. Similarly, in *Emerson's Pragmatic Vision: The Dance of the Eye* (University Park: Pennsylvania State University Press, 1993), David Jacobsen points out that "*to do*, in Emerson, primarily means to see, to make visible" (37). Carolyn Blinder, indeed, finds this absorption in the visual so definitive as to make Emerson America's first theorist of photography. Blinder finds in "Emerson's dictum that 'The act of seeing and the thing seen, the seer and the spectacle [. . .] are one,'" evidence that "the transcendental ethos is aligned with the camera's ability to capture the real and the spiritual, the native and the universal simultaneously." See Carolyn Blinder, "'The Transparent Eyeball: On Emerson and Walker Evans," *Mosaic* 37: 4 (2004): 139–63.

For the best-articulated argument that Emersonian transcendentalism constitutes a form of political quietism, see John Carlos Rowe, *At Emerson's Tomb: The Politics of Classic American Literature* (New York: Columbia University Press, 1996); for a full-throated reply, see Len Gougeon, "'Fortune of the Republic': Emerson, Lincoln, and Transcendental Warfare," *ESQ* 45: 3–4 (1999): 259–324. Gougeon's *Virtue's Hero: Emerson, Antislavery, and Reform* (Athens and London: University of Georgia Press, 1990) painstakingly describes Emerson as an active social reformer who "fired the artillery of sympathy, emotion, and idealism, in the hope of precipitating a cultural revolution that would have the effect of elevating the civilization of America to a higher moral plane" (337). For the further argument that Emersonian thought is implicitly racist, see Anita Haya Patterson, *From Emerson to King: Democracy, Race, and the Politics of Protest* (New York and Oxford: Oxford University Press, 1997), especially pp. 131–32; for opposing argument, see my chapter 1, earlier in this volume; Ian Finseth, "Evolution, Cosmopolitanism, and Emerson's Antislavery Politics," *American Literature* 77: 4 (December 2005): 729–60; or Susan Castillo, "'The Best of Nations'? Race and Imperial Destinies in Emerson's *English Traits*," *Yearbook of English Studies* 34 (2004): 100–11.

49. "Village and Farm Cottages," *North American Review* 84: 174 (January 1857): 173.

50. Ibid., 172.

51. Quoted in "Slavery and Freedom: Mr. Seward's Speech on the Compromise Bill," *Liberator* (July 19, 1850): 116.

52. "The Churches North and South in Their Relation to the Union of the States," *Christian Review* 15: 60 (April 1, 1850), 276.

53. Ibid., 275.

54. Ibid., 274.

55. Hawthorne, "Chiefly About War-Matters," *Atlantic Monthly* 10: 57 (July 1862): 49–50, 53.

56. "The Battle of Antietam," *Harper's Weekly* (October 18, 1862): 663; "Brady's Photographs: Pictures of the Dead at Antietam," *New York Times*, October 20, 1862, 5.

57. Much work has been undertaken by Americanist scholars of Civil War photography. Since William Frassanito demonstrated that many of these documentary images were manipulated, much of this scholarship has insisted that the images press upon their viewer a set of epistemological problems—for instance, in the antebellum photograph's implicit or explicit claims to authentic reportage alongside its commitment to a Unionist ideological encampment. See William Frassanito, *Gettysburg: A Journey in Time* (Gettysburg, PA: Thomas Publications, 1975), 187–92; Alan Trachtenberg, *Reading American Photographs: Images as History, Matthew Brady to Walker Evans* (New York: Noonday Press, 1989), 71–118; and Timothy Sweet, *Traces of War: Poetry, Photography, and the Crisis of the Union* (Baltimore: Johns Hopkins University Press, 1990), passim. In her incisive work, Franny Nudelman argues, "In light of the tradition of postmortem photography, viewers may not have been shocked to learn that photographers posed battlefield corpses." See Franny Nudelman, *John Brown's Body: Slavery, Violence, and the Culture of War* (Chapel Hill: University of North Carolina Press, 2004), 123. More recent historians of Civil War photography examine the extent to which such photographs perturbed antebellum conceptions of death. See, for example, chapter 6 of Mark S. Schantz, *Awaiting the Heavenly Country: The Civil War and America's Culture of Death* (Ithaca, NY: Cornell University Press, 2008), especially 184–96; and Drew Gilpin Faust, *This Republic of Suffering: Death and the American Civil War* (New York: Alfred Knopf, 2008), xvi–xvii.

Chapter 4

1. Austen's engagements with picturesque aesthetics and theory went well beyond Elizabeth Bennet's sally of wit on the vogue of triadic groupings. (Declining to join Darcy, Miss Bingley, and Mrs. Hurst on their walk at Netherfield Park, Elizabeth remarks, "The picturesque would be spoilt by a fourth.") See Jane Austen, *The Novels of Jane Austen*, 6 vols. (Oxford: Oxford University Press, 1966), 2: 53. For an assessment of Austen's transformation of the picturesque into a set of narrative principles, see chapter 2 of Peter Knox-Shaw, *Jane Austen and the Enlightenment* (Cambridge: Cambridge University Press, 2004), 73–107.

2. Gilpin, *Observations on the Western Part of England*, 328; emphasis original.

3. Gilpin, *Observations, on Several Parts of England, Particularly the Mountains and Lakes of Cumberland and Westmoreland, Relative Chiefly to Picturesque Beauty*, 3rd ed., 2 vols. (London: T. Caldwell and W. Davies, 1808), 2: 44.

4. Uvedale Price, *Essays on the Picturesque, as Compared with the Sublime and the Beautiful* (London: J. Mawman, 1810), 1: 63.

5. Ibid., 2: 367, 68.

6. Malcolm Andrews, *The Search For the Picturesque: Landscape, Aesthetics and Tourism in Britain, 1760–1800* (Stanford, CA: Stanford University Press, 1989), 59.

7. Gary Lee Harrison, *Wordsworth's Vagrant Muse: Poetry, Poverty, and Power* (Detroit, MI: Wayne State University Press, 1994), 62. Similarly, Wendy Bullion points out, "Implicated in the constructions of social and ethnic difference and deployed in the interest of maintaining the status quo," the aesthetic comprised "a powerful discourse, one that served to draw (and persistently redraw) boundaries between the haves and the have-nots." See Bullion, *Citizen-Spectator: Art, Illusion, and Visual Perception in Early National America* (Chapel Hill: University of North Carolina, 2011), 144.

8. For more on the picturesque as a conservative response to the problem of poverty, see John Barrell, *The Dark Side of Landscape: The Rural Poor in English Painting, 1730–1840* (Cambridge: Cambridge University Press, 1980); and Ann Bermingham, *Landscape and Ideology: The English Rustic Tradition, 1740–1860* (Berkeley and Los Angeles: University of California Press, 1989). For Bermingham, the picturesque landscape was "[a]n appropriately elegiac background for the laborer dispossessed by the agrarian revolution . . . whose preindustrialized character demodernized his plight and whose charms compensated him for it." At the same time, "[t]he pathos of such a landscape cut two ways. On the one hand, the picturesque landscape celebrated a way of life as that which had been, or was being, lost. On the other hand, the manifest desolation of the landscape could work as a justification for transforming it to a more efficient, vital one" (69).

9. John Barrell, *The Dark Side of the Landscape*, 1.

10. Harrison, *Wordsworth's Vagrant Muse*, 62. Writing in the inaugural issue of the *Atlantic* in 1857, Emerson recognized the tendency of picturesque "illusion" to sentimentalize poverty, even to an extent that shapes the consciousness of the impoverished themselves. "Bare and grim to tears is the lot of the children in the hovel I saw yesterday," he wrote, "yet not the less they hung it round with frippery romance, like children of the happiest fortune, and talked of 'the dear cottage where so many joyful hours had flown.' Well, this thatching of hovels is the custom of the country. . . . They see through Claude-Lorraines." Though the sentimentalizing of impoverishment is for Emerson a picturesque "stage effect" akin to the distorting views beheld in a Claude glass, he nevertheless asks, "And how dare anyone, if he could, pluck away the *coulisses*, stage effects, and ceremonies, by which they live? Too pathetic, too pitiable, is the region of affection, and its atmosphere always liable to *mirage*." See Emerson, "Illusions,"*Atlantic Monthly*, November 1857, 59–60.

11. See Sarah Burns, *Pastoral Inventions: Rural Life in Nineteenth-Century Art and Culture* (Philadelphia: Temple University Press, 1989), 77–89. Indeed, Burns quotes from Whittier's "The Panorama" (1856), which urges its reader to "Look once again! The moving canvas shows/A slave plantation's slovenly repose,/Where, in rude cabins rotting midst their weeds,/The human chattel eats, and sleeps, and breathes" (84).

12. Angela Miller, *The Empire of the Eye: Landscape Representation and American Cultural Politics, 1825–1875* (Ithaca, NY, and London: Cornell University Press, 1993), 233–38. Miller argues convincingly that landscape painters of the antebellum period were beset with the problem of formulating landscapes that could represent the entire nation in the face of increasing sectionalism—which is not to say that many were compelled to actually sojourn in the South. Instead, artists such as Cole, Church, and Alexander Wyant formed an iconology of sublimity (associated with Niagara, for example) in order to efface sectional division. When such painters chose southern subjects, they often chose "those that carried associations with the Revolution and the ensuing federal period: the Great Falls of the Potomac [. . .] linked to the nation's capital; the Pedee River in North and South Carolina, associated with the revolutionary hero Francis Marion; the Natural Bridge in Virginia [. . .]; and the Alleghany, Blue Ridge, and Cumberland mountains, crossed by the nation's first western emigrants" (234). So, while "Nature, a resource possessed, in theory, by all Americans, presented a solution to regional and later sectional disputes by offering a nonspecific and expansive symbol of nationalism," Nature "could also be enlisted in the shadow play of sectional loyalties being enacted before the

war," becoming "covertly politicized" (216). One of the rare art historians to deal with sectionalism, Miller nevertheless deals primarily with northern painters, examining for instance their reluctance to deal with southern subjects as itself an expression of their sectionalism.

13. See Joshua Shaw et al., *Picturesque Views of American Scenery* (Philadelphia: M. Carey & Son, 1821).

14. Rebecca Sokolitz, "Picturing the Plantation," in *Landscape of Slavery: The Plantation in American Art*, eds. Angela D. Mack and Stephen Hoffius (Charleston: University of South Carolina Press, 2008), 42–43. For a more thorough overview of plantation painting during the first half of the nineteenth century, see John Michael Vlach, *The Planter's Prospect: Privilege and Slavery in Plantation Paintings* (Chapel Hill and London: University of North Carolina, 2001).

15. Thomas Addison Richards, "The Landscape of the South," *Harper's New Monthly Magazine* 6: 36 (May 1853): 722.

16. Frank H. Alfriend, "A Southern Republic and a Northern Democracy," *Southern Literary Messenger* 37: 5 (May 1, 1863): 289.

17. William Harper, James Henry Hammond, William Gilmore Simms, and Thomas Roderick Dew, *The Pro-Slavery Argument; As Maintained by the Most Distinguished Writers of the Southern States, Containing the Several Essays, on the Subject* (Charleston, SC: Walker, Richards and Company, 1852), 254.

18. John Pendleton Kennedy, *Swallow Barn: or, Life in the Old Dominion*, 2 vols. (Philadelphia: Carey and Lea, 1832), iv. Forthcoming parenthetical citations of *Swallow Barn* will refer either to the first, 1832 edition or the revised, 1851 edition (New York: George P. Putnam, 1851).

19. Harriet Martineau, *Society in America*, 2 vols. (London: Saunders & Otley, 1837), 2: 305.

20. William Gilpin, *Three Essays on Picturesque Beauty* (London: R. Blamire, 1792), 57.

21. Ibid., 24.

22. Ibid; emphasis original.

23. Gilpin, *Observations, Relative to Chiefly to Picturesque Beauty, Made in the Year 1772, on Several Parts of England, Particularly the Mountains, and Lakes of Cumberland, and Westmoreland*, 3rd ed. (London: R. Blamire, 1792), 10–11.

24. Gilpin, *Three Essays on Picturesque Beauty*, 24.

25. Ibid., 58.

26. Price, *Essays on the Picturesque*, 1: 51–52.

27. In the 1851 version of the passage, Kennedy changed the phrase "an old steeple" to "the buttress of an old steeple."

28. John Conron, *American Picturesque* (University Park, PA: Pennsylvania State University Press, 2000), 77.

29. Ibid., 128–30.

30. See Price, *Essays on the Picturesque*, 1: 196–97: "The same distinctions which have been remarked in other objects, are equally observable in trees. The ugliest, are not those in which the branches, whether from nature or accident, make sudden angles, but such as are shapeless from having been long pressed by others, or from having been regularly stripped of their boughs before they are allowed to grow on. Trees that are torn by winds, or shattered by lightning, are deformed, and at first seem very strikingly so; and as the crudeness of such deformity is gradually softened by new boughs and foliage, they often

become in a high degree picturesque." Also see Price's note on 1: 375: "Among the various ill effects occasioned by the prevailing system of making the ground every where, and in all cases smooth and even, none is more lamented by the painter then that of covering up the picturesque roots of old trees, which seems to fasten upon the earth with their dragon claws. . . . The trunk then loses one of the most marked and striking parts of its character, and looks like an enormous post stuck into the ground."

31. Gilpin, *An Essay on Prints, Containing Remarks upon the Principles of Picturesque Beauty* (London: J. Robson, 1768), 2.

32. For a suggestive reading of the swamp as a zone of contact with "non-human forces" (341) and shifting barriers, both of which produce subjects capable of resistance, see Monique Allewaert, "Swamp Sublime: Ecologies of Resistance in the American Plantation Zone," *PMLA* 123: 2 (March 2008): 340–57. For more on the swamp as a challenge to Romantic iconography, see David C. Miller, *Dark Eden: The Swamp in Nineteenth-Century American Culture* (New York: Cambridge University Press, 1989). Miller examines the swamp phenomenologically, arguing that "the energy and intricacy of jungle vegetation," for instance, tended to "undermine [the] inherently moralizing conventions" of the "pastoral or instructive conventions" of "the Romantic approach to landscape" (4).

33. Jan Bakker sees in the journey through Goblin Swamp a "subtle criticism of plantation pastoral" with its "gothic inversion of the details of the traditional pastoral setting" resulting in a "good/bad dichotomy." Though the sequence is tinged with foreboding gloom, I would maintain that Bakker's emphasis upon individual words making up Kennedy's description of the swamp—"lurid shade," "chilling vapor," the "hoarse scream" of a hawk, for instance—extracts these elements from the lushness of the moment to which they contribute. It is a reading, in other words, that finds hideousness in detail not fully absorbed into panorama, much in the tradition of Gilpin's picturesque. See Jan Bakker, "Time and Timelessness in Images of the Old South: Pastoral in John Pendleton Kennedy's *Swallow Barn* and *Horse-Shoe Robinson*," *Tennessee Studies in Literature* 26 (1981), 79–80.

Chapter 5

1. Quoted in Andrew Whitmore Robertson, *The Language of Democracy: Political Rhetoric in the United States and Britain, 1790–1900* (Ithaca, NY: Cornell University Press, 1995), 84.

2. Political rhetorics of electricity in America have been well examined by Americanist cultural historians. In *A Most Amazing Scene of Wonders: Electricity and Enlightenment in Early America* (Cambridge, MA: Harvard University Press, 2006), James Delbourgo demonstrates that "[e]lectricity lent itself readily to political use because it provided a language of power through which to articulate the meaning of revolution" (132) while also tracing the extent to which such political rhetorics of electricity were grounded, as it were, in figurations of electricity that proliferated among evangelicals active in antebellum awakenings (133–34). In his treatment of Catherine Sedgwick's *The Linwoods* (1835), Jeffrey Insko finds such notions of "electrical politics" in Sedgwick's assumption that "liberty and equality pass like fire or currents of electricity from one body to another, linking together those who receive, conduct, and transmit its current" while also acknowledging that "the meanings ascribed to the electric chain in the 1830s, 1840s, and 1850s also have roots in the eighteenth century—especially in the period of the American and French revolutions—and the political valences

then attributed to the power of electricity." Jeffrey Insko, "Passing Current: Electricity, Magnetism, and Historical Transmission in *The Linwoods*," *ESQ* 56: 3 (2010): 298. In *Mesmerism, Monsters, and Machines: Science Fiction & the Cultures of Science in the Nineteenth Century* (Kent, OH: Kent State University Press, 2006), Martin Willis traces the extent to which discourses calling upon electricity as a medium for sympathetic identification drew upon scientific debates over whether electricity was an organic fluid—controversies not only over whether electrical charges animated the muscles of the body, but whether galvanism transmitted a kind of "*spiritus animus*" among all living things. As Willis shows, this question would preoccupy the romantic response to more materialist conceptions of the nature of electricity (71–72). Similarly, Paul Gilmore, "Romantic Electricity, Or the Materiality of Aesthetics," *American Literature* 76.3 (September 2004): 467–94, argues, "By the mid-eighteenth century, electricity functioned as a powerful metaphor of emotional connection, bodily excitement, and artistic power, connotations that were given further impetus as American romantics built on developments in electrical science and technology" (474). In Gilmore's account, "romantic electricity works counter to the nationalizing tendency—the idea of culture as creating or voicing a particularized national self," thus allowing antebellum Americans "to imagine aesthetics as a sensual experience of the individual body, embedded in specific social situations, that somehow leads to the individual's momentary suspension in a sense of a larger whole" (473). Also see Gilmore, "Aesthetic Power: Electric Words and the Example of Frederick Douglass," *American Transcendental Quarterly* 16.4 (2002): 291–311.

   3. Reprinted in "Deadly Assault on Charles Sumner," *National Era*, May 29, 1856, 86; *New York Observer and Chronicle*, May 29, 1856, 174.

   4. *Brooklyn Circular*, May 29, 1856, 74; "Deadly Assault on Charles Sumner," *National Era*, May 29, 1856, 86; *Littell's Living Age*, September 13, 1856, 704; "Fracas in the United States Senate," *Times* (London), June 7, 1856, 12.

   5. Quoted in Charles Sumner, *The Works of Charles Sumner*, 15 vols. (Cambridge, MA: Welch, Bigelow and Company, 1871), 277; emphasis original.

   6. John Mitchell in Trouble," *National Era*, October 1857, 563; "Gutta Percha Religion," *Liberator*, September 26, 1856, 158.

   7. As James Dawes relays in his own sketch of the Sumner assault, some accounts of the assault also highlighted the gold head of Brooks's cane, though mention of this detail appears far less frequently than that of the cane's gutta-percha construction. See James Dawes, *The Language of War: Literature and Culture in the U.S. from the Civil War Through World War II* (Cambridge, MA: Harvard University Press, 2002), 5.

   8. William Dowe, "The Sea-Serpents: A Romance of the Ocean-Soundings," *Graham's American Monthly Magazine of Art, Literature, and Fashion*, September 1855, 239–40. Ralph Waldo Emerson, *The Collected Works of Ralph Waldo Emerson*, 10 vols., eds. Joseph Slater, Douglas Emory Wilson, et al. (Cambridge, MA, and London: Harvard University Press, 1971–2013), 7: 81. Further references to this edition are cited parenthetically as *CW* and include volume and page number.

   9. "Gutta Percha," *New York Daily Times*, June 16, 1853, 4.

   10. Dawes, *Language of War*, 5.

   11. The *London Anti-Slavery Reporter* documented the presentation of both canes while also relaying a series of public resolutions made in southern towns implicitly connecting the assault to a form of argument or eloquence. See "Preston S. Brooks," *Anti-Slavery Reporter and Aborigine's Friend*, November 1, 1856, 262–63.

   12. Ibid., 262.

13. Ralph Waldo Emerson, "Eloquence," *Atlantic Monthly*, September 1858, 386. Further references to this version of "Eloquence" are cited parenthetically in the text as *E*.

14. Emerson continues: "The Scandinavians in her race still hear in every age the murmurs of their mother, the ocean; the Briton in the blood hugs the homestead still" (*CW* 5: 28).

15. Ralph Waldo Emerson, *The Complete Works of Ralph Waldo Emerson*, 12 vols., ed. Edward Waldo Emerson (Boston: Houghton Mifflin, 1903–1904), 11: 248.

16. Emerson's 1847 lecture notes for "Eloquence" are housed with the Ralph Waldo Emerson Memorial Association deposit, Houghton Library, Harvard University (bMS Am 1280.199 [11]). Not to be reproduced in whole or in part without permission. See also Ralph Waldo Emerson, "Orator" in *Complete Works*, 9: 291.

17. *Congressional Globe* (Appendix), 34th Congress, 1st Session, 343. Further references to *Congressional Globe* are cited parenthetically in the text as *CG* and include Congress, session, and page number. References to the *Congressional Globe Appendix* are cited as *CGA*. A number of historians make the case that Sumner mocked a speech defect of Butler's through his references to the "loose expectoration" of Butler's speech. See, for instance, Williamjames Hull Hoffer, who suggests that Sumner's remarks were "likely a veiled reference to the fact that Butler had developed a speech impediment, possibly from a mild stroke"; as well as T. Lloyd Benson, who states that Sumner lampooned "the South Carolinian's deformed lip and speech impediment." See Williamjames Hull Hoffer, *The Caning of Charles Sumner: Honor, Idealism, and the Origins of the Civil War* (Baltimore: Johns Hopkins University Press, 2010), 58; T. Lloyd Benson, *The Caning of Senator Sumner* (Toronto: Thomson Wadsworth, 2004), 116; and also Mark S. Weiner, *Black Trials: Citizenship from the Beginnings of Slavery to the End of Caste* (New York: Random House, 2004), 226.

18. Robert Connors, *Composition-Rhetoric: Backgrounds, Theory, & Pedagogy* (Pittsburgh, PA: University of Pittsburgh, 1997): 45–46.

19. Much more in concert with that enthusiasm was Emerson's initial response to the cable's activation, recorded in his poem "The Adirondacs," where Emerson describes the news of the first transmissions as "great news . . . the report/For which the world had waited, now firm fact,/Of the wire-cable laid beneath the sea,/And landed on our coast, and pulsating/With ductile fire." See *Complete Works* 9: 191.

20. The image was reprinted in altered form eight years later on the front page of *Harper's Weekly*, apropos of the completion of the Atlantic Cable. See *Harper's Weekly* 2: 85 (August 14, 1858): 513.

21. See "The Atlantic Telegraph: Messages of the Queen and President Buchanan," *John Bull and Britannia*, August 22, 1858, 544.

22. "Completion of the Atlantic Telegraph," *Englishwoman's Review*, August 7, 1858, 50.

23. "The Great Atlantic Telegraph," *John Bull and Britannia*, July 27, 1857, 474.

24. *Times* (London), August 26, 1858, 8.

25. Frederick Townsend, *Ghostly Colloquies* (New York: D. Appleton & Co., 1857), 5–11.

26. "Mr. Beecher on the Atlantic Telegraph," *Independent*, August 19, 1858, 2.

27. Ibid.

28. "Eloquence," 385.

29. Christopher Cranch, "An Evening with the Telegraph Wires," *Atlantic Monthly*, September 1858, 490. Further references are cited in the text as *ETW*.

30. See Robert Luther Thompson, *Wiring a Continent: The History of the Telegraph Industry in the United States, 1932–1866* (Princeton, NJ: Princeton University Press, 1947); and Daniel Czitrom, *Media and the American Mind: From Morse to McLuhan* (Chapel Hill: University of North Carolina Press, 1982). Paul Gilmore suggests that the extreme veneration of the telegraph in the United States was underwritten by "an unequivocal racial logic" entailed in the popular notion that telegraphy would unite disparate sections of the nation into a singular body. See Paul Gilmore, "The Telegraph in Black and White," *ELH* 69 (2002): 805–833.

31. "The Anglo-Saxon Twins, Connected by the Atlantic Telegraph," *Punch*, August 14, 1858, 72.

32. Ibid.

33. "The Song of the Telegraph," *Liberator*, January 28, 1853, 16.

34. Ibid.

35. Ibid.

36. Mr. Yerrinton, "Speech of Wendell Phillips, Esq.," *Liberator*, January 30, 1857, 18. Further references are cited in the text as *WP*.

37. Henry David Thoreau, *Walden: An Annotated Edition*, ed. Walter Harding (Boston: Houghton Mifflin Harcourt, 1995), 49.

38. Ibid., 425.

39. For a penetrating reading of such unsettling epistemological effects of telegraphy, see Gilmore, "The Telegraph in Black and White," 810–13.

40. "The International Telegraph," *Saturday Evening Post*, August 1, 1857, 2.

41. *The Examiner*, August 2, 1856, 482.

42. See Butler, *Congressional Globe* (Appendix), 34th Congress, 1st Session, 630: "What is the meaning of the provision of the Constitution, which says that a Senator, or a member of the House, for any speech or debate in either House, shall not be questioned in any other place? Does it not mean to give the Congress of the United States the power of deciding what is privilege without the courts deciding it? If so, it goes far beyond the settled doctrine in Great Britain at this day, which was maintained by Chief Justice Denman, in the case of Stackdale *vs.* Hansard; and that case has much to do with the matter now under consideration. Hansard had undertaken, under the authority of Parliament, to publish a book which contained a libel. Without such license or privilege, all agreed that he was responsible. The English House of Commons said that having granted him the license, it was their privilege. Chief Justice Denman took cognizance of the case, on the broad ground that the courts could determine what was privilege under the laws of England. He said: '[. . .] Can it be maintained . . . that the House of Commons, by claiming a privilege, shall thereby appropriate it to themselves, and screen a villain from the consequences of his libel?'"

43. A number of commentators have focused upon the interplay between speech and writing in the formation of democratic eloquence in American colonial and early republican public discourse. In *Eloquence Is Power: Oratory and Performance in Early America* (Chapel Hill and London: University of North Carolina, 2000), Sandra Gustafson demonstrates that extemporaneous speech and the written word subsisted in complex interplay beginning with the witch trials in Salem and through the eighteenth century, when "[p]reachers and political orators signified unmediated access to truth in extemporaneous

speeches, or they dramatized the stability of their spiritual or political intent by reading from a manuscript or referring to foundational documents" (xvii). The rhetorical theorization that resulted from this interplay, Gustafson argues, resulted in "a complex system of meaning . . . that understood the oral and textual bodies of language, not as fixed categories, but as figures for competing constructions of the social body" (xvi). Gustafson's account is meant as a corrective to teleological accounts of the history of language representing written political discourse as merely displacing "primitive" oral traditions, thus obscuring this more dynamic relationship between the spoken and the written determining not only American semiotic myths over the role of the word in democracy, but also pressuring the gendered and racial social body. The teleological view, for Gustafson, too often positions the white male communicator as the exponent of protestant written knowledge without acknowledging the extent to which the early republic privileged extemporaneous eloquence as the acme of novel, generative language. See also Christopher Looby, *Voicing America: Language, Literary Form, and the Origins of the United States* (Chicago: University of Chicago Press, 1996), and Jay Fliegelman, *Declaring Independence: Jefferson, Natural Language, and the Culture of Performance* (Stanford, CA: Stanford University Press, 1996), both of which examine the oratorical voice in the early republic as "the instrument and embodiment of a new Anglo-American republican authority" (Fliegelman, *Declaring Independence*, 35), bound to "the illusion that spoken language was the medium of unconstrained willful subjectivity, an instrument wholly subservient to the intentional expressive control of the speaker," but also the concession "that subjectivity, agency, and intentionality were in some measure the controlled effects of a prior impersonal linguistic system" (Looby, *Voicing America*, 26).

44. Though Burlingame presented the Massachusetts resolutions to the House on June 10, they appear reprinted in *Congressional Globe* as put before the Senate on June 11. The resolutions passed the Massachusetts House of Representatives on May 29 and declare Brooks's assault "a gross breach of parliamentary privilege—a ruthless attack upon the liberty of speech—an outrage of the decencies of civilized life, and an indignity to the Commonwealth of Massachusetts." See *Congressional Globe*, 34th Congress, 1st Session, 1386. The same session of Congress to resolve the Sumner investigation witnessed another case of Congressional assault when Fayette McMullin of Virginia attacked Amos P. Granger of New York while the two debated policy during their commute toward the Capitol. Like Brooks, McMullin declared his attack to be a response to the impolite spoken words of his (northern) victim, but as the offending phrases were spoken directly to McMullin outside the Capitol, the case was never construed as involving issues of free speech. See *Congressional Globe*, 34th Congress, 2nd session, 33–34, as well as coverage in "Disgraceful Assault on Mr. Granger by McMullen [*sic*] of Virginia," *New York Times*, August 19, 1856, 1.

45. *Southern Literary Messenger*, September 1, 1857, 236.

46. Ibid., 237.

47. Ibid.

48. Meredith L. McGill argues that deliberations in Congress over international copyright during the 1830s and '40s intensified tensions over federal power, since the 1790 statute (eventually nullified in 1891) framed international copyright in terms of a negative freedom: Congress, in other words, was forbidden to pass laws restricting any American's ability to import and sell foreign works. Thus the 1790 statute, which limited the right to literary piracy to American citizens, "allows for political difference alongside cultural continuity" (81) but

also forced domestic authors to compete with inexpensive and market-proven reprints of successful English books" (83). See McGill, *American Literature and the Culture of Reprinting, 1834–1853* (Philadelphia: University of Pennsylvania Press, 2003).

49. Extract published in "Deadly Assault on Charles Sumner," *National Era*, May 29, 1856, 86.

50. Ibid.

51. Ibid.

Chapter 6

1. See "Speech of Hon. S. P. Chase," *Congressional Globe*, Appendix, 33rd Congress, 1st Session, 134.

2. Frederick Douglass, *The Frederick Douglass Papers, Series One: Speeches, Debates, Interviews*, 5 vols., eds. John W. Blassingame and John R. McKivigan (New Haven, CT, and London: Yale University Press, 1979–92), 3:167.

3. Amy Kaplan, "Left Alone with America: The Absence of Empire in the Study of American Culture," in *Cultures of United States Imperialism*, eds. Amy Kaplan and Donald Pease (Durham, NC: Duke University Press, 1993), 11.

4. Kaplan, "Left Alone with America," 4.

5. Donald Pease, "New Perspectives on U.S. Culture and Imperialism," in *Cultures of United States Imperialism*, 24.

6. Quoted in Kaplan, "Left Alone with America," 11–12. While developing around a myriad of topoi, antebellum New Americanist scholarship nevertheless cohered as a rejoinder to an earlier, triumphalist tradition of critical discourse while rejecting decisively Chase's view of American literary culture as benignly aloof to the machinations of European Empire. Following a model indicated by Richard Slotkin and Annette Kolodny, who discerned beneath the narratives of the myth and symbol school an "alternative primal scene" of "Indian removal, frontier violence, government theft, and devastation, class cruelty, racial brutality, and misogyny" (Pease, "New Perspectives," 25), New Americanists elaborated an anti-imperial set of critical practices intended similarly to supplant the apolitical accounts of the myth and symbol school. As Kaplan put it in her introduction to *Cultures*, the collection "takes for its subject . . . the multiple histories of continental and overseas expansion, conquest, conflict, and resistance which have shaped the cultures of the United States and the cultures of those it has dominated within and beyond its geopolitical boundaries" (4). Priscilla Wald describes her project in *Constituting Americans* (1995) around a similar impulse to scrutinize the transformation "of contestable geopolitical boundaries and plural ethnic and racial peoples into a community whose origins predates those contests," while in *Literary Culture and U.S. Imperialism* (2000), John Carlos Rowe, noting that "the geopolitical map of the United States changes dramatically in the 150 years framing this study," describes his aim "to give prominence to 'literary culture' as a constitutive force in U.S. imperialism." See Priscilla Wald, *Constituting Americans: Cultural Anxiety and Narrative Form* (Durham, NC: Duke University Press, 1995), 2; and John Carlos Rowe, *Literary Culture and U.S. Imperialism* (Oxford: Oxford University Press, 2000), 14, 15. In her 1998 presidential address to the American Studies Association, Janice Radway provided an overview of the "rich body of work" to follow Kaplan and Pease's *Cultures of United States Imperialism*, as a "turn to the question of American imperialism"

(7), what she described as a "work of reconceptualization [that] should be now placed at the heart of the field's agenda" and which the ASA "should itself seek ways to foster . . . through every means possible." See Janice Radway, "What's in a Name? Presidential Address to the American Studies Association, 20 November, 1998," *American Quarterly* 51: 1 (March 1999): 1–32.

The sheer magnitude of influence exercised by anti-imperial Americanist criticism of the antebellum period makes it impracticable to attempt anything like a full bibliography here. Some of the more signal book-length examples include Wai Chee Dimock, *Empire for Liberty: Melville and the Poetics of Individualism* (Princeton, NJ: Princeton University Press, 1991); Mary Louise Pratt, *Imperial Eyes: Travel Writing and Transculturation* (New York: Routledge, 1992); Angela Miller, *Empire of the Eye: Landscape Representations and American Cultural Politics, 1825–1875* (Ithaca, NY: Cornell University Press, 1993); Eric Wertheimer, *Imagined Empires: Incas, Aztecs, and the New World of American Literature, 1771–1876* (Cambridge: Cambridge University Press, 1999); Amy Kaplan, *The Anarchy of Empire in the Making of U.S. Culture* (Cambridge, MA: Harvard University Press, 2002); Davis Kananjian, *The Colonizing Trick: National Culture and Imperial Citizenship in Early America* (Minneapolis: University of Minnesota Press, 2003); Andy Doolen, *Fugitive Empire: Locating Early American Imperialism* (Minneapolis: University of Minnesota Press, 2005); and Eric J. Sundquist, *Empire and Slavery in American Literature, 1820–1865* (Jackson: University Press of Mississippi, 2006).

7. Michael Hardt and Antonio Negri, *Empire* (Cambridge, MA: Harvard University Press, 2000), xii.

8. Edward W. Said, *Culture and Imperialism* (New York: Vintage, 1994), 9.

9. Martin Brückner and Hsuan L. Hsu, "Introduction," in *American Literary Geographies: Spatial Practice and Cultural Production, 1500–1900*, eds. Martin Brückner and Hsuan L. Hsu (Newark: University of Delaware Press, 2007), 16. Carolyn Porter noted early on the ways in which emergent transnational critical models challenged some suppositions of the New Americanists in her assertion that a "radically enlarged context" for American Studies itself erodes the very nationalist paradigms Americanists since the late 1970s had been submitting to thick description. A "quite proper acknowledgment of the nation as the limit within which the 'new Americanists' have operated," Porter explains, "underscores simultaneously the limited capacities of any new Americanist studies that does not question the most fundamental assumption in both the old and the new field-imaginaries as described by Pease—that the nation itself is the basic unit of, and frame for, analysis." See Carolyn Porter, "What We Know That We Don't Know: Remapping American Literary Studies," *American Literary History* 6: 3 (Autumn 1994), 470.

10. John Carlos Rowe, "Culture, US Imperialism, and Globalization" in *Exceptional State: Contemporary U.S. Culture and the New Imperialism*, eds. Ashley Dawson and Malini Johar Schueller (Durham, NC: Duke University Press, 2007), 37.

11. Ibid.

12. Rowe, "Nineteenth-Century United States Literary Culture and Transnationality," *PMLA* 118: 1 (January 2008): 79; Paul Jay, "Beyond Discipline? Globalization and the Future of English," *PMLA* 116: 1 (January 2001): 39; Giles Gunn, "Introduction: Globalizing Literary Studies," *PMLA* 116: 1 (January 2001): 22. I read Rowe's disenchantment with the transnational turn in American Studies as an expression of umbrage at the ways the critique of globalization has diverged from his own recommendations for the field in 1998: "A common

purpose linking [differing] versions of American Studies should be the critical study of the circulation of 'America' as a commodity of new cultural imperialism and the ways in which local knowledges and arts have responded to such cultural importations—the study of what some have termed 'coca-colonization." See Rowe, "Post-nationalism, Globalism, and the New American Studies," *Cultural Critique* 40 (Autumn 1998): 17.

13. John Dewey, "Imperialism Is Easy," *New Republic*, March 23, 1927, 133.

14. Ibid.

15. Brückner and Hsuan, "Introduction," 14.

16. Thomas Peyser, *Utopia and Cosmopolis: Globalization in the Era of American Literary Realism* (Durham, NC: Duke University Press, 1998), 25.

17. Gretchen Murphy, *Hemispheric Imaginings: The Monroe Doctrine and Narratives of U.S. Empire* (Durham, NC: Duke University Press, 2005), 156. John Carlos Rowe operates from similar suspicions as he suggests that "[i]f we identify transnationalism only with postmodern forces of globalization or with resistances to them, such as creolization and hybridization, then we are likely to forget the roots of these postmodern economic and cultural practices in modernization" (79). See Rowe, "Nineteenth-Century United States Literary Culture and Transnationality," 79.

18. Henry Timrod, *Poems of Henry Timrod* (Richmond, VA: B. F. Johnson, 1901), 6–7. Further citations to this edition appear as *PHT*.

19. For Timrod's political stance during the nullification crisis, see Walter Brian Cisco, *Henry Timrod: A Biography* (Madison, NJ: Farleigh Dickinson University Press, 2004), 27–29.

20. Edgar Allan Poe, *The Complete Works of Edgar Allan Poe*, 10 vols., ed. Charles F. Richardson (New York: G. P. Putnam's Sons, 1902), 3: 183–84. Further references are cited parenthetically in the text as *CWP* and include volume and page number. In her fascinating examination of John Cleves Symmes, Hester Blum suggests that nineteenth-century arctic space constitutes a "verge" marking the limits of transnational modes of appropriation—whether imperial or globalist—zones toward which state-sponsored expeditions race but in which an absence of resources and people prompt reconsideration of the economic and geopolitical terms motivating conquest. Thus, "[t]he face of blankness seemingly presented to the world by the North and South Poles should not be perceived as metaphorical (as it has been, for example, in the baffling ending of Poe's *Narrative of Arthur Gordon Pym*) but as a geophysical given." See Hester Blum, "John Cleves Symmes and the Planetary Reach of Polar Exploration," *American Literature* 84: 2 (June 2012): 245–46, 248.

21. Indeed, this facet of Timrod's poem is in some ways definitive for Coleman Hutchison, who refers to the "agro-literary" agenda of Timrod's work, a joining of the Confederacy's aspirations as producer of two-thirds of the world's cotton supply with its legitimacy as a cultural entity. See Coleman Hutchison, *Apples and Ashes: Literature, Nationalism, and the Confederate States of America* (Athens and London: University of Georgia Press, 2012), 9.

22. Another clarification to add concerning my distinction between the expansionist and globalist models of nationhood I attach to the South during different stages of the antebellum period must acknowledge that global economics had long shaped U.S. deliberations over national territorial expansion, as of course global economics are always at issue in international disputes over territory. The "other" territorial conflict of the 1840s (for most current Americanists eclipsed by the annexation of Texas), between the United States

and Britain over the Oregon territory, relocates Anglo-American geopolitical economics to a transpacific space, with the American slogan "Fifty-four fifty or fight!" as well as British insistence upon an American border south of the Columbia River far less animated by abstractions over manifest destiny as by concerns over the solvency of the Hudson's Bay Company (on the British side) and access to the deep-water port of the Columbia River (on the U.S.). For an intriguing assessment of the Oregon dispute as well as the ramifications of its neglect in literary history, see Paul Giles, "Transnationalism and Classic American Literature," *PMLA* 118: 1 (2003): 62–77.

23. John C. Calhoun, "South Carolina Exposition and Protest," in *John C. Calhoun: Selected Writings and Speeches*, ed. H. Lee Creek, Jr. (Washington, DC: Regnery Publishing, 2003), 273–74.

24. Ibid., 274.

25. For more on the Calhoun's relations with the nullifiers of the Free Trade Association, see Robert Ellis, *The Union at Risk: Jacksonian Democracy, States' Rights, and the Nullification Crisis* (Oxford: Oxford University Press, 1987): 64–66.

26. On the passage of the compromise tariff and the Force Bill, see Ellis, *Union at Risk*, 158–77.

27. Quoted in Laura Amanda White, *Robert Barnwell Rhett: Father of Secession* (New York: American Historical Association, 1965), 27.

28. For more on Simms's nationalist views during the nullification crisis, see Sean R. Busick, *A Sober Desire for History: William Gilmore Simms as Historian* (Columbia: University of South Carolina Press, 2005), 12.

29. William Gilmore Simms, *Poems: Descriptive, Dramatic, Legendary, and Contemplative*, 2 vols. (Charleston, SC: John Russell, 1853), 1: 133. Further references are cited in the text as *WS* and include volume and page number.

30. "New Publications: Poems—by Henry Timrod," *New York Times*, February 22, 1860, 7. *The Knickerbocker* reiterated the praise of the *Times*, calling Timrod's *Poems* "a welcome offering to the common literature of the country." See "Poems by Henry Timrod," *Knickerbocker, or New York Monthly Magazine* 55: 3 (March 1860): 252.

31. "Ode on Occasion of the Meeting of the Southern Congress, by Henry Timrod," *Littell's Living Age* (March 30, 1861): 824.

32. See "William Gilmore Simms," *De Bow's Review* (May 1856): 606–607.

33. See "Atalantis. A Story of the Sea," *Philadelphia Album and Ladies Literary Portfolio* 6: 45 (November 17, 1832): 365–66; and "Southern Passages and Pictures," *Southern Literary Messenger* 17: 5 (May 1851): 289–96.

34. See "W. G. Simms," *Cincinnati Weekly Herald and Philanthropist* 10: 35 (May 13, 1846): 1.

35. Coleman Hutchison points out that "[s]outhern elites before, during, and after the Civil War were constantly considering the 'relative standing of nations.' They were anxious to 'catch up' and convinced that the war had finally . . . provided an opportunity to do so," a mindset that informed a sensibility of a "vanishing present" in much Civil War–era southern writing. See Hutchison, 7–8.

36. John Henry Hammond, Speech in U.S. Senate, *Congressional Globe*, 35th Congress, 1st Session, 961.

37. Alphonse Esquiros, "L'exposition universelle de 1862," *Revue des deux Mondes*, July–August 1862, 62.

38. For more on the London World's Exhibition, see John Hollingshead, *A Concise History of the International Exhibition of 1862: Its Rise and Progress, Its Building and Features and a Summary of All Former Exhibitions* (London: Printed for her Majesty's Commissioners, 1862).

39. Alfred Lord Tennyson, *Poems*, 2 vols. (Boston: James R. Osgood, 1872), 1: 499.

40. Ibid., 1: 500.

41. "Manchester Athenæum Soiree," *Times* (London), November 20, 1847, 8.

42. Ibid.

43. Robert Hunt, *Handbook to the Industrial Department of the International Exhibition* (London: Edward Stanford, 1862), 167. Further references are cited in the text as *H*.

44. "The Supply of Cotton," *Times* (London), August 14, 1862, 12.

45. Ibid.

46. "Southern Planters Convention," *Southern Cultivator*, May/June 1862, 104.

47. W. H. Chase, "The Secession of the Cotton States," *De Bow's Review*, January 1861, 93, 94; original emphasis.

48. "Keep Back the Cotton," *Charleston Mercury*, January 25, 1861, 1.

49. "Can Europe Do Without Our Cotton?" *Charleston Mercury*, October 3, 1861, 1.

50. Frederick Law Olmsted, *The Cotton Kingdom: A Traveller's Observations on Cotton and Slavery in the American Slave States*, 2 vols. (New York: Mason Brothers, 1861), 1: 5.

51. "The Resources of the South," *Southern Literary Messenger*, February/March 1862, 189.

52. *Congressional Globe*, 35th Congress, 1st Session, 961.

53. "Is England Anti-Slavery?" *Independent*, October 3, 1861, 4.

54. "The Reign of King Cotton," *Atlantic Monthly*, April 1861, 459–60.

55. Ibid., 460.

56. For a penetrating overview and analysis of American abolitionists' deference to English models of antislavery, see chapter 3 of Elisa Tamarkin, *Anglophilia: Deference, Devotion, and Antebellum America* (Chicago and London: University of Chicago Press, 2007), 178–246.

57. R. J. M. Blackett recounts Samuel Fielden's recollections of his childhood in the 1850s, when he acquired his political education by listening to former American slaves such as Henry "Box" Brown address the textile workers. As Blackett explains, "Textile workers' reactions to developments in the United States, Fielden insisted, were to a significant degree framed by the accounts that African Americans gave of their experiences as slaves and their encounters with racial discrimination. More importantly, these contacts, sustained over thirty years, provided a unique opportunity for wide-ranging discussion between the visitors and their hosts about the meaning and nature of oppression and about the best means to attain freedom." "Collectively," Blackett says, "these African Americans played a pivotal role in the effort to win popular support for the Union." See R. J. M. Blackett, "Pressure from Without: African Americans, British Public Opinion, and Civil War Diplomacy," in *The Union, the Confederacy, and the Atlantic Rim*, ed. Robert E. May (West Lafayette, IN: Purdue University Press, 1995), 70–71.

58. Resolution of the Reverend Charles Rattray, printed in "Frederick Douglass in Newcastle-Upon-Tyne," *Douglass' Monthly*, April 1860, 247.

59. See "King Cotton Bound; or, the Modern Prometheus," *Punch* (November 2, 1861): 176; and *Littell's Living Age* (December 14, 1861): 500.

60. "The Civil War in America," *Times* (London), May 22, 1861, 10.

61. "The Southern Confederacy," *Times* (London), May 22, 1861, 12.

62. "Lincoln," *Times* (London), January 19, 1863, 10.

63. Quoted in Blackett, "Pressure from Without," 74.

64. "British Sympathy with America," *American Theological Review*, July 1862, 492. Further references are cited parenthetically within the text.

65. "Anthony Trollope on America," *Continental Monthly*, February 1863, 309.

66. Ralph Waldo Emerson, *The Complete Works of Ralph Waldo Emerson*, 12 vols., ed. Edward Emerson (Boston: Houghton Mifflin, 1903–04), 11: 147, 125.

67. Ralph Waldo Emerson, *The Late Lectures of Ralph Waldo Emerson, 1843–1871*, 2 vols., eds. Ronald A. Bosco and Joel Myerson (Athens and London: University of Georgia Press, 2001), 2: 323. Further references to this edition will be cited parenthetically in the text as *LL* and include volume and page number. For another overview of Emerson's views of England during the war—including his anxiety that the South might issue its own emancipation proclamation so as to secure English support, and also detailing his conflict with Carlisle—see Len Gougeon, *Virtue's Hero: Emerson, Antislavery, and Reform* (Athens and London: University of Georgia Press, 1990), 289–310.

68. For more on the working conditions of Lancashire mill operatives, both adult and child, during the 1840s and '50s, see John K. Walton, *Lancashire: A Social History, 1558–1939* (Manchester: Manchester University Press, 1987), 174–80.

69. One would not want to overstate the liberalism of the Lancashire operatives, however. As P. F. Cark and John K. Walton document, several Liberal MPs who had supported the Union during the Civil War later lost their seats in a backlash expressing frustration with the economic hardship the blockade had inflicted upon the textile mills and their operatives. See P. F. Clark, *Lancashire and the New Liberalism* (Cambridge: Cambridge University Press, 1971), 45; and Walton, *Lancashire*, 257.

70. See "Voices of British Working Men" (*London Daily News*), reprinted in *Living Age*, February 14, 1863, 329.

71. Ibid., 330. In her landmark 1972 study of Lancashire attitudes toward the Civil War, Mary Ellison, pointing to pro-South editorials in newspapers published in the hardest hit areas of Lancashire during the cotton famine, argued that Lancastrian support for the Union was much softer than indicated by the 1862 Manchester Address—itself more of a carefully orchestrated simulation of popular sentiment than a spontaneous display of political conviction. See Ellison, *Support for Secession: Lancashire and the American Civil War* (Chicago: University of Chicago Press, 1972), 80–81. Ellison's depiction of the attitudes of Lancaster's working class are challenged, however, by R. J. M. Blackett, who points out that while the cotton famine "influence[d] the way textile workers saw the war," persuading many that "the solution to the crisis lay in recognition of the Confederacy and the reopening of the Cotton trade," many others "insisted that normalcy would only return when the United States was reunited." In Blackett's account, the Confederacy drew its English support primarily from the aristocracy, those who were angered by either the Trent affair or the Morris Act, some free traders, and those who were simply invested too heavily in the South to abandon it. See Blackett, *Divided Hearts: Britain and the American Civil War* (Baton Rouge: Louisiana State University Press, 2001), 172, 90–94.

72. Cobden's remarks were paraphrased in "Manchester Athenæum Soiree," *Times* (London), November 20, 1847, 8.

73. Richard Cobden to Charles Sumner, Dec 3, 1861, quoted in John Atkinson Hobson, *Richard Cobden: The International Man* (New York: Henry Holt, 1919), 350. For more on

Cobden's correspondence with Sumner and his hopes for free trade and pacifism, see Martin Ceadel, "Cobden and Peace," and Stephen Meardon, "Richard Cobden's American Quandary," both in *Rethinking Nineteenth-Century Liberalism: Richard Cobden Bicentenary Essays*, eds. Anthony Howe and Simon Morgan (Surrey, UK, and Burlington, VT: Ashgate, 2006), 189–207, 208–28.

74. Richard Cobden to Charles Sumner, November 27, 1861 (quoted in Hobson, *Richard Cobden*, 342).

75. Ralph Waldo Emerson, *The Collected Works of Ralph Waldo Emerson*, 10 vols., eds. Joseph Slater et al. (Cambridge and London: Harvard University Press, 1971–2013), 7: 44–45. Further references to this edition are cited parenthetically as *CW* and include volume and page number.

76. "The Cotton Kingdom," *Scottish Review*, April 1862, 100.

77. Goldwin Smith, "England and America," *Atlantic Monthly*, December 1864, 751–52. Further references to this text are cited parenthetically in the text as *GS*.

78. Abraham Lincoln, *Complete Works of Abraham Lincoln*, 12 vols., eds. John G. Nicholay and John Hay (1894; repr. New York: Francis D. Tandy, 1905), 8: 196.

79. See "The Cotton-Burners' Hymn" in *War Poetry of the South*, ed. William Gilmore Simms (New York: Richardson and Company, 1867), 349–51.

80. John R. Thompson, "England's Neutrality," *Southern Literary Messenger*, November/December 1863, 654. Thompson's poem would also be included in Simms's *War Poetry of the South*, 181–87.

81. Ibid.

82. On Britain's preparations for war with the United States during the *Trent* affair, see Ephraim Douglass Adams, *Great Britain and the American Civil War*, 2 vols. (London: Longmans, Green and Company, 1925), 1: 213; and Gordon H. Warren, *Fountain of Discontent: The Trent Affair and Freedom of the Seas* (Boston: Northeastern University Press, 1981), 132–33.

83. Thompson, "England's Neutrality," 655.

84. Hardt and Negri, *Empire*, 151.

Coda

1. See Peter Adams, *The Bowery Boys: Street Corner Radicals and the Politics of Rebellion* (Westport, CT: Praeger, 2005), xvi; and Sean Wilentz, *Chants Democratic: New York City & the Rise of the American Working Class, 1788–1850* (New York and Oxford: Oxford University Press, 1984), 300–301. While early Bowery b'hoys fashioned themselves as working-class dandies, by the 1850s their dominance of New York fire departments cemented the association. As Adams explains, fire companies in lower Manhattan over the course of the 1840s and '50s became "vehicle[s] for gang intimidation and power"—in fact, fire brigades run by rival factions of b'hoys occasionally brawled while responding to alarms (xvii).

The ramifications entailed in the imagery of Weingärtner's fire brigade become still more complex in light of other events that unfolded the evening of the September 1 celebrations, when approximately one thousand arsonists burned the Staten Island quarantine hospital. The presence of the hospital had been the subject of ire among Staten Island citizens (who claimed to have endured outbreaks of pestilence as well as economic decline since its opening), and it now appears that conspirators chose the evening of celebration, when many of Manhattan's fire brigades would be on parade, as an opportune moment to burn it down. Anna Hope, writing for the *National Era*, described a "torch-light procession of . . . firemen" in Manhattan as "a splendid affair," and of a piece with a very ether of multinational harmony, something like much of the imagery of Weingärt-ner's lithograph: "Flags of all nations floated on the breeze," she writes. "I have never witnessed so magnificent a celebration; nor indeed has there ever been its peer in this country. Its tendency was all peaceful; there was nothing warlike about it, except the mil-itary display." Hope's wonderment turns to horror, however, as she realizes that the glow on the deepening evening's horizon is not the electrical display promised by the mayor (who had passed resolutions through the city council providing for the lighting of Broad-way), but rather the flames of a burning Staten Island. See Anna Hope, "Letter from New York," *National Era* 12: 610 (September 9, 1858): 143. Other commentators in the months to follow covered this event—and the second arson of what remained standing after the first attack—in outrage, but the editorials grew more rancorous when it was revealed that the ringleader of the mob was himself chief of a Staten Island fire brigade. "An example like this," wrote the Boston *Flag of Our Union*, "of mob violence; so broad and glaring; so utterly reckless of consequences; so wasteful of property and destruction of innocent life; so evidently premeditated and planned by powerful and influential conspirators; so plainly encouraged by official sanction of local authorities; so boldly and unabashedly rejoiced over by its perpetrators; if not visited with a punishment as prompt and exem-plary as the crime was cowardly and cruel, will go far to destroy all respect for laws for the protection of property and life." See "Mob Law by Wholesale," *Flag of Our Union* (Octo-ber 2, 1858): 316.

2. David Dudley Field, "Reform in the Legal Profession and the Law: Address to the Graduating Class of the Albany Law School," March 23, 1855, in *Speeches, Arguments, and Miscellaneous Papers of David Dudley Field*, ed. A. P. Sprague (New York: D. Appleton and Co., 1884), 1: 516.

3. Stanley Cavell, *Philosophical Passages: Wittgenstein, Emerson, Austin, Derrida* (Oxford, UK: Blackwell, 1995), 13.

4. Joint Statement by President Roosevelt and Prime Minister Churchill (August 14, 1941), in U.S. Department of State, *Foreign Relations of the United States* 1 (1941): 368. For an examination of the Anglo-American context for the formulation of the charter as well as its position in relation to Roosevelt's declaration of the "four freedoms" in January 1941, see Glenn Tatsuya Mitoma, "Civil Society and Human Rights: The Commission to Study the Organization of Peace and the UN Human Rights Regime," *Human Rights Quarterly* 30: 3 (August 2008), 607–30.

5. See Laura Doyle, *Freedom's Empire: Race and the Rise of the Novel in Atlantic Moder-nity, 1640–1940* (Durham, NC, and London: Duke University Press, 2008), 446.

{ INDEX }

CPSIA information can be obtained at www.ICGtesting.com
Printed in the USA
BVOW05s2054060316

439267BV00002B/1/P